K-Pop Lyrics:

Word for Word in English and Spanish

Letras de K-Pop:

Palabra por Palabra en inglés y español

Includes Korean grammar tips in English

Kyung Kyle LEE

K-Pop Lyrics: Word for Word in English and Spanish
Letras de K-pop: Palabra por Palabra en inglés y español

Copyright © 2021, Kyung Lee.

Published by Kyung Lee, Edmonton, Canada

ISBN
Paperback: 0-978-1-77354-308-6
eBook: 978-1-77354-309-3

PageMaster PUBLISHING
PageMasterPublishing.ca

Dedication / Dedicación

Me gustaría expresar mi sincero agradecimiento a mi amiga, Álvarez González Elsa, a quien conocí en las Naciones Unidas en Ginebra, Suiza. Gracias, Elsa, por darme la inspiración para escribir este libro para los aficionados de K-Pops de todo el mundo. Nunca había esperado que me enviaras mensajes en coreano tantos años después de mi partida de Ginebra.

-

I would like to express my sincere gratitude to my friend, Elsa Álvarez González, who I met at the United Nations in Geneva, Switzerland. Thank you, Elsa, for giving me the inspiration to write this book for aficionados of K-Pops around the World. I had never expected you to send me messages in Korean so many years after I left Geneva.

About the Author / Sobre el Autor

Kyung Kyle LEE was born in the Republic of Korea, and has lived across the world, including the U.S.A, Switzerland, Korea, and Canada. He received formal education from the George Washington University in D.C., U.S.A., where he received a Master of Business Administration (MBA). Throughout his career he held stewardship positions with a National Bank in Korea, United Nations Economic Commission for Europe (UN ECE), and the POS Research Institute in Seoul. Today he is semi-retired while continuing to manage a small business. Kyung is a published author and researcher, including the following books and reports:

- Iron and Steel Scrap Report (United Nations)
- Directory of the Steel Industry and the Environment (United Nations)
- Analysis of the Privatization Process of Countries in Transition (POS Research Insutitute)

Kyung now enjoys a relaxed life in Alberta, where he takes in the beautiful Rocky Mountains, and spends time walking his dog, a labradoodle named Lincoln. Kyung's passion for the Korean language and Koren Pop Culture will shine through in this book, illustrating his desire to educate learners on the basics of the Korean language, writing system, and the deeper meaning of each lyric. Kyung hopes this book will be just the first edition of a growing collection.

Table of Contents / Contenido

Introduction

Currently, the Korean language is the fastest growing in the world by the number of learners. This kind of the rapid growth seems to be owed to three major factors: economic and industrial importance of the country, K-Culture and the ease of the writing system.

Korean language has the easiest writing system in the world, which is called Hangeul (한글). Motivated people can learn Hangeul within a matter of hours. Basically, it requires you to know only eight (8) symbols to understand the structure of the writing system. Many foreigners who started to learn Hangeul by themselves during their flight to Seoul are surprised to find themselves reading all the signs at the Incheon International Airport upon arrival.

The majority of new learners of Korean are motivated by their affection for K-culture, especially K-Pop. During K-Pop concerts, the audience sing along to the Korean songs with the artists. One major reason that makes this phenomenon possible is that the Korean writing system is so easy to use that many people read the lyrics in the Korean alphabet, Hangeul. However, non-Korean audiences have only a vague idea of what each song implies and do not understand the exact meaning of each word in the lyrics.

While the writing system is easy, the Korean language itself is not at all easy to master. Actually, it is known to be one of the hardest languages to learn. The major reason is that its grammatical structure is quite different from other languages and the conjugation of its verbs and adjectives are incredibly complicated. Thus, for foreigners the Korean language remains to be the one that is easy to start with, but hard to be in its good command.

Keeping the above in mind, I wrote this book based upon the following principles:

[1] I repeatedly translated all the words in the selected lyrics into English and Spanish. This book is designed to save time and effort of readers referring to dictionaries and/or any grammar book. Instead of explaining the complicated rules of Korean grammar, I simply chose the repetition technique to show the grammatical structure of Korean sentences. Accordingly, readers can understand the logic and structure of Korean language without much stress of memorizing various rules of the Korean grammar.

[2] Readers also can master the Korean markers through repetition. I repeatedly explained every single Korean mark in the chosen lyrics. Accordingly, readers could automatically learn by heart all the Korean marks without labour.

[3] Considering all the verbs and adjectives, I always started with the original form, which means the infinitive form. Then, I progress step by step with each conjugation process. Thus, readers can understand all the steps and logics in the conjugation process of the Korean verbs and adjectives. With this technique, readers can learn the infinitive form and its conjugation rules of every single verb and adjective used in the chosen lyrics. In addition, they could conjugate any Korean verb and adjective by themselves in the end.

[4] Although the grammatical explanation is minimized, even when an explanation is unavoidable, I did it in a way that readers can understand with minimal knowledge of English or Spanish grammar. In reality, readers could feel that Korean grammar is not so different from European languages in its basic logic and concept.

[5] Concerning shortened words, I displayed the original form in full to show readers the contraction process step by step. Thus, readers can easily understand the contraction process and logic of Korean words and expressions.

[6] YouTube readers can understand the overall meaning of K-pop lyrics with translated lines. In many cases those translations are more liberal than literal. In this respect, those translations are not always grammatically accurate or exactly corresponding in their meaning, confusing the artists verbatim intentions of their lyrics. I don't mean those translations are wrong. What I mean is that in case of the liberal translation, it is unavoidable to twist some words or phrases to fit into a natural pattern of a translated language. On the other hand, a literal translation tends to be absurd and awkward and does not make much sense. In my case, I did the literal translation of every single word in the lyrics to show readers how exactly the original Korean sentences are composed. Subsequently, I tried to reconstruct them in natural English and Spanish without twisting or abandoning their original meaning and expressions. In that respect, this book will assist K-Pop fans and Korean language learners with understanding the deeper meaning, both literally and figuratively in English and Spanish translations.

[7] The Korean alphabet, Hangeul, is supposed to be pronounced as it is written. As such, in principle, phonetic symbols are not needed. However, in order to pronounce Hangeul perfectly without referring to phonetic symbols, readers should know the various rules of reading Korean words. Instead of explaining the rules, I transcribed the phonetic sounds of every word whose pronunciation is different from the written characters. By reading them, readers will be able to acquire the pronunciation rules as theirs in a natural way like native Korean speakers.

In conclusion, this book is written for the learners of Korean around the world who are also aficionados of K-Pop songs. It is designed to provide its readers with so many "Eureka!" moments while they leisurely enjoy reading and listening to the equivalent K-Pop song at the same time. By taking advantage of the writer's repetition technique, in the end, most thorough readers would be able to be in good command of one of the hardest languages without much stress. Korean is also a human language that happens to have a quite rich cultural background. Once readers understand its structure and logic that are repeatedly shown in this book. I hope you enjoy the book and have ease learning the Korean language and song lyrics within!

Kyung Kyle LEE

한글 (Hangeul, Korean Alphabet)

The Hangeul, the easiest and most efficient writing system in human history, was created by King Sejong (1397 ~ 1450) in the year 1493. He let his sons and scholars to test the usefulness of the writing system for three years and let them publish several books in Hangeul. After the testing period of three years and the confirmation of its usefulness, he proclaimed his invention on October 9, 1446 [한글날, Hangeul Day].

He original invented a set of eight (8) basic symbols which are composed of five (5) consonants and three (3) vowels.

[A] Five (5) basid symbols for consonants

   (1) G = ㄱ [palatal sound] = copied the shape of the inner upper **palate**

   (2) N = ㄴ [lingual sound] = copied the shape of the **tongue**

   (3) M = ㅁ [labial sound] = copied the shape of the **lips**

   (4) S = ㅅ [dental sould] = copied the shape of the **tooth**

   (5) Ng = ㅇ [gutteral sound] = copied the shap of the **throat**

[B] Three (3) basic symbols for vowels

Vowels are made of three (3) essetials of Korean philosophy: Heaven / Earth / Human

   (1) · = **Heaven** = The original sound was between [a] and [ʌ].
              [Not in use in modern Korean.]

   (2) ㅡ = **Earth** = pronunciation [ə] as in «Le» or «De» in French

      This is marked as 'eu' in Romanification Alphabet [example: 한글 = Hangeul]

   (3) ㅣ = **Human** = pronunciation [í] as in «India» or «Italy»

With these eight (8) symbols, we can expand numerously the number of sounds as follows and more.

[C] Expansion of consonants

ㄱ = G / ㅋ = K in English and German / ㄲ = K in Russian and Roman languages

ㄴ = N / ㄷ = D / ㅌ = T in English and German / ㄸ = T in Roman languages and Russian

ㄹ = R / ㄹㄹ = L as in «Cola» [콜라]

ㅁ = M / ㅂ = B / ㅍ = P in English and German / ㅃ = P in Roman languages and Russian

ㅅ = S in Spanish / ㅆ = S or SS in most other European languages / ㅈ = J in English /

ㅊ = Ch as in English and Spanish / ㅉ = Z in German or Cz in Russian

ㅇ = Ng as in «Doing» or «Going» at the end of a character, while it is silent at the beginning

of a character. For example, «앙» is pronounced as «Ahng».

ㅎ = H

King Sejong also made symbols for 'V' 'F' 'Z (in English and French)' 'Ñ or Gn'
and 'Ch (in German)'and several others. However, they are not in use in modern Korean.

[D] Expansion of vowels

Currently '·' is used only in combination with other vowels.

[ㅣ + ·] = ㅏ = A

[ㅣ + ··] = ㅑ = Ya

[· + ㅣ] = ㅓ = eo [ʌ] = as 'U' in «Sun» or «Up» in English or «서울 (Seoul)» in Korean

[·· + ㅣ] = ㅕ = Yeo [jʌ] = Pronuncation as in English «Young»

[· + ─] = ㅗ = O [o] = This is not [ou]

[·· + ─] = ㅛ = Yo

[─ + ·] = ㅜ = U

[─ + ··] = ㅠ = Yu

[ㅏ + ㅣ] = ㅐ = Ae or Ä in German

[ㅑ + ㅣ] = ㅒ = Yae or Jä in German

[ㅓ + ㅣ] = ㅔ = [é] / This is the only mistake done by King Sejong, because

[é] is not a combination of ㅓ [ʌ] and ㅣ [í].

[ㅕ + ㅣ] = ㅖ = «Yes» or «Yet» in English

[─ + ㅣ] = ㅢ = French [ə] + [í] at the same time / Russian 'ы' or Polish 'Y' can be

somewhat similar, but 'ㅢ' should be pronounced more distinctively and clearly than them.

[ㅗ + ㅣ] = ㅚ = Ö in German or French 'eu' [ø] as in «Europe»

[ㅗ + ㅏ] = ㅘ = Wa or «What» in English

[ㅗ + ㅐ] = ㅙ = Wae

[ㅜ + ㅣ] = ㅟ = «Win» or «Will» in English

[ㅜ + ㅓ] = ㅝ = «Won» or «War» in English

[ㅓ + ㅔ] = ㅞ = «Went» or «West» in English

1. IONIQ: I'm on it

***Artist:* BTS**

< Line 1 > **When I look into your eyes, all I see is you filling my mind.**
새로운 만남들은 나를 충전해.

새롭다 = [pronunciation] 새롭따 = [infinitive of adjective] be new [fresh] / ser nuevo [fresco]

새로운 = present tense of 새롭다 = (that is) new / fresh / (que es) nuevo / fresco

새롭던 = [pronunciation] 새롭떤 = past tense of 새롭다 = that was new / that was fresh / que fue nuevo / que era fresco

새로울 = future tense of 새롭다 = that will be new [fresh] / que será nuevo [fresco]

만남들은 = [pronunciation] 만남드른 = 만남(encounter, encuentro) + 들[plural] + 은[marker for subject] = encounters / encuentros

나를 = 나 (I, yo) + 를 [marker for object] = me

충전하다 = [infinitive of verb] charge up / make a charge / energize / replenish / cargar / recargar / dar energía / rellenar

충전해 = [expresión tuteando de] familiar (relationship) ending of 충전하다

새로운 만남들은 나를 충전해. = New encounters energize me. /
Los nuevos encuentros me dan energía.

< Line 2 > **Tho' bump into something. New possibility.**
어떤 날 발견할지 두근대.

어떠하다 = [infinitive of adjective] how it is / be such / be like / cómo es / ser así / ser como

어떠한 = **어떤** = present tense of 어떠하다 = a certain / some (kind of) / any (kind of) / what type of / un cierto / algún (tipo de) / cualquier (tipo de) / qué clase de

날 = 나를 = 나 (I, yo) + 를 [marker for object] = me

어떤 날 = what kind of me / what type of me / qué clase de yo / qué tipo de mí

발견하다 = [infinitive of verb] discover / find out / encounter / descubrir / encontrar

발견할 = (future) adjective form of 발견하다

발견할지 = [pronunciation] 발견할찌 = noun form of 발견하다 = the incident to encounter / the incident becoming to discover / lo que se va a encontrar / lo que llegar a descurbrir / lo que volverse a descubrir

● '지' was originally an independent word, whose meaning is «uncertainty», «probability» or «whether». Now it is combined with a verb for making a noun form.

● In Korean, the pronunciation of the first consonant after '르' tends to become hard.
[발견할지 = 발견할 + 지 → 발견할찌]

두근대다 = [infinitive of verb] feel nervous / be excited / beat fast / throb / palpitate / sentirse nervioso / estar emocionado / latir rápido / palpitar
두근대 = [expresión tuteando] familiar (relationship) ending of 두근대다

어떤 날 발견할지 (보려고) 두근대.
Excited to see what kind of me, I am going to discover. /
My heart is beating fast to see what kind of new me, I am going to encounter.

Estoy emocionado de saber qué tipo de mí, voy a descubrir. /
Mi corazón late rápido para saber qué clase de nuevo yo, voy a encontrar.

● In the original Korean lyric line, «to see / para saber» is missing.

< Line 3 > Full energy, higher esteem. Better focus on what's charging me.
가끔 길을 잃을 때면, (I got you) 영혼의 지돌 따라가.

가끔 = [adverb] at times / now and then / once in a while / a veces / de vez en cuando
길을 = [pronunciation] 기를 = 길 (way, path, route, camino, calle, ruta) + 을 [marker for object]
잃다 = [pronunciation] 일타 = [infinitive of verb] lose (oneself) / miss / go astray / perderse / extraviarse / desviarse

● When 'ㅎ' combines with a consonsant, the consonant becomes aspirated.
[ㄱ + ㅎ → ㅋ] [ㄷ + ㅎ → ㅌ] [ㅂ + ㅎ → ㅍ] [ㅈ + ㅎ → ㅊ]
[잃다 → 일 + ㅎ + 다 → 일타]

잃을 = [pronunciation] 일을 → 이를 = (future) adjective form of 잃다 = getting to be lost / going astray / be going to miss / extraviandose / estando perdido

● In case of Korean (future) adjective forms, sometimes it is more natural to translate them into the present tense or the infinitive form in European languages.

때 = [noun] time / occasion / moment / when / tiempo / ocasión / momento / cuando

이다 = [infinitive of marker that conjugates] be / ser

● «이다» is the only marker that conjugates like verbs or adjectives.

● Markers are not regarded as an independent word. That is why there is no space in front of them.

때면 = 때 + 이면 (if it is, si es) = if it is (the case) that ~ / in the occasion that ~ / when / si es (el caso) que ~ / en caso de que ~ / cuando

잃을 때면 = at the time to lose (myself) / in the occasion that (I) miss / when I go astray / en el momento de despitarse / en caso de que me pierdo / cuando me extravío

가끔 길을 잃을 때면 = In the occasion that I miss the route / At times when I'm lost / En la ocasión en que me pierda la ruta / A veces cuando estoy perdido

영혼의 = [pronunciation] 영혼에 → 영호네 = 영혼 (soul, spirit, alma, espíritu) + 의 [marker for possession] = of soul / de alma

● «의 [marker for possession]» is pronounced as «에». However, in case that it is a part of

an independent word, it is pronounced as «의».

[정의 (justice)] [의미 (meaning)] [거의 (almost)]

지돌 = 지도를 = 지도 (map, mapa) + 를 [marker for object]

따라가다 = [infinitive of verb] follow / go after / refer to / seguir / ir tras / referirse a

따라가 = familiar or poetic ending of 따라가다

영혼의 지돌 따라가 = I follow [refer to] the map of the soul. / Sigo [Me refiero a] el mapa de mi alma.

가끔 길을 일을 때면, 영혼의 지돌 따라가.
At times when I'm lost, I follow [refer to] the map of the soul. /
A veces cuando estoy perdido, sigo [me refiero a] el mapa de mi alma.

< Line 4 > 쉼없이 달려가다 네가 지칠 땐, 내가 네 휴식이 되어 줄께.

쉼 = [noun] pause / rest / recess / temporary stop / pausa / descanso / receso / parada temporal

없이 = [pronunciation] 업씨 = [adverb] without / not having / sin / no teniendo

쉼 없이 = [adverb phrase] without pause / without rest / sin pararse / sin descanso

달려가다 = [infinitive of verb] run / dash / rush / correr / recorrer

달려가다(가) = while running / dash, and / rush, and / mientras corriedo / recorrer, y

네가 = 너 + 이가 = 너 (you, tú) + 이가 [marker for subject]

● Many Korean speakers including BTS pronounce «네가» as «니가». That is not correct.

지치다 = [infinitve of verb] grow tired / get exhausted / become fatigued /
estar exhausto / cansarse / agotarse / fatigarse

지칠 = (future) adjective form of 지치다 = that will be growing tired / that (will) become exhausted / getting to be fatigued / que estés cansado / que estarás exhausto / ir a agostarse

● In case of Korean (future) adjective forms, sometimes it is more natural to translate them into the present tense or the infinitive form in European languages.

땐 = 때는 = 때에는 = 때 (time, moment, tiempo, momento) + 에는 (at, en) = at that time / at the moment / when / in case that ~ / en ese tiempo / en el momento / cuando / en caso de que ~

쉼없이 달려가다(가) 네가 지칠 땐,
At the moment that you will become tired by continued running, /
When you get exhausted while running without pause,

En este momento que te cansarás por seguir corriendo, /
Cuando te agotas mientras corres sin pausa,

내가 = 나 + 이가 = 나 (I, yo) + 이가 [marker for subject]

네 = 너의 = 너 (you, tú) + 의 [marker for possession] = of you / your / tu

휴식이 = 휴식 (rest, repose, relaxation, descanso, reposo, desahogo) + 이 [marker for subject]

되다 = [infinitive of verb] become / turn into / volverse / convertirse / resultar / terminarse / hacerse / ser

주다 = [infinitive of verb] kindly do / give as a favour / willing to do / please, / amablemente hacer / dar con gusto / dispuesto a hacer / por favor,

되어 주다 = kindly become / willing to become / amablemente covertiré / estoy dispuesto a llegar a ser

줄께 = familiar ending for commitment of 주다 = I am willing / I promise / I do with pleasure / Estoy despuesto / Prometo / (Lo) hago con placer

되어 줄께 = [familiar ending for commitment] of 되어 주다 =
I am willing to be / I promise to be / I become with pleasure / I shall become happily / Estoy despuesto a ser / Prometo ser / Me convierte con placer / Seré con gusto

내가 네 휴식이 되어 줄께. = I am willing to be your relaxation. /
Me convertiré en tu descanso con gusto.

쉼없이 달려가다 네가 지칠 땐, 내가 네 휴식이 되어 줄께.

When you become exhausted while running without pause, I am willing to be your relaxation. /
Cuando te agotas mientras corres sin pausa, me convertiré en tu descanso con gusto.

< Line 5 > I'm on it. Chasing my chance. IONIQ takes me there.
내가 원하는 건 simple. 멀리보단 늘 함께 가고 싶어. Show you the way.

내가 = 나 + 이가 = 나 (I, yo) + 이가 [marker for subject]

원하다 = [infinitive of verb] = want / desire / wish / querer / desear

원하는 = present adjective form of 원하다 = wanting / desiring / that I wish / queriendo /
deseando / que deseo

건 = 것은 = 것 (the thing that ~, the fact that ~, la cosa que ~, el hecho que ~, lo que ~)

+ 은 [marker for subject]

내가 원하는 건 **simple** = The thing that I want is simple. / What I desire is simple. /
La cosa que quiero es simple. / Lo que deseo es simple.

멀리 = [adverb, also used as noun] far / afar / in the distance / lejos / a lo lejos / a distancia

보단 = 보다는 = 보다 (than, more than, más que) + 는 [marker for emphasis]
= rather than / más bien que

늘 = [adverb] always / all the time / the whole time / siempre / todo el tiempo

함께 = [adverb] together / along with / in company with / contigo / junto con / en compañía de

가다 = [infinitive of verb] go (away) / move away / ride / ir / irse / marchar / alejarse

가고 = a noun-type conjugation of 가다 = to go (away) / to move away / irse

● «noun form» can be regarded as a noun, «adverb-form» can be regarded as an adverb, while
«a noun-type conjuation» or «an adverb-type conjugation» is regarded as a verb.

● In Korean, when two verbs combine, there is a tendency that the first verb does either a
noun-type or an adverb-type conjugation. By doing so, the first verb serves like an object for
the second verb [in case that the second verb is a transitive verb], or modifies the second verb
like an adverb [in case that the second verb is an intransitive verb].

싶다 = [pronunciation] 십다 → 십따 = [infinitive of adjective] feel like / would like /

want / wish / desire / querer / gustar

가고 싶다 = [verb phrase] feel like going / would like to go away / want [wish, desire] to go / tengo ganas de irse / me gustaría ir / quiero [deseo] ir
가고 싶어 = [pronunciation] 가고 시퍼 = familiar ending of 가고 싶다

● [가고 싶다 = want to go] By doing a noun-type conjugation the first verb can serve like an object of the second verb. Thus, «가고 (to go)» is the object of «싶다 (want)».

● Other examples of a noun-type cojugation that is used in English: «get going», «giving up smoking», «ended up buying» or «keep on running».

멀리보단 늘 함께 가고 싶어. = Rather than going far, I feel like going together with you, always. / Me gustaría ir siempre contigo, más bien que irse lejos.

< Line 6 > I see a sign, saying "slow it down." I've pushed myself too hard.
몰아세우기보단 나아갈 힘을 줄래? Cheer up!

몰아세우다 = [infinitive of verb] lash out / scold away / put into a corner / drive into / be hard on / reprimand / bombardear / arrinconar / reprender fuerte / amonestar / regañar
몰아세우기 = noun form of 몰아세우다
● «noun form» can be regarded as a noun, «adverb-form» can be regarded as an adverb, while «a noun-type conjuation» or «an adverb-type conjugation» is regarded as a verb.

보단 = 보다는 = [marker phrase] 보다 (than, more than, más que) + 는 [marker for emphasis]
= rather than / instead of / más bien que / en lugar de
나아가다 = [infinitive of verb] go forward / move forward / proceed / advance / adelantar / proseguir / marchar / avanzar
나아갈 = (future) adjective form of 나아가다 = to go forward / to proceed / para avanzar / para seguir

● In case of Korean (future) adjective forms, sometimes it is more natural to
translate them into the present tense or the infinitive form in European languages.

힘을 = 힘 + 을 = 힘 (power, strength, energy, fuerza, energía) +을 [marker for object]
주다 = [infinitive of verb] give / bestow / provide / supply / present / dar / conceder / otorgar / ofrecer / presentar
줄래? = familiar ending for questioning of 주다 = will you give me, please? / me darías, por favor?
힘을 줄래? = will you give me energy? / will you encourage me? / ¿me darías energía, por favor?

몰아세우기보단 나아갈 힘을 줄래?

Rather than scolding me away, will encourage me to move forward? /
Instead of lashing me out, will you give me energy to proceed, (please)?

En lugar de regañarme, ¿me animará a seguir adelante? /
En lugar de amonestarme, ¿me darías energía para avanzar, (por favor)?

< Line 7 > When we're together, I get may energy. The memory, it makes me go again.
실바람 소리가 들려와, 그 위에 내 목소릴 실어, 난.

새로운 음악으로 만들어 가. Make it loud. Make it right.

실바람 = [noun] light breeze / light air / a wisp of breeze / brisa ligera / aire ligero /
una voluta de brisa

소리가 = 소리 (sound, sonido) + 가 [marker for subject]

들려오다 = [infinitive of verb] come into hearing / be heard / fall on one's ears /
llegar a oír / ser escuchado / entrar en la audición

들려와(서) = be heard, so / can hear, thus / ser escuchado, y / oírse, así [por lo tanto]

실바람 소리가 들려와(서) = The sound of a light breeze is to be heard, so / I feel a light
breeze, and / Porque se oye el sonido de una ligera brisa, / Siento una ligera brisa así que

그 = [determiner] the / that / those / ese / esos / tal

● A determiner is an adjective that does not conjugate.

위 = [noun] the top / the upper side / la cima / la parte superior

위에 = 위 + 에 (on, at, sobre, en) = on top of / encima de

내 = 나의 = 나 (I, yo) + 의 [marker for possession] = of me / my / mi

목소릴 = 목소리를 = 목소리 (voice, voz) + 를 [marker for object]

● Markers are not regarded as an independent word. That is why there is no space in
front of them.

싣다 = [pronunciation] 싣따 = [infinitive of verb] load (onto) / take [have] on board /
let carry / llevar / cargar / montar

실어, = [pronunciation] 시러 = familiar or poetic ending of 싣다

난 = 나는 = 나 (I, yo) + 는 [marker for subject]

그 위에 내 목소릴 실어, 난. = I load my voice on top of it. / I load my voice onto the breeze. /
I let it carry my voice. / Cargo mi voz encima. / Cargue mi voz encima de la brisa. /

Dejo que lleve mi voz.

새롭다 = [pronunciation] 새롭따 = [infinitive of adjective] be new [fresh] / ser nuevo [fresco]

새로운 = present tense of 새롭다 = (that is) new / fresh / (que es) nuevo / fresco

음악으로 = [pronunciation] 음아그로 = 음악 (the music, la música) + 으로 (into, as, en, como)

만들다 = [infinitive of verb] make / produce / create / build / producir / crear / componer

만들어 = an adverb-type of cojugation of 만들다

가다 = [infinitive of verb] go (away) / move away / ride / ir / irse / marchar / alejarse / llevarse

만들어 가다 = [present progressive] be gradually making it into / compose little by little / be in the process of producing / gradualmente haciéndolo en / componer gradualmente / estar en el proceso de producir

만들어 가 = familiar or poetic ending of 만들어 가다

새로운 음악으로 만들어 가. = I gradually make it into a new music. / Little by litte I compose it as a new music. / Graualmente lo convierto en una nueva música. / Poco a poco lo compongo como una nueva música.

< Line 8 > 거의 다 왔어 where I am heading for. It's finally one step away.

거의 = [adverb] almost / nearly / practically / approximately / casi / aproximadamente

다 = [adverb] all / everything / everyone / totally / completely / todo(s) / totalmente / completamente

거의 다 = [adverb phrease] almost / almost all / casi / casi todo(s)

오다 = [infinitive of verb] come / come to / approach / arrive / venir / venir a / acercarse / llegar (a)

왔다 = [pronunciation] 왔다 → 왇따 = past tense of 오다 = have come / reached / arrived / hemos llegado / hemos venido / arribamos

왔어 = [pronunciation] 와써 = familiar ending of 왔다

거의 다 왔어 = We are almost there. / Estamos casi allí.

< Line 5 > I'm on it. Chasing my chance. IONIQ takes me there.
내가 원하는 건 simple. 멀리보단 늘 함께 가고 싶어. Show you the way.

내가 원하는 건 simple.

The thing that I want is simple. / What I desire is simple.

La cosa que quiero es simple. / Lo que deseo es simple.

멀리보단 늘 함께 가고 싶어.
Rather than going far, I feel like going together with you, always.

Me gustaría ir siempre contigo, más bien que ir lejos.

2. Autumn Outside the Post Office (가을 우체국 앞에서)

Artist: YB (*윤도현 밴드*)

Lyric Writer: 김현성

< **Line 1** > 가을, 우체국 앞에서 그대를 기다리다,
노오란 은행잎들이 바람에 날려가고, 지나는 사람들같이 저 멀리 가는 걸 보네.

● The basic format of this line is as follows: "While waiting for A, I observe B and C."

가을, = [noun] autumn / the fall / otoño
우체국 = [noun] post office / Correos

● In principle, a comma (,) is necessary here to clarify «가을 (autumn)» is not a word modifying «우체국 (the post office, Correos) ».

앞에서 = [pronunciation] 아페서 = 앞 (the front, el frente) + 에서 (at, in, en) =
in front of / outside / frente a / delante de
우체국 앞에서 = in front of the post office / outside the post office / delante de Correos

그대 = [pronoun] poetic expression of you, dear, tú, amado, amada
그대를 = 그대 + 를 [marker for object]
기다리다 = [infinitive of verb] wait (for) / await / hold on / expect / esperar / aguardar / esperanzar
기다리다(가) = be waiting, and / while waiting for / esperando, y / mientras te estoy esperando

가을 우체국 앞에서 그대를 기다리다(가),
Autumn, outside the post office, while wating for you, /
Autumn, outside the post office, I was waiting for you, and

Otoño, fuera de la oficina de Correos, mientras te esperaba, /
Otoño, delante de Correos, esperando a mi amada, y

● The original line of this part is written in the present tense. However, the following lines turn into the past tense. Therefore, tenses are not an issue in this lyric.

노랗다 = [pronunciation] 노라타 = [infinitive of adjective] be yellow / be golden / ser dorado
노랗던 = [pronunciation] 노라턴 = past tense of 노랗다 = that was yellow [golden] /

15

que era amarillo [dorado]

노오란 = 노란 = present form of 노랗다 = yellow / that is golden / amarillo / that is dorado

은행잎들이 = [pronunciation] 은행닙뜨리 = 은행 (ginko) + 잎 (leaf, hoja) + 들 [suffix for plural] +이 [marker for subject]

● «은행잎» is the combination of two independent words 은행 and 잎. In that case, a sound-linking (or liaison) is not allowed as «은행입». The correct pronunciation is «은행닙».

● All the vowels and four consonants (ㄴ, ㄹ, ㅁ, ㅇ) are voiced sounds, which are soft. A consonant that is not between any two of them becomes hard (or fortis). ㄷ of '들' is located between ㅂ and ㅡ. 'ㅂ' is a voiceless sound. Therefore, this ㄷ becomes hard as ㄸ. [은행잎들 → 은행닙들 → 은행닙뜰]

바람에 = [pronunciation] 바라메 = 바람 (the wind) +에 (by, in, por, en) = by the wind / por el viento

날리다 = [infinitive of verb] be blown / fly / flutter / ser soplado / volar

가다 = [infinitive of verb] go (away) / move away / ride / ir / irse / marchar / alejarse / llevarse

날려가다 = [phrase phrase] be blown away / fly away / flutter away / ser soplado lejos / volándose llevar / revolotear

날려가고 = be blown away, and / fly away, and / volarse, y / ser soplado lejos, y / volándose llevar, y

노오란 은행잎들이 바람에 날려가고, = The golden leaves of ginko are blown away by the wind, and / Las hojas doradas del ginko volándose llevadas por el viento, y

지나다 = [infinitive of verb] pass by / go by / go past / pasar (por) / marchar / caminar

지나는 = adjective form of 지나다 = passing by / that goes by / pasando / que marchan

사람들 = 사람 (person, human, persona, ser humano) + 들 [suffix for plural] = people / persons / la gente / personas

● All the vowels and four consonants (ㄴ, ㄹ, ㅁ, ㅇ) are voiced sounds, which are soft. A consonant that is between any two of them becomes soft as well. The above ㄷ of '들' is located between ㅁ and ㅡ. So, this ㄷ becomes soft. Because of that, the word is pronounced as «사람들», not «사람뜰».

지나는 사람들 = people passing by / passers-by / los pasantes

같이 = [pronunciation] 가치 = [marker for similarity] like / such as / similar to / como / similar a

● In Korean, the pronunciation of the first consonant just after '2' tends to become hard. However, this does not apply to Markers. Therefore, the above is pronounced as «사람들가치», not «사람들까치».

지나는 사람들같이 = like people passing-by / como los pasantes

저 = [determiner] that / those / over there / aquel / allí
● A determiner is an adjective that does not conjugate.

멀리 = [adverb] far / afar / in the distance / lejos / a lo lejos / a distancia
저 멀리 = [adverb phrase] far away / that far / tan lejos / así de lejos / lejano

가다 = [infinitive of verb] go (away) / move away / ride / ir / irse / marchar / alejarse / llevarse
가는 = adjective form of 가다 = going / that goes away / yendo / que van / se alejando
걸 = 것을 = 것 (the scene that ~, the fact that ~, el hecho que ~, lo que ~) + 을 [marker for object]
가는 걸 = the scene that they go away / el hecho que se van
보다 = [infinitive of verb] see / watch / look at / observe / ver / mirar / observar
보네 = poetic ending of 보다

저 멀리 가는 걸 보네. = (I) observe the scene that (they) are going far away / Observo el hecho que se van tan alejando

지나는 사람들같이 저 멀리 가는 걸 보네.
(I) observe that (they) are going far away like passers-by.
Observo que se van alejando como los pasantes.

가을 우체국 앞에서 그대를 기다리다
노오란 은행잎들이 바람에 날려가고, 지나는 사람들같이 저 멀리 가는 걸 보네.

Autumn, outside the Post Office, while waiting for you,
I observe that the golden leaves of ginko are I blown by the wind,
thus, they are going far away like passers-by.

Otoño, delante de Correos, esperando a mi amada,
observo que las hojas doradas del ginko volándose llevadas por el viento,
y así que se alejando como los pasantes.

< Line 2 > 세상에 아름다운 것들이 얼마나 오래 남을까?

세상에 = 세상 (the world, el mundo) + 에 (in, on, en) = in the world / en el mundo

아름답다 = [pronunciation] 아름답따 = [infinitive of adjective] be beautiful / be pretty / be lovely / ser bello / ser hermoso

● All the vowels and four consonants (ㄴ, ㄹ, ㅁ, ㅇ) are voiced sounds, which are soft. A consonant that is not between any two of them becomes hard (or fortis). The ㄷ of '다' is located between ㅂ and ㅏ. Therefore, this ㄷ becomes hard. [아름답다 → 아름답따]

아름답던 = [pronunciation] 아름답떤 = past tense of 아름답다 = that was beautiful / that was pretty / que fue bello / que era hermoso

아름다운 = present tense of 아름답다 = beautiful / that is pretty / lovely / bello / que es hermoso

것 = [pronunciation] 걷 = [noun] thing / stuff / fact / case / cosa / hecho / caso / algo

것들이 = [pronunciation] 걷드리 → 걷뜨리 = 것 + 들 [suffix for plural] + 이 [marker for subject]

아름다운 것들이 = the things that are beautiful / beautiful things / all the beauty / las cosas que son hermosas / cosas hermosas / toda esta belleza

얼마나 = [adverb] how much / how many / cuánto / cuántos

오래 = [adverb] for long / for a long time / por mucho tiempo

얼마나 오래 = [adverb phrase] for how long / por cuanto tiempo

남다 = [infinitive of verb] remain / last / sustain / permanecer / durar / sostener / quedarse

남을까? = [soliloquy questioning] will remain? / will last? / will sustain? / ¿permanecerá? / ¿durará? / ¿se mantendrán?

세상에 아름다운 것들이 얼마나 오래 남을까 ?
For how long all this beauty will remain in the world? /
¿Cuantó tiempo permanecerá toda esta belleza en el mundo?

● This lyric line seems to imply his realization that their love would not last very long.

< Line 3 > 한여름 소나기 쏟아져도 굳세게 버틴 꽃들과
지난 겨울 눈보라에도 우뚝 서 있는 나무들같이
하늘 아래 모든 것이 저 홀로 설 수 있을까?

● The basic format of this line is as follows; "Like A and B, can C do it?"

한여름 = [pronunciation] 한녀름 = 한 (mid, high, culmination, media, pleno, culminación)
+ 여름 (summer, verano) = [noun, also used as adverb] mid-summer / high summer /
in the middle of summer / pleno verano / en medio del verano

● «한여름» is the combination of two independent words 한 and 여름. In that case, a sound-linking (or liaison) is not allowed as «하녀름». The correct pronunciation is «한녀름».

소나기 = [noun] a shower / the pouring rain / chaparrón / las lluvias torrenciales
쏟아지다 = [pronunciation] 쏘다지다 = [infinitive of verb] pour / heavily fall down /
derramarse / desgarrarse el cielo
쏟아져도 = [pronunciation] 쏘다져도 = in spite of pouring / in spite of falling down heavily /
a pesar de derramarse / incluso de caso de que desgarrarse el cielo

굳세다 = [pronunciation] 굳쎄다 = [infinitive of adjective] be firm / be strong / be stout /
ser firme / ser fuerte / ser resistente
굳세게 = [pronunciation] 굳쎄게 = adverb form of 굳세다 = firmly / undauntedly /
stoutly / unflinchingly / firmemente / con firmeza / sin desalentar / sin desanimarse

버티다 = [infinitive of verb] withstand / endure / bear (up) / get over / overcome / soportar
버틴 = past adjective form of 버티다 = withstood / endured / that has overcome /
que ha soportado
꽃 = [pronunciation] 꼳 = [noun] flower / blossom / flor
꽃들과 = [pronunciation] 꼳들과 → 꼳뜰과 = 꽃 (flower, flor) + 들 [suffix for plural]
+ 과 (and, y) = the flowers, and / las flores, y

● All the vowels and four consonants (ㄴ, ㄹ, ㅁ, ㅇ) are voiced sounds, which are soft. A
consonant that is not between any two them becomes hard (or fortis). The ㄷ of '들' is located
between ㄷ and ㅡ. Therefore, it becomes hard. [꽃들 → 꼳들 → 꼳뜰]

굳세게 버틴 꽃들 = the flowers that endured undauntedly /
the blossoms that firmly withstood / las flores que soportaron sin desalentar /
las flores que resistieron firmemente

한여름 소나기 쏟아져도 굳세게 버틴 꽃들과 =

[pronunciation] 한녀름 소나기 쏘다져도 굳쎄게 버틴 꼳뜰과
The flowers that endured undauntedly the pouring showers in the midsummer, and /
Esas flores que soportaron firmemente las lluvias torrenciales en medio del verano, y

지나다 = [infinitive of verb] pass by / go by / go past / pasar (por) / marchar / caminar

지나는 = present adjective form of 지나다 = passing by / that goes by / pasando / que marchan

지난 = past adjective form of 지나다 = that has gone / past / last / que pasado / anterior

겨울 = [noun] winter / winter season / invierno

눈보라 = [noun] blizzard / snowstorm / tormentas de nieve / nevada fuerte

눈보라에도 = 눈보라 + 에도 (in spite of, a pesar de) = in spite of the snowstorms /
a pesar de las tormentas de nieve

우뚝 = [adverb] high / aloft / lofty / towering / en lo alto / altísimo / empinado

서다 = [infinitive of verb] stand / estar / levantarse / mantenerse / seguir erecto

있다 = [pronunciation] 읻다 → 읻따 = [infinitive of verb] there is / be / exist / stay / remain /
stand / hay / estar / existir / quedarse / permanecer / pararse

우뚝 서 있다 = stand aloft / stand towering / estar en lo alto / pararse altísimo

우뚝 서 있는 = present adjective form of 서 있다 = standing aloft /
that stands towering / estando en lo alto / que siguen erectos altísimo

있는 = [pronunciation] 읻는 → 인는 = present adjective form of 있다

나무들 = 나무 (tree, árbol) + 들 [plural] = trees / árboles

같이 = [pronunciation] 가치 = [marker for resemblance] like / similar to / como / similar a

지난 겨울 눈보라에도 우뚝 서 있는 나무들같이
Like the trees that stand aloft in spite of the snowstorms of last winter /
Like the trees that maintain a high figure after enduring the blizzards of last winter

Como los árboles que están en lo alto a pesar de las tormentas de nieve del invierno pasado /
Parecidas los árboles que siguen erectos altísimo después de soportar las tempestades del
invierno pasado

하늘 = [noun] the sky / the heaven / el cielo

아래 = [noun] the bottom / the foot / under / el pie / debajo

하늘 아래 = [noun phrase] under the sky / bajo el cielo

20

모든 = [determiner] all / every / whole / entire / todo(s) / cada / entero

것(들) = [noun] thing / stuff / cosa / hecho / caso + 들 [plural]

모든 것이 = [pronunciation] 모든 거시 = all the things / everything / todas las cosas + 이 [marker for subject]

저 = [pronoun] oneself / self / it / uno mismo / eso

홀로 = [adverb] alone / single / on one's own / solo / sin (la) ayuda de nadie

저 홀로 = [adverb phrase] by itself / single-handedly / independently / por sí mismo

서다 = [infinitive of verb] stand (on its own feet) / estar / levantarse / mantenerse / seguir erecto

서는 = present adjective form of 서다 = standing / estando / que se levanta / que se mantiene

설 = (future) adjective form of 서다 = will stand / to stand / se levantará / se mantendrá

수 = [noun] means / resource / possibility / likelihood / medio / recurso / posibilidad / probabilidad

있다 = [pronunciation] 읻다 → 읻따 = [infinitive of verb] there is / be / exist / stay / remain / stand / hay / estar / existir / quedarse / permanecer / pararse

(할) 수 있다 = [pronunciation] 할 쑤 읻따 = [verb phrase] can do / poder hacer = [action]

설 수 있다 = It is possible to stand / can stand / es posible mantenerse / puede estar de pie

(할) 수 **있을까?** = Is it possible (to do)? / Can it do? / ¿Es posible hacer? / ¿Puede hacer?

설 수 있을까? = [pronunciation] 설 쑤 이쓸까? = Is it possible to stand? / Can it stand? / ¿Es posible mantenerse? / ¿Puede estar de pie?

● In Korean, the pronunciation of the first consonant just after ' ㄹ ' tends to become hard.
[할 수 → 할 쑤] [설 수 → 설 쑤]

저 홀로 설 수 있을까? = Is it possible to stand alone? / Can it stand by itself? / ¿Es posible mantenerse solo? / ¿Puede estar de pie por sí mismo? / ¿Puede sostenerse por sí mismo?

하늘 아래 모든 것이 저 홀로 설 수 있을까?
Is it possible that everything under the sky stands independently by itself? / ¿Puede todo lo que hay bajo el cielo mantenerse en pie por sí mismo?

한여름 소나기 쏟아져도 굳세게 버틴 꽃들과

지난 겨울 눈보라에도 우뚝 서 있는 나무들같이
하늘 아래 모든 것이 저 홀로 설 수 있을까 ?

Like the flowers that endured undauntedly the pouring showers in the midsummer and
the trees that stand aloft in spite of snowstorms of last winter,
can everything under the sky stand independently by itself?

Como esas flores que soportaron firmemente las lluvias torrenciales del verno, y
los árboles que siguen erectos a pesar de las tempestades del pasado invierno,
¿Puedo todo bajo el cielo mantenerse en pie por sí mismo?

< Line 4 > 가을, 우체국 앞에서 그대를 기다리다,
우연한 생각에 빠져 날 저물도록 몰랐네.

가을, 우체국 앞에서 그대를 기다리다(가),
Autumn, outside the Post Office, while waiting for you, /
Otoño, delante de Correos, esperando a mi amada,

우연히 = [adverb] by accident / by accident / accidentally / con casualidad / accidentalmente
우연한 = adjective form of 우연히 = randomly coming to mind / that occurs by chane /
accidental / casual / que viene a la mente al azar
생각에 = [pronunciation] 생가게 = 생각 (thought, consideration, pensamiento, consideración)
+ 에 (into, en)

빠지다 = [infinitive of verb] be lost / fall into / be submerged in / drift into / absorber /
perderse / perderse / caer en / derraparse en
빠져(서) = an adverb-type conjugation of 빠지다 = by being lost / owing to falling into /
while being drifted into / por perderse / debido a caer en / mientras me derrapé en

날 = [noun] day / daytime / time / día / diurno / tiempo
저물다 = [infinitive of verb] get dark / grow dark / (sun) sets / be over / ponerse / terminar
날 저물도록 = until it gets dark / while growing dark / until the sun sets /
hasta que se oscurezca / hasta que se ponga el sol / hasta que hacerse de noche
모르다 = [infinitive of verb] not know [aware, realize, notice, understand, learned] /
no saber [aprendí] / desconocer / no darse cuenta
모르네 = present form of poetic ending of 모르다
몰랐다 = [pronunciation] 몰란다 → 몰란따 = past tense of 모르다 = didn't realize /
didn't notice / didn't know / no me di cuenta / no sabía
몰랐네 = [pronunciation] 몰란네 → 몰란네 = past tense of poetic ending of 몰랐다

우연한 생각에 빠져 날 저물도록 몰랐네

I happened to drift into a certain thought, so I didn't realize it until the sun sets.

Absorto en mis pensamientos que vino con casualidad, no me di cuenta que se hizo de noche.

< Line 2 > 세상에 아름다운 것들이 얼마나 오래 남을까?

For how long all this beauty will remain in the world?

¿Cuantó tiempo permanecerá toda esta belleza en el mundo?

● Some people interpret that his dear girl didn't show up until it got dark. In the meantime, something came up to his mind while watching the autumn scenery. And he realized that their love would not last for long. Maybe it was too beautiful to last.

우연한 생각에 빠져 날 저물도록 몰랐네

3. Seesaw

Artist: *Suga of BTS*
Lyric Writers: *Suga, Slow Rabbit*

< Line 1 > 시작은 뭐 즐거웠었네. 오르락 내리락 그 자체로.

시작은 = [pronunciation] 시자근 = 시작 (the beginning, el pricipio) + 은 [marker for subject]

뭐 = [interjection] well / uh / bueno

즐겁다 = [pronunication] 즐겁따 = [infinitive of adjective] be pleasant [joyful, cheerful] / be fun / ser entretenido [divertido]

즐거웠었다 = [pronunciation] 즐거워썼다 → 즐거워썼따 = past tense of 즐겁다 = was [pleasant, joyful, cheerful] / was a fun / fue entretenido [divertido]

즐거웠었네 = [pronunciation] 즐거워썼네 → 즐거워썬네 = poetic ending of 즐거웠었다

오르락 내리락 = [mimetic adverb] movement of going up and down / movimiento de subir y bajar

그 = [determiner] the / that / those / ese / esos / tal

자체로 = 자체 (itself, its own, per se, sí mismo, lo propio) + 로 (as, by, como, por)

그 자체로 = [adverb phrase] as it is / as itself / tal como es / por sí mismo

시작은 뭐 즐거웠었네. 오르락 내리락 그 자체로.
Well, the beginning was fun. Just with the movement of going up and down itself.
Bueno, el principio fue entretenido. Solo con tal movimiento de subir y bajar por sí mismo.

● < markers for subject > [가 / 이 / 는 / 은]

«가 (after vowels)» «이 (after consonants)» **vs.** «는 (after vowels)» «은 (after consonants)»

In general, Koreans use «이 (or 이가)» and «가» as principal markers for subject.

On the other hand, «은» and «는» are used for the following cases:

[1] In case of indicating the contrast of ideas or concepts.
　　시작**은** 좋았다. 그러나, 끝**은** 나빴다. The beginning was good. But the ending was bad.

[2] In case of introduciton.
　　저**는** 제임스입니다. 저**는** 음악가입니다. [polite expression]
　　I am James. I am a musician.

24

[3] In case of stating a general fact that is accepted by everyone.

사과**는** 과일입니다 [polite expression]. Apples are fruits.

[4] In case that there are two subjects in a sentence, «는» or «은» becomes the subject of the whole sentence, while «가» or «이» becomes only the subject of a verb.

나는 네가 좋아 = I like you. / To me, you are likeable.

나는 네가 좋아 = Yo te quiero. / Para mí, tú eres agradable.

[5] When «는» or «은» is combined with an adverb, it becomes an emphasizing form or a stronger expression. [이제 (now) → 이제는] [아직 (not yet) → 아직은] [보다 (more than) → 보다는] [더 (more) → 더는] [약간 (a little) → 약간은]

< Line 2 > 어느새 서로 지쳐버렸네, 의미없는 감정 소모에.

어느새 = [adverb] without one's knowledge / while not realizing / sin darse cuenta

서로 = [adverb] each other / one another / reciprocally / (we) together / uno al otro / recíprocamente / (nosotros) juntos

지치다 = [infinitve of verb] grow tired / get exhausted / be fatigued / estar cansado [exhausto] / cansarse

지쳐버리다 = stronger expression than 지치다

지쳐버렸다 = [pronunciation] 지쳐버런다 → 지쳐버럳따 = past tense of 지쳐버리다 = broke down from exhaustion / got tired [exhausted, fatigued] / nos cansamos

지쳐버렸네 = [pronunciation] 지쳐버럳네 → 지쳐버런네 = poetic ending of 지쳐버렸다

어느새 서로 지쳐버렸네, = Both of us got tired, while not realizing it. / We got tired of each other, while not realizing it. / Sin darnos cuenta nos cansamos, los dos. / Sin darnos cuenta nos cansamos el uno del otro.

의미 = [noun] meaning / sense / signification / point / sifnificado / sentido / significación / punto vital

없다 = [pronunciation] 업다 → 업따 = [infintive of adjective] there is no / not exist / be absent / be without / no hay / no existir / estar ausente / estar sin

없는 = [pronunciation] 업는 → 엄는 = present tense of 없다 = that is absent / que es sin

의미 없는 = (that is) meaningless / without sense / pointless / (que es) sin sentido

감정 = [noun] feeling(s) / emotion / sentiment / emoción

소모에 = 소모 (exahustion, waste, consumption, use up, desperdicio, consumición) + 에 (by, owing to, por, debido a)

의미 없는 감정 소모에 = Owing to the meaningless waste of emotion /
Debido al desperdicio sin sentido de la emoción

< Line 3 > 반복된 시소 시소 게임, 이쯤되니 지겨워 지겨워졌네.

반복하다 = [pronunciation] 반보카다 = [infinitive of verb] repeat / reiterate / repetir / reiterar
반복하는 = [pronunciation] 반보카는 = present adjective form of 반복하다 = repeating /
repitiendo
반복되다 = [pronunciation] 반복뙤다 = [infinitive of passive verb] be repeated /
become repetaed / ser repetido
반복되는 = [pronunciation] 반복뙤는= present adjective form of 반복되다 =
being repeated / that is repeated / siendo repetido / que es repetido
반복된 = [pronunciation] 반복뙨 = past adjective form of 반복되다 = that was repeated /
that have been repeated / que fue repetido / que se ha repetido
시소 = [in Korean]널 = [noun] seesaw / balancín
게임 = [in Korean] 경기 = [noun] game / juego

반복된 시소 (시소) 게임 = repeated seesaw game / repetido balancín [juego de balancín]

이쯤 = [noun] approximately now [here] / approximately this far /
aproximadamente ahora [aquí]
되다 = [infintive of verb with time or situation] become / get near / reach / ser / llegar / pasar
이쯤되니 = [adverb phrase] coming this far / reaching this point / llegado a este punto

지겨워지다 = [infinitive of verb] get bored [browned off, fed up] / volverse aburrimiento /
hartarse / llegar a ser saciado [harto]
지겨워지었다 = 지겨워졌다 = [pronunciation] 지겨워졜따 = past tense of 지겨워지다 =
grew tired of / got bored / se volvió aburrimiento [saciado, harto]
지겨워졌네 = [pronunciation] 지겨워졜네 → 지겨워젼네 = poetic ending of 지겨워졌다

이쯤되니 (지겨워) 지겨워졌네.
After coming this far it turned into boredom. / By now we've got bored. /
Llegado a este punto se volvió aburrimiento. / A estas alturas ya nos aburrimos.

< Line 4 > 반복된 시소 시소 게임, 우린 서로 지쳐서 지겨워졌네.

반복된 시소 시소 게임 = repeated seesaw seesaw game / repetido balancín [juego de balancín]

우린 = 우리 [pronoun] + 는 = 우리 (we, nosotros) + 는 [marker for subject]

서로 = [adverb] each other / one another / reciprocally / (we) together / uno al otro / recíprocamente / (nosotros) juntos

지치다 = [infinitve of verb] grow tired / get exhausted / become fatigued / estar cansado [exhausto] / cansarse

지쳐서 = grew tired, and / because exhausted / as having been fatigued / volverse cansado [exhusto], y / porque estamos cansados

지겨워지다 = [infinitive of verb] get bored [browned off, fed up] / volverse aburrimiento / hartarse / llegar a ser saciado [harto]

지겨워지었다 = 지겨워졌다 = [pronunciation] 지겨워졛따 = past tense of 지겨워지다 = grew tired of / got bored / se volvió aburrimiento [saciado, harto]

지겨워졌네 = [pronunciation] 지겨워졛네 → 지겨워젼네 = poetic ending of 지겨워졌다

우린 서로 지쳐서 지겨워졌네. = We grew tired of each other, thus became bored. / Estamos cansados el uno del otro, y nos aburrimos [y nos volvimos aburrimientos].

< Line 5 > 사소한 말다툼이 시작이었을까? 내가 너보다 무거워졌었던 순간

사소하다 = [infinitive of adjective] be petty [trivial, trifling] / ser nimio [trivial, insignificante]

사소한 = present tense of 사소하다 = petty / trifling / that is trivial / nimio / pequeño / leve / que es insignificante

말다툼 = 말 (words, palabras) + 다툼 (quarrel, pelea) = argument / bickering / discusión / disputa

말다툼이 = [pronunciation] 말다투미 = 말다툼 (argument, discusión) + 이 [marker for subject]

시작 = [noun] the beginning / the start / the motive / el inicio / el principio

이다 = [infinitive of marker that conjugates] be / ser

● «이다» is only marker that conjugates like verbs or adjectives.

이었다 = [pronunciation] 이얻따 = past tense of 이다 = was / has been / fue / ha sido

이었을까? = [pronunciation] 이어쓸까? = was it? / I wonder if ~ / ¿fue eso? / Me pregunto si ~

사소한 말다툼이 시작이었을까? = Was the petty argument the beginning of all this? / I wonder if our first trivial bickering is to blame for all this.

¿Fue esa nimia discusión el principio de todo esto? /
Me pregunto si nuestra primera disputa trivial es la culpable de todo esto.

● Here, the petty arugument means that the cause of the argument was trivial. The arugument itself was not insigficant.

내가 = 나 [pronoun] + 이가 = 나 (I, yo) + 이가 [marker for subject]

너보다 = 너 (you, tú) + 보다 (more than, más que) = more than you / más que tú

무겁다 = [infinitive of adjective] be heavy / be weighty / ser pesado

무거워지다 = [present tense] grow heavy / become weighty / volverse pesado

무거워졌다 = [pronunciation] 무거워졑다 → 무거워졑따 = [past or present perfect tense] grew to be heavy / have become weighty / se volvió pesado / se ha vuelto pesado

무거워졌었다 = [pronunciation] 무거워져썬따 = [past perfect tense] = (I) had become heavier / (Yo) me babía vuelto más pesado

무거워졌었던 = [pronunciation] 무거워져썬던 → 무거워져썬떤 = adjective form of 무거워졌었다 = that I had become heavier / que se babía vuelto más pesado

순간 = [noun] moment / instant / momento / instante

내가 너보다 무거워졌었던 순간 = The moment that I had become heavier than you / The moment that I felt that I belonged to a higher league than you / The moment that we thought each one is above the other

El momento en el que me había vuelto más pesado que tú /
En el momento en que sentí que pertenecía a una liga superior a la tuya /
El momento en el que creímos que estábamos por encima del otro

● Verb tenses are less strict in Korean than in most European languages. In principle, Korean has only three verb tenses which are present, past and future. Korean language, however, has diverse expressions that are equivalent to the various verb tenses of European languages.

< Line 6 > 애초에 평행은 존재한 적이 없기에, 더욱이 욕심내서 맞추려 했을까?

애초에 = 애초 (beginning, principio) + 에 [marker] = from the very beginning / desde el principio

평행은 = 평행 (equilibrium, parallel, balance, equilibrio, paralelismo, balanza) + 은 [marker for subject]

존재하다 = [infinitive of verb] exist / subsist / existir

존재하는 = present adjective form of 존재하다 = existing / that subsists / existiendo / que existe

존재한 = past adjective form of 존재하다 = that has exsited / that subsisted / que ha existido / que existía

적이 = [pronunciation] 저기 = 적 (time, occasion, case, when, tiempo, ocasión, caso, cuando) + 이 [marker for subject]

없다 = [pronunciation] 업다 → 업따 = [infintive of adjective] there is no / not exist / be absent / be without / no hay / no existir / estar ausente / estar sin

없기에 = [pronunciation] 업끼에 = not existed, thus / because not existed / porque no existido

애초에 평행은 존재한 적이 없기에,

Because, from the beginning, there has never been an occasion that an equilibrium existed, / From the very beginning, an equilibrium has never existed between us, accordingly

Porque, desde el principio, nunca ha habido una ocasión en la que existió un equilibrio, / Desde el principio, nunca ha existido un equilibrio entre nosotros, por lo tanto

더욱이 = [pronunciation] 더우기 = [adverb] even harder / much more / más aún / más y más

욕심 = [noun] greed / avarice / eagerness / desire / condicia / ansias / anhelo / deseo / entusiasmo

내다 = [infinitive of verb] exert / gather / muster / manifest / display / put out / ejercitar / juntar / mostrar / sacar / extraer

욕심내다 = [infinitive of verb] do with greed / muster greed / display one's desire / hacer con codicia / acumular ansias / mostrar nos deseo

욕심내서 = with much greed [avarice, eagerness, desire] / con mucha codicia [ansias, entusiasmo]

(평행을) = 평행 (equilibrium, parallel, balance, equilibrio, paralelismo) + 을 [marker for object]

맞추다 = [pronunciation] 맏추다 = [infinitive of verb] achieve / get / lograr / ajustar / alcanzar

맞추려 = [pronunciation] 맏추려 = a noun-type conjuagation of 맞추다

하다 = [infinitive of verb] do / act / make / hacer / realizar

(평행을) 맞추려 하다 = [pronunciation] 맏추려 하다 = try to achieve a balance / try to get an equilibrium / intentar lograr una balanza / intentar alcanzar al equilibrio

(평행을) 맞추려 했을까? = [pronunciation] 맏추려 해쓸까? = [questioning] Did (we) try to achieve an equilibrium? / ¿Intentamos lograr un equilibrio?

더욱이 욕심내서 (평행을) 맞추려 했을까? = Did we try even harder to achieve an equilibrium? / Is that the reason why we tried with much eagerness to get an equilibrium?

¿Nos esforzamos aún más para lograr un equilibrio? /
¿Es esa la razón por la que intentamos con mucho entusiamo alcanzar un equilibrio?

< Line 7 > 사랑이었고, 이게 '사랑'이란 단어의 자체면, 굳이 반복해야 할 필요 있을까?

사랑 = [noun] love / amor

이다 = [infinitive of marker that conjugates] be / ser

이었다 = [pronunciation] 이얻따 = past tense of 이다 = was / has been / fue / ha sido

이었고 = [pronunciation] 이얻꼬 = was, and / has been, and / fue, y / ha sido, y

사랑이었고, = This has been our love, and / Este ha sido nuestro amor, y

이게 = 이것이 = 이것 (this, this thing, esto) + 이 [marker for subject]

'사랑' = [noun] 'love' / 'amor'

이다 = [infinitive of marker that conjugates] be / ser

이라는 = **이란** = that is called (as) / so-called / that is named as / being known as / that they call / que se llama (como) / así se llama / que se conoce como / que la gente llama / tal como

단어의 = [pronunciation] 단어에 = 단어 (word, vocabulary, palabra, vocablo) + 의 [marker for possession] = of the word / de la palabra

● «의 [marker for possession]» is pronounced as «에». However, in case that it is a part of an independent word, it is pronounced as «의».

[정의 (justice)] [의미 (meaning)] [거의 (almost)]

자체 = [noun] itself / oneself / its own / per se / sí mismo / uno mismo / lo propio

면 = 이면 = 이다 (be, ser) + 면 = if it is / si es

단어의 자체이다. = It is the word itself. / It is identical to the definition of the word itself. / Es la palabra misma. / Es idéntica a la definición de la palabra misma.

이게 '사랑'이란 단어의 자체면, = if this it is identical to the definition of the word itself / si esto es idéntica a la definición de la palabra misma

굳이 = [pronunciation] 구디 → 구지 = [adverb] in spite of that / nevertheless / nonetheless / a pesar de eso / sin embargo

반복하다 = [pronunciation] 반보카다 = [infinitive of verb] repeat / reiterate / repetir / reiterar

반복해야 = [pronunciation] 반보캐야 = must repeat / have to reiterate / debe repetir / tener que reiterar

해야 하다 = must do / have to do / should do / deber hacer / tener que hacer

할 = adjective form of 하다 = to do / to make / para hacer

필요가 = [pronunciation] 피료가 = 필요 (necessity, necesidad) + 가 [marker for subject]

있다 = [pronunciation] 읻다 → 읻따 = [infinitive of verb] there is / be / exist / stay / remain / stand / hay / estar / existir / quedarse / permanecer / pararse

있을까? = [pronunciation] 이쓸까? = [questioning] is it? / is there? / does it exist? / ¿lo es? / ¿lo está? / ¿existe?

필요(가) 있을까 ? = Is it necessary? / Is there a necessity? / ¿Es necesario?

굳이 반복해야 할 필요(가) 있을까? = Is it necessary that we should repeat, nevertheless? / ¿Es necesario que debemos repetir, sin embargo?

< Line 8 > 서로 지쳤고, 같은 카드를 쥐고 있는 듯해. 그렇다면 뭐 ...

서로 = [adverb] each other / one another / reciprocally / (we) together / uno al otro / recíprocamente / (nosotros) juntos

지치다 = [infinitve of verb] grow tired / get exhausted / become fatigued / estar cansado [exhausto] / cansarse

지쳤다 = [pronunciation] 지쳗다 → 지쳗따 = past tense of 지치다 = grew tired / got fatigued / became exhausted / estuvimos exhaustos / nos cansábamos

지쳤고 = [pronunciation] 지쳗꼬 = grew tired, and / got fatigued, and / became exhausted, and / estuvimos exhaustos, y / nos cansábamos, y

서로 지쳤고 = Both of us grew tired, and / Estuvimos exhaustos los dos, y

같다 = [pronunciation] 갇다 → 갇따 = be the same / be identical / ser el mismo / ser idéntico

같은 = [pronunciation] 가튼 = present form of 같다 = same / identical / mismo / idéntico

카드를 = 카드 (cards, cartas) + 를 [marker for object]

쥐다 = [infinitive of verb] hold / grasp / grip / seize / clench / tomar / sostener / agarrar / apretar

쥐고 = an adverb-type conjugation of 쥐다

● an adverb-type conjugation combines with an intransitive verb to imply a simultaneous action or the aim of an action.

● «noun form» can be regarded as a noun, «adverb-form» can be regarded as an adverb, while «a noun-type conjugation» or «an adverb-type conjugation» is regarded as a verb.

있다 = [pronunciation] 읻다 → 읻따 = [infinitive of verb] there is / be / exist / stay / remain / stand / hay / estar / existir / quedarse / permanecer / pararse

쥐고 있다 = [simultaneous action] be holding / be grasping / estar tomando / estar sosteniendo

● An simultaneous action using the verb «있다» can be also the present progressive tense.

있는 = [pronunciation] 읻는 → 인는 = adjective form of 있다 [verb] = being / staying / estando / quedando

듯 = [pronunciation] 듣 = [noun] possibility / probability / posbilidad / probabilidad

하다 = [suffix] do / act / make / hacer / realizar

듯하다 = [pronunciation] 듣하다 → 드타다 = [adjective phrase] it seems that / it looks like / it appears / parece que / verse quizá

● The independent verb '하다' means 'do'. However, this '하다' is not an independent verb. This '하다' is a suffix which is attached to a noun and makes it act like a verb.

듯해 = [pronunciation] 듣해 → 드태 = familiar ending of 듯하다

쥐고 있는 듯하다 = [pronunciation] 쥐고 인는 듣타다 = seems to be holding / looks like holding / parece que estamos tomando

같은 카드를 쥐고 있는 듯해. = We seem to be holding the same type of cards. / It seems to me that we are holding the same sort of cards.

Parece que estamos tomando el mismo tipo de cartas /
Me parece que tenemos el mismo tipo de cartas.

● If players hold the same type of cards, no one can win.

그러하다 = 그렇다 [그러타] = [infinitive of adjective] be (like) such / be like that / ser así / ser como tal

그러하다면 = **그렇다면** [그러타면] = an adverb-type conjugation of 그렇다 = in that case / if it is the case / if so / en ese caso / si es el caso / si así es

뭐 = [interjection] well / uh / bueno

그렇다면, 뭐 … = in that case, well … / if it is the case, then … / if so, well / en ese caso, bueno .., / si es el caso, bueno … / entonces, bueno …

< Line 9 > All right. 반복된 시소 게임, 이제서야 끝을 내보려 해.

All right! = ¡Vale!

반복된 시소 게임 = (This) repeated seesaw game / (Este) repetido juego de balancín

이제 = [noun, also used as adverb] now / the current moment / at this time / ahora /
en este momento

이제서야 = 이제 + 서야 [emphasis] now at last / eventually now / ahora por fin /
eventualmente ahora

끝을 = [pronunciation] 끄틀 → 끄츨 = 끝 (the end, closing, el final) + 을 [marker for object]

내다 = [infinitive of verb] exert / gather / muster / manifest / display / put out / ejercitar /
mostrar / sacar / extraer

끝을 내다 = [verb phrase] finish / finalize / terminate / complete / finalizar / terminar /
completar

끝을 내보려 하다 = intend to finish / get an intention to finalize / be considering termination /
tener [obtener] la intención de finalizar / está considerando la terminación

끝을 **내보려 해** = familiar ending of 끝을 내보려 하다

이제서야 끝을 내보려 해. = Eventually now, I intend to finish it. /
Ahora por fin, tengo la intención de terminarlo.

< Line 10 > All right. 지겨운 시소 게임, 누군간 여기서 내려야 돼. 할 순 없지만 ...

지겹다 = [verb] feel tedious [sick of, tiresome, wearisome, fed up] /
sentirse tedioso [harto, saciado / cansado]

지겨운 = ajective form of 지겹다 = tedious / sick of / tiresome / wearisome / tedioso /
harto / saciado / cansado

시소 게임 = [noun phrase] seesaw game / juego de balancín

지겨운 시소 게임 = (This) tedious seesaw game / (Este) cansado juego de balancín

누구인가는 = 누군가는 = **누군간** = 누구 (someone, alguien) + 인가 + 는 [marker for
subject] = someone whoever he is / anyone among us / alguien quien que sea /
alguien entre nosotros [ellos]

● «이다 (be, ser)» is the only marker that conjugates. «인가» is a noun form of «이다» for
uncertainty. «누구인가» indicates someone who is uncertain or undesignated.

여기 = [pronoun, also used as adverb] this spot / this place / here / now / esto / este lugar /
aquí / ahora

여기서 = 여기 + (에)서 [from, out of, desde, fuera de] = out of here / fuera de aquí

내리다 = [infinitive of verb] get off / get down / dismount / go out of / bajar / salir

내려야 = a noun-type conjugation of 내리다

(해야) 되다 = [infinitive of verb with another verb] have to (do) / should (do) / tener que (hacer) / deber (hacer)

되어 = 돼 = familiar ending of 되다

내려야 돼 = should do dismounting / should dismount / have to get off / tiene que bajar / deber salir

누군간 여기서 내려야 돼.
One of us us has to get off now. / Whoever it is, someone has to get off here.

Alguien entre nosotros tiene que bajarse ahora./
Quienquiera que sea, alguien tiene que salir aquí.

하다 = [infinitive of verb] do / act / make / hacer / realizar

할 = ajective form of 하다 = doing / to do / making / to make / haciendo

순 = 수 (way, method, manera, modo, means) + 는 [maker for subject]

● In Korean, the pronunciation of the first consonant just after '리' tends to become hard.
[할 수 → 할 쑤] [할 순 → 할 쑨]

있다 = [pronunciation] 읻다 → 읻따 = [infinitive of verb] there is / be / exist / stay / remain / stand / hay / estar / existir / quedarse / permanecer / pararse = [action]

없다 = [pronunciation] 업다 → 업따 = [infintive of adjective] there is no / not exist / be absent / be without / no hay / no existir / estar ausente / estar sin = [situation or status]

없지만 = [pronunciation] 업지만 → 업찌만 = although there is no / even though (it) does not exist / aunque no hay / a pesar de que no existe

할 수 있다 = [pronunciation] 할 쑤 읻따 = [verb phrase] can do / poder hacer = [action]

할 수 없다 = [pronunciation] 할 쑤 업따 = There is no means to do. / Hay no forma de hacerlo. = [situation or status]

● In Korean, a 'verb' means an action and an 'adjective' means a situation or status. In case of «없다 (no exist)», it is always an adjective. However, «있다 (be, exist, estar)» can be either a verb or an adjective.

- 그는 방에 없다. = He is not in the room. He is not to be found in the room. = [status]

- 그는 방에 있다. = He is in the room. He is staying in the room. = [action]

- 그는 자고 있다. = He is sleeping. = [action]

- 꽃이 피어 있다. = A flower has bloomed. It is in the status of being bloomed. = [status]

할 순 없지만 … = [pronunciation] 할 쑨 업찌만

Although there is no way to do it … / Although it is (almost) impossible … / Aunque no hay manera de hacerlo … / Aunque es (casi) imposible …

< Line 11 > 누가 내릴지 말진, 서로 눈치 말고.
그저 맘 가는대로, 질질 끌지 말고.

누가 = 누구 [pronun] + 가 = 누구 (who, which person, quién) + 가 [marker for subject]

내리다 = [infinitive of verb] get off / get down / dismount / go out of / bajar / salir

말다 = [verb] quit doing / refrain from doing / not do any longer / dejar de hacer / no hacer

● All the vowels and four consonants (ㄴ, ㄹ, ㅁ, ㅇ) are voiced sounds, which are soft. A consonant that is between any two of them becomes soft as well. Therefore, the above two words become soft. [내리다 → 내리다] [말다 → 말다]

● '지' was originally an independent word, whose meaning is «uncertainty», «probability» or «whether». Now it is combined with a verb for making a noun form.

● In Korean, the pronunciation of the first consonant after 'ㄹ' tends to become hard. [내릴지 = 내릴 + 지 → 내릴찌] [말지 = 말 + 지 → 말찌]

내릴지 말진 = [pronunciation] 내릴찌 말찐 = 내릴지 말지 (whether to get off or not, si se vaje or no) + 는 (about, regarding, concerning, sober, acerca de, conrespecto a)

누가 내릴지 말진 = About which one will get off, or not / Whether someone is to get off or not / Sobre quién va a irse o no / Si alguien debe bajarse o no

서로 = [adverb] each other / one another / reciprocally / (we) together / uno al otro / recíprocamente / (nosotros) juntos

눈치 = [noun] reading the face [countenance, mind] / lo leer la cara [mente, pensamiendo]

눈치보다 = [infinitive of verb] try to read the face [countenance] / try to read the mind / tratar leer la corazón / intentar adivinarlo en la cara [mente]

눈치보지 = [pronunciation] 눈치보지 = a noun-type conjugation of 눈치보다

● Here, «눈치보지» has nothing to do with the original noun '지' for «uncertainty», «probability» or «whether». [cf. 눈치볼지 (whether ~) = 눈치볼 + 지 → 눈치볼찌]

말다 = [verb] quit doing / refrain from doing / not do any longer / dejar de hacer / no hacer

말고. = familiar or poetic ending of 말다

● In Korean, the pronunciation of the first consonant just after '르' tends to become hard. However, this is not usually applicable within a word. [말다, 말고, 말지, 말게, 말도록]

눈치보지 말다 = Quit trying to read the mind. / Dejar de intentar leer la mente.

서로 눈치(보지) 말고. = Without attempts to read each other's mind! / ¡Sin intentos de leer la mente del otro!

● In Korean, if there is no intention of emphasis, an exclamation mark (!) can be omitted.

그저 = [adverb] just / only / simply / simplemente / solamente

맘 = 마음 = [noun] mind / heart / feelings / caring heart / mente / corazón

가다 = [infinitive of verb] go (away) / move away / ride / ir / irse / marchar / alejarse / llevarse

가는대로 = as it goes / as it leads us / como va / como nos guía

그저 맘 가는대로 = Just as the heart leads us / Simplemente como el corazón nos guía

질질 = [mimetic adverb] dragging / arrastrando

끌다 = [infinitive of verb] drag / pull / draw / procrastinate / arrastrar / procastinar / retrasar

질질 끌다 = drag with toil / procrastinate lengthy / keep postponing / arrastrar con esfuerzo / procrastinar largo / seguir posponiendo

질질 끌지 = [pronunciation] 질질 끌지 = a noun-type conjugation of 질질 끌다

● In Korean, the pronunciation of the first consonant just after '르' tends to become hard. However, this is not usually applicable within a word. [끌다, 끌고, 끌지, 끌게, 끌도록]

● Here, «끌지» has nothing to do with the original noun '지' for «uncertainty», «probability» or «whether».

말다 = [verb] quit doing / refrain from doing / not do any longer / dejar de hacer / no hacer

말고. = [pronunciation] 말고 = poetic ending of 말다 [ending conjugation]

질질 끌지 말고. = No further procrastination! / No more being indecisive! / ¡Sin más dilación / ¡No más procrastinación! / ¡No más ser indeciso!

● In Korean, if there is no intention of emphasis, an exclamation mark (!) can be omitted.

< Line 12 > 이젠 내릴지 말지, 끝을 내보자고!
반복되는 시소 게임, 이젠 그만 해!

이제 = [noun, also used as adverb] now / the current moment / at this time / ahora / en este momento

이젠 = 이제 (now, ahora) + 는 [marker for emphasis] = (on the contrary) now / now at last / eventually now / coming to now / (al contrario) ahora / ahora por fin / llegando a ahora

내리다 = [infinitive of verb] get off / get down / dismount / go out of / bajar / salir

말다 = [verb] quit doing / refrain from doing / not do any longer / dejar de hacer / no hacer

내릴지 말지 = [pronunciation] 내릴찌 말찌 = whether getting off or not / va a bajarse o no

● '지' was originally an independent word, whose meaning is «uncertainty», «probability» or «whether». Now it is combined with a verb for a noun-type conjugation.

● In Korean, the pronunciation of the first consonant after 'ㄹ' tends to become hard.
[내릴지 = 내릴 + 지 → 내릴찌] [말지 = 말 + 지 → 말찌]

끝을 = [pronunciation] 끄틀 → 끄츨 = 끝 (the end, closing, el final) + 을 [marker for object]

끝을 내(보)다 = [verb phrase] finish / finalize / terminate / complete / finalizar / terminar / completer

끝을 내보자! = familiar ending for persuasion of 끝을 내보다 = Let's finalize! / ¡Vamos a finalizar!

끝을 내보자고! = poetic ending of 끝을 내보자! = Let's finish up! / Let's finalize! / ¡Terminemos! / ¡Vamos a finalizar!

이젠 내릴지 말지, 끝을 내보자고!
Now at last, let's decide whether getting off, or not! Let's finalize! /
Ahora por fin, ¡decidamos si bajar o no! ¡Vamos a finalizar!

반복하다 = [infinitive of verb] repeat / reiterate / repetir / reiterar

반복하는 = present adjective form of 반복하다 = repeating / repitiendo

반복되다 = [infinitive of verb] be repeated / become repetaed / ser repetido

반복되는 = present adjective form of 반복되다 = being repeated / siendo repetido

시소 = [in Korean] 널 = [noun] seesaw / balancín

게임 = [in Korean] 경기 = [noun] game / juego

반복되는 시소 (시소) 게임 = seesaw game being repeated / juego de balancín siendo repetido

이젠 = 이제 (now, ahora) + 는 [marker for emphasis] = (on the contrary) now / now at last / eventually now / coming to now / (al contrario) ahora / ahora por fin / llegando a ahora

그만 = [adverb] no more / no further / no más

하다 = [infinitive of verb] do / act / make / hacer / realizar

그만 해! = familiar for imperative of 하다 = Quit it! / Stop it! / ¡Dejalo! / ¡Para!

반복되는 시소 게임, 이젠 그만 해! = This repeated seesaw game, stop it now! / Este repetitive juego de balancín. ¡Paremos ya!

< Line 13 > 사람이 참 간사하긴 하지! 한 명이 없음 다칠 걸 알면서(도)

사람이 = 사람 (person, human, persona, ser humano) + 이 [marker for subject]

참 = [adverb] really / truly / indeed / actually / realmente / verdaderamente / de hecho / en realidad

간사하다 = [infinitive of adjective] be shrewd [astute, cunning, clever] / ser astuto [taimado, avispado]

간사하기 = noun form of 간사하다

간사하긴 = 간사하기 + 는 [marker for subject]

사람이 참 간사하긴 = 사람인 참 간사하기는 = (The fact) that a man is indeed shrewd
Lo que un ser humano es realmente es realmente astuto

하다 = [infinitive of verb] do / act / make / they say that ~ / be correct / hacer / realizar / dicen que ~ / es correcto

하지 = soliloquy or familiar ending of 하다

사람이 참 간사하긴 하지!
It might be correct to say that a human being is indeed shrewd. /
How astute a human being can be! /

Podría ser correcto decir que un ser humano es realmente astuto. /
¡Que taimado puede ser el ser humano! /

한 명이 = 한 명 (one person, one player, una persona) + 이 [marker for subject]

없다 = [pronunciation] 업다 → 업따 = [infintive of adjective] there is no / not exist / be absent / be without / no hay / no existir / estar ausente / estar sin

없음 = [pronunciation] 업씀 = 없으면 = [pronunciation] 업쓰면 = if (one) is absent / if disappears / if (one) gets off / si no está ausente / si uno desaparece / si uno se baja

(상대방이) = 상대방 (the other person, the other player, el otro persona) + 이 [marker for subject]

다치다 = [infinitive of verb] get hurt / be injured / be wounded / ser herido / lastimarse

다칠 = (future) adjective form of 다치다 = getting to be hurt / becoming injured / llegando a ser herido / se lastimará

걸 = 것을 = 것 (the thing that ~, the fact that ~, el hecho que ~, lo que ~) + 을 [marker for object]

다칠 걸 = the fact that he will get hurt / el hecho de que va a salir lastimado

알다 = [infinitive of verb] know / be aware of / recognize / notice / saber / conocer / notar

알면서(도) = even though (we) know that ~ / in spite of knowing that ~ / aunque saber que ~ / a pesar de saber que ~

한 명이 없음 (상대방이) 다칠 걸 알면서(도)
Even though we know that if one player disappears, (the other) would get hurt /
A pesar de que sabemos que si uno salta primero, (el otro) se lastimará

< Line 14 > 서로 나쁜 새끼 되기 싫기에, 애매한 책임 전가의 연속에 Umm Umm

서로 = [adverb] each other / one another / reciprocally / together / uno al otro / recíprocamente / juntos

나쁘다 = [infinitive of adjective] be bad / be guilty / be wrong / ser malo / ser culpable

나빴던 = [pronunciation] 나빧던 → 나빤떤 = past tense of 나쁘다 = that was bad / que was guilty / que era malo / que fue culpable

나쁜 = present tense of 나쁘다 = bad / that is wicked / guilty / wrong / malo / que es culapble

나쁠 = (future) adjective form of 나쁘다 = that will be bad [guilty] / que será malo [culpable]

새끼 = 새끼 (guy, bloke, brat, chico, tipo) + 는 [marker for subect]

되다 = [infinitive of verb] become / turn into / volverse / convertirse / resultar / terminarse / hacerse / ser

되기 = noun form of 되다 = becoming / to become / turning into / ser lo

● «noun form» can be regarded as a noun, «adverb-form» can be regarded as an adverb, while «a noun-type conjuation» or «an adverb-type conjugation» is regarded as a verb.

되기(가) = 되기 [noun form] + 가 [marker for subject]

싫다 = [pronunciation] 실타 = be not likeable / does not appeal / no ser agradable / ser desagrable => dislike / hate / don't want (to) / disgustar / odiar

● When 'ㅎ' combines with a consonsant, the consonant becomes aspirated.

[ㄱ + ㅎ → ㅋ] [ㄷ + ㅎ → ㅌ] [ㅂ + ㅎ → ㅍ] [ㅈ + ㅎ → ㅊ]

[싫다 → 실 + ㅎ + 다 → 실타] [싫기에 → 실 + ㅎ + 기에 → 실키에]

되기(가) **싫기에,** = [pronunciation] 되기(가) 실키에
becoming so is not likeable, therefore / because getting to be so doesn't appeal to me / on the reason not wanting to become it

no quiere ser lo, por lo tano / porque no quiere convertirse en eso / sobre la razón de no querer ser lo, así

서로 나쁜 새낀 되기 싫기에, = Neither of us wants to be a bad guy to the other, thus / Because neither of us wanted to be a bad guy to the other,

Ninguno de los dos quiere ser un chico malo con el otro, por lo tanto / Porque ninguno de los dos quería ser un mal tipo para el otro,

애매하다 = [infinitive of adjective] be ambigous [noncommittal, vague, hesitant] / ser ambiguo [evasio, vago, vacilante]
애매한 = present form of 애매하다 = that is ambiguuous / noncommittal / vague / que es ambiguo / vago / vacilante
책임 = [noun] resposibility / liability / accountability / responsabilidad
전가 = [noun] imputation / imputación
책임 전가 = [noun phrase] buck-passsing / imputación de responsibilidad
책임 전가**의** = 책임 전가 + 의 [marker for possession] = [pronuication] 채김 전가에 = of buck-passing / de la imputación

● «의 [marker for possession]» is pronounced as «에». However, in case that it is a part of an independent word, it is pronounced as «의».

[정의 (justice)] [의미 (meaning)] [거의 (almost)]

연속에 = 연속 (continuity, repetition, continuidad, repetición) + 에 (with, by, con, por)

애매한 책임 전가의 연속에, Umm Umm
By continuously using the noncommittal buck-passing tactics, umm umm /
Por empleando continuamente las tácticas para la imputación ambigua, umm umm

< Line 15 > 지칠 만큼 지쳐서 되레 평행이 됐네. 이런 평행을 바란 건 아닌데 ...

지치다 = [infinitve of verb] grow tired / get exhausted / be fatigued /
estar cansado [exhausto] / cansarse

지칠 = adjective form of 지치다 = getting to be tired / becoming fatigued / llegando a estar
cansado / se volviendo exhausto

만큼 = [noun, also used as adverb] as much as / tanto como

지쳐서 = grew tired, and / because exhausted / as having been fatigued /
porque estamos cansados

지칠 만큼 지쳐서 = Because we become exahusted as much as we are / Being exhausted so
much, thus / Porque nos volvemos exhaustos tanto como estamos / Estando exhaustos tanto, así

되레 = 도리어 = [adverb] on the contrary / rather / instead / ironically / al contrario /
irónicamente / antes bien

평행이 = 평행 (equilibrium, parallel, balance, equilibrio, paralelismo) + 이 [marker for subject]

되다 = [infinitive of verb] become / turn into / volverse / convertirse / resultar / terminarse /
hacerse / ser

되었다 = [pronunciation] 되얻다 → 되얻따 = past tense of 되다 = became / has become /
turned into / se convirtió / se ha convertido = 됐다 = [pronunciation] 됃다 → 됃따

되었네 = **됐네** = [pronunciation] 됃네 → 됃네 = poetic ending of 됐다

되레 평행이 됐네. = on the contrary, (it) has become an equilibrium. /
ironnically, we've got an equilibrium between us. / al contrario, se ha convertido en un
equilibrio /irónicamente esto resultó en un equilibrio.

이런 = 이러한 = [determiner] such / this kind of / this type of / este tipo de

평행을 = 평행 (equilibrium, parallel, balance, equilibrio, paralelismo) + 을 [marker for object]

바라다 = [infinitive of verb] desire / expect / hope / want / wish / querer / desear

바라는 = present adjective form of 바라다 = desiring / expecting / wanting / queriendo /
deseando

바란 = past adjective form of 바라다 = that desired [expected, wanted] / que quise [deseaba]

건 = 것은 = 것 (the thing that ~, the fact that ~, la cosa que ~, el hecho que ~, lo que ~)
+ 은 [marker for subject]

바란 건 = The thing that (I) desired / what (I) wanted / lo que desaba

아니다 = [infinitive of adjective] be not / be no / be not correct / no ser / no ser correcto

아닌데 … = [familiar ending with discontent] actually (it) is not … / ya ves, no ser …

이런 평행을 바란 건 아닌데 … = Actually, what I wanted is not this kind of equilibrium … / Ya ves, lo que yo deseaba no es este tipo de equilibro …

< Line 16 > 처음에는 누가 더 무거운지 자랑하며 서롤 바라보며 웃지.
이제는 누가 무거운지를 두고 경쟁을 하게 되었네. 되레 싸움의 불씨.

처음에는 = 처음 (beginning, the start, principio) + 에는 (in, at) = in the beginning /
al prinicipio
누가 = 누구 [pronoun] + 가 = 누구 (who, which person, quién) + 가 [marker for subject]
더 = [adverb] more / further / additionally / más / adicionalmente
무겁다 = [pronunciation] 무겁따 = [infinitive of adjective] be heavy / be weighty /
ser pesado
더 무거운지 = noun form of 무겁다 = the issue who is heavier / being more weighty /
whether heavier or not / el problema quién pesa más / lo ser más pesado /
si sea más pesado o no

● '지' was originally an independent word, whose meaning is «uncertainty», «probability» or «whether». Now it is combined with a verb for making a noun form.

● This '지' does not become hard when it comes after 'ㄴ' instead of 'ㄹ'.
[무거운지 = 무거운 + 지 → 무거운지] [무거울지 = 무거울 + 지 → 무거울찌]

자랑 = [noun] brag / boasting / showing off / presunción / alarde
자랑하다 = [infinitive of verb] = brag / boast of / make a boast of / presumirse / alardear de
자랑하며 = an adverb-type conjugation of 자랑하다 = [simultaneous action] while bragging /
while making a boast of / mientras alardeando de

● an adverb-type conjugation combines with an intransitive verb to imply a simultaneous action or the aim of an action.

웃다 = [pronunciation] 욷다 → 욷따 = [infinitive of verb] laugh / grin / smile / reír / sonreír
자랑하며 웃다 = laugh while bragging / reímos mientras presumimos /
reímos mientras alardeamos

서로 = [adverb] each other / one another / reciprocally / (we) together /
uno al otro / recíprocamente / (nosotros) juntos
서롤 = 서로 + 를 [marker for object]

바라보다 = look / look at / see / view / watch / mirar / ver / observar

바라보며 = an adverb-type conjugation of 바라보다 = [simultaneous action] while looking (on) / while seeing [viewing] / mientras mirando [viendo]

웃다 = [pronunciation] 욷다 → 욷따 = [infinitive of verb] laugh / grin / smile / reír / sonreír

웃지 = [pronunciation] 욷지 → 욷찌 = familiar or poetic ending of 웃다

처음에는 누가 더 무거운지(를) 자랑하며 서롤 바라보며 웃지.
In the beginning, we used to laugh seeing each other while bragging who is heavier. /
Al principio, solíamos al vernos, mientras alardeábamos de quién era más pesado.

이제는 = 이제 (now, ahora) + 는 [marker for emphasis] = (on the contrary) now / now at last / eventually now / coming to now / (al contrario) ahora / ahora por fin / llegando a ahora

누가 = 누구 [pronoun] + 가 = 누구 (who, which person, quién) + 가 [marker for subject]

(더) = [adverb] more / further / aditionally / más / adicionalmente

무겁다 = [infinitive of adjective] be heavy / be weighty / ser pesado

(더) **무거운지를** = (더) 무거운지 + 를 [marker for object]
the issue who is heavier / being more weighty / whether heavier or not /
el problema quién pesa más / lo ser más pesado / si sea más pesado o no

두다 = [infinitive of verb] pull / place / set (forth) / take out / bring up / sacar / colocar (adelante) / traer

두고 = [sequential action] having set up, and / after taking out / by brining up / después de sacar

경쟁을 = 경쟁 (competition, competencia) + 을 [marker for object]

하다 = [infinitive of verb] do / act / make / hacer / realizar

경쟁을 하다 = vie with each other / compete / contend / competir / contender

하게 = an adverb-type conjugation of 하다

되다 = [infinitive of verb] become / turn into / volverse / convertirse / resultar / terminarse / hacerse / ser

하게 되다 = [infinitive of verb] become to do / get to do / venir a hacer / llegar a hacer

경쟁을 하게 되다 = become to compete / get to vie with / venir a [llegar a] competir

되었다 = [pronunciation] 되얻따 = past tense of 되다 = came to do / has become to do / venimos a hacer / llegamos a hacer

되었네 = [pronunciation] 되얻네 → 되언네 = 됐네 [댄네] = poetic ending of 되었다

이제는 누가 (더) 무거운지를 두고 경쟁하게 되었네.
Now we came to vie with each other by bringing up the issue of who is heavier. /
Now we have become to vie with each other about who is heavier.

Ahora llegamos a competir después de sacar el tema de quién es más pesado. /
Ahora nos hemos vuelto a competir el uno con el otro sobre quién pesa más.

되레 = 도리어 = [adverb] on the contrary / rather / instead / ironically / al contraio /
irónicamente / antes bien
● Many Korean speakers including BTS pronounce «되레» as «되려». That is not correct.

싸움의 = 싸움 (conflict, argument, feud, discusión) + 의 [marker for possession] = of conflict
불씨 = [noun] embers / cause / brasas / causa

되레 싸움의 불씨. = Ironically it has (rather) become the embers of our conflicts. /
Irónicamente se ha convertido (antes bien) en las brasas de nuestros conflictos.

< Line 17 > 누군가는 결국 이곳에서 내려야 끝이 날 듯하네.
가식 섞인 서롤 위하는 척 더는 말고. 이젠 결정해야 돼.

누구인가는 = **누군가는** = 누군간 = 누구 (someone, alguien) + 인가는 [marker for
uncertainty] = someone whoever he is / anyone among us / alguien quien que sea /
alguien entre nosotros [ellos]

● «이다 (be, ser)» is the only marker that conjugates. «인가» is a noun form for questioning
of «이다». «누구인가» indicates someone who is uncertain or undesignated.

결국 = [pronunciation] 결국 = [noun, also used as adverb] eventually / finally / at last /
in the end / al final / por fin

이곳 = [pronunciation] 이곧 = [pronoun] this place / this point / this spot / este lugar /
este punto
이곳에서 = [pronunciation] 이고세서 = 이곳 + 에서 (form, out of, de)

내리다 = [infinitive of verb] get off / get down / dismount / go out of / bajar / salir de
내려야 = only after getting off / only after going out of / sólo después de bajarse /
cuando dejar de

끝이 = [pronunciation] 끄티 → 끄치 = 끝 (the end, closing, el final) + 이 [marker for subject]

나다 = [infinitive of verb] come out / spring up / occur / producirse / brotarse / hacerse

끝이 나다 = come to an end / be over / be finished / llegar al fin / terminarse / acabar

끝이 날 = [adjective phrase] coming to an end / to be over / llegando al fin / yendo a terminar

듯 = [pronunciation] 듣 = [noun] possibility / probability / posbilidad / probabilidad

듯하다 = [pronunciation] 듣하다 → 드타다 = [adjective phrase] it seems that / it looks like / it appears / parece que / verse quizá

● The independent verb '하다' means 'do'. However, this '하다' is not an independent verb. This '하다' is a suffix which is attached to a noun and makes it act like a verb.

듯해 = [pronunciation] 듣해 → 드태 = familiar ending of 듯하다

듯하네 = [pronunciation] 듣하네 → 드타네 = familiar ending of 듯하다

끝이 날 듯하다 = [pronunciation] 끄티 날 뜯하다 → 끄치 날 뜨타다 = It seems like to end. / Parece que v a terminar.

● In Korean, the pronunciation of the first consonant just after 'ㄹ' tends to become hard. This rule applies only between two independent pure Korean words.

끝이 날 듯하네 = [pronunciation] 끄치 날 뜨타네 = poetic ending of 끝이 날 듯 하다

누군가는 결국 이곳에서 내려야 끝이 날 듯하네.
It looks like to be over finally only after someone goes out of this (seesaw). /
This situation might end only when one of us gets off (of the seesaw).

Parece que finalmente terminará sólo después de que alguien salga (de este balancín). /
Esta situación quizá acabará solamente cuando uno de los dos se baja (del balancín).

가식 = [noun] pretence / hypocracy / afectación / hipocresía

섞다 = [pronunciaton] 석다 → 석따 = [infintive of verb] mix / blend / combine / mezclar

섞인 = [pronunciation] 서낀 = adjective form of 섞다 = mixed / blended / combined / mezclado

서로 = [adverb] each other / one another / reciprocally / together / uno al otro / recíprocamente / juntos

서롤 = 서로 + 를 [marker for object]

위하다 = [infinitive of verb] do for the good of / do in behalf of / care for / hacer por el bien de / hacer para / cuidar de

위하는 = adjective form of 위하다 = doing for the good of / caring for / cuidando / haciendo para

척 = [noun] action with pretence / faking action / acción con afectación / acción fingida

더 = [adverb] more / further / additionally / más / adicionalmente

더는 = 더 + 는 [marker for emphasis] = not any longer / ya no más

말다 = [verb] quit doing / refrain from doing / not do any longer / dejar de hacer / no hacer

말고 = familiar or poetic ending of 말다

더는 말고 … = [poetic ending] not doing any longer / doing no more / no hacer más

가식 섞인 서롤 위하는 척 더는 말고 …
No further faking actions mixed with hypocracy pretending to care for each other … /
Ya no más acciones fingidas mezcladas con hipocresía pretendiendo que nos amamos …

이젠 = 이제는 = 이제 (now, ahora) + 는 [marker for emphasis] = (on the contrary) now / now at last / eventually now / coming to now / (al contrario) ahora / ahora por fin / llegando a ahora

결정 = [pronunciation] 결쩡 = [noun] decision / determination / decisión / determinación

결정하다 = [infitive of verb] decide / determine / make a decision / conclude / decidir

되다 = [infinitive of verb] have to / must / should / deber / tener que

돼 = 되어 = familiar ending of 되다

결정하게 돼 = come to decide / get to a decision-making / venimos a dedicir / llegar a decidir

결정해야 돼 = have to decide / should make a decision / deber decider / tenemos que dedicir

이젠 결정해야 돼 = And now, (we) have to make a decision. / Y ahora, es el momento de decidir.

< Line 18 > 서로 마음이 없다면, 서로 생각 안 했다면, ay 우리가 이리도 질질 끌었을까?

서로 = [adverb] each other / one another / reciprocally / together / uno al otro / recíprocamente / juntos

마음이 = 마음 (mind, heart, feelings, caring heart, mente, corazón) + 이 [marker for subject]

없다 = [pronunciation] 업다 → 업따 = [infintive of adjective] there is no / not exist / be absent / be without / no hay / no existir / estar ausente / estar sin

없다면 = if absent / if there is no / if don't have / if do without / si no estár / si no tener

서로 마음이 없다면 = If we are not laking of caring heart for each other /
Si no tenemos corazón el uno para el otro / Si no nos cuidamos

생각(을) = 생각 (thought, consideration, pensamiento, consideración) + 을 [marker for oject]

아니 = 안 = [adverb] not / be not / do not / no / no ser / no hacer

하다 = [infinitive of verb] do / act / make / hacer / realizar

생각 안 하다 = do not think / do not consider / no pensar / no nos preocupamos

생각 안 했다 = [pronunciation] 생각 안 핻따 = past tense of 생각 안 하다 = did not think /
have not thought [considered] / no pensábamos / no ha habido consideraciones

생각 안 했다면 = if did not think / if have not thought / si no pensábamos / si no nos
preocupamos / si no ha habido consideraciones

서로 생각 안 했다면 = if we did not think enough for each other, /
if there have not been enough considerations for each other,

si no nos preocupamos lo suficiente el uno para el otro, /
si no ha habido suficientes consideraciones el uno para el otro,

우리가 = 우리 (we, nosotros) + 가 [marker for subject]

이러하다 = [infinitive of adjective] be like this [this way, as follows] /
ser así [éste, la siguiente]

이러하게 = adverb form of 이러하다 = 이렇게 [이러케] = 이리 = so / like this /
like such / como éste / como tal

이러하게도 = 이렇게 +도 [marker for emphasisi] = **이리도** = stronger expression

than 이리 = as much as like this / tan mucho como éste

질질 = [mimetic adverb] dragging / arrastrando

끌다 = [infinitive of verb] drag / pull / draw / procrastinate / arrastrar / procastinar

질질 끌다 = drag with toil / procrastinate lengthy / keep postponing / restrasar continuamente /
procrastinar largo / seguir posponiendo

질질 끌었다 = past tense of 질질 끌다

질질 끌었을까? = [questioning] Did we procrastinate? / Did we drag? /
¿Procrastinamos? / ¿Nos retrasamos contiuamente?

우리가 이리도 질질 끌었을까?

Did we procrastinate (our decision) like this? /
¿Procrastinábamos (nuestra decisión) durante tanto tiempo?

< Line 19 > 이제 마음이 없다면, 이 시소 위는 위험해, 위험해.
내 생각 더는 말고!

이제 = [noun, also used as adverb] now / the current moment / at this time / ahora /
en este momento

마음이 = 마음 (mind, heart, feelings, caring heart, mente, corazón) + 이 [marker for subject]

없다 = [pronunciation] 업다 → 업따 = [infintive of adjective] there is no / not exist /
be absent / be without / no hay / no existir / estar ausente / estar sin

없다면 = [pronunciation] 업다면 → 업따면 = if there is no / if not exist / is be absent /
if be without / si no hay / si no existir / si no estar / si estar sin

이제 마음이 없다면, = Now, if there are no caring hearts (between us), /
Ahora, si no hay corazón cariñoso (entre nosotros),

이 = [determiner] this / these / este / estos

시소 = [in Korean]널 = [noun] seesaw / balancín

위는 = 위 (the top, the upper side, la cima, la parte superior) + 는 [marker for subject]

위험하다 = [infinitive of verb] be dangerous / be risky / be perilous / ser peligroso

위험해 = familiar ending of 위험하다

이 시소 위는 위험해, 위험해 = The top of this seesaw is dangerours, dangerous /
La cima de este balancín es peligrosa, peligrosa.

내 = 나 (I, yo) + 의 [marker for possession] = my / mi

생각 = [noun] thought, consideration, pensamiento, consideración

더는 = [adverb phrase] 더 (more, más) + 는 [marker for emphasis]

• «더는» is not negative as it is, but one can expect that a negative word would come along.

말다 = [verb] quit doing / refrain from doing / not do any longer / dejar de hacer / no hacer

말고 = familiar or poetic ending of 말다

생각(하지) 말다 = stop thinking / quit considering / deja de pensar / deja de considerar

내 생각 더는 말고.
I should stop thinking (of other things). / No more considerations for myself! /
Debería dejar de pensar (en otras cosas). / ¡No más consideraciones para mí mismo!

● The above original Korean line can be translated either way. Please pick up your preference.

< Line 9 > All right. 반복된 시소 게임, 이제서야 끝을 내보려 해.

반복된 시소 게임,
(This) repeated seesaw game /
(Este) repetido juego de balancín

이제서야 끝을 내보려 해.
Eventually now, I intend to finish it. /
Ahora por fin, tengo la intención de terminarlo.

< Line 10 > All right. 지겨운 시소 게임, 누군간 여기서 내려야 돼. 할 순 없지만 ...

지겨운 시소 게임,
(This) tedious seesaw game /
(Este) cansado juego de balancín

누군간 여기서 내려야 돼.
Someone between us has to get down now. /
Alguien entre nosotros tiene que bajarse ahora.

할 순 없지만 ... = [pronunciation] 할 쑨 업찌만
Although there is no way to do it ... / Although it is (almost) impossible ... /
Aunque no hay manera de hacerlo ... / Aunque es (casi) imposible ...

< Line 20 > (Hol' up, Hol' up) 네가 없는 이 시소 위를 걸어, 네가 없던 처음의 그 때처럼. 네가 없는 이 시소 위를 걸어. 네가 없는 이 시소에서 내려.

네가 = 너 (you, tú) + 이가 [marker for subject]

● Many Korean speakers including BTS pronounce «네가» as «니가». That is not correct.

없다 = [pronunciation] 업다 → 업따 = [infintive of adjective] there is no / not exist /
be absent / be without / no hay / no existir / estar ausente / estar sin
없는 = [pronunciation] 업는 → 엄는 = present tense of 없다

이 = [determiner] this / these / este / estos
시소 = [in Korean] 널 = [noun] seesaw / balancín

네가 없는 이 시소 = this seesaw on which you don't exist / este balancín en el que no existes

위 = [noun] the top / the upper side / la cima / la parte superior

위를 = 위 (the top) + 를 [marker for object]

걷다 = [pronunciation] 걷따 = [infinitive of verb] walk / tread / tramp / hike / caminar / pisar / vagar

걸어 = [pronunciation] 거러 = familiar or poetic ending of 걷다

네가 없는 이 시소 위를 걸어.
I walk on this seesaw where you don't exist. /
Camino en este balancín donde tú no existes.

네가 = 너 (you, tú) + 이가 [marker for subject]

없다 = [pronunciation] 업다 → 업따 = [infintive of adjective] there is no / not exist / be absent / be without / no hay / no existir / estar ausente / estar sin

없는 = [pronunciation] 업는 → 엄는 = present tense of 없다

없던 = [pronunciation] 업떤 = past tense of 없다

처음의 = [pronunciation] 처음에 → 처으메 = 처음 (beginning, previous, original, inicio, anterior) + 의 [marker for possession]

그 = [determiner] the / that / those / ese / esos / tal

때 = [noun] time / days / occasion / moment / when / tiempo / época / ocasión / momento / cuando

처럼 = [adverb] like / as if / as / como

네가 없던 처음의 그 때처럼.
Like during the original days when you didn't exist beside me. /
Like those old days that I didn't know you yet.

Como en los tiempos originales cuando no existías a mi lado. /
Parecidas esos viejos tiempos que aún no te conocía.

이 시소에서 = 이 (this) + 시소 (seesaw, balancín) + 에서 (from, out of, de)

내리다 = [infinitive of verb] get off / get down / dismount / go out of / bajar / salir

내려 = familiar or poetic ending of 내리다

네가 없는 이 시소에서 내려. = I get off of the seesaw that you have already left. /
Me bajo del balancín que ya te has ido.

< Line 9 > All right. 반복된 시소 게임, 이제서야 끝을 내보려 해.

(This) repeated seesaw game /
(Este) repetido juego de balancín

Eventually now, I intend to finish it. /
Ahora por fin, tengo la intención de terminarlo.

< Line 10 > All right. 지겨운 시소 게임, 누군간 여기서 내려야 돼. 할 순 없지만 …

(This) tedious seesaw game /
(Este) cansado juego de balancín

Someone between us has to get down now. /
Alguien entre nosotros tiene que bajarse ahora.

Although there is no way to do it … /
Aunque no haya modo de hacerlo …

< Line 11 > 누가 내릴지 말진, 서로 눈치 말고.
그저 맘 가는대로, 질질 끌지 말고.

About which one will get off, or not /
Sobre quién va a irse o no

Without attempts to read each other's mind /
No intentemos adivinarlo en nuestras mentes

Just as the heart leads us /
Simplemente como el corazón nos guía

No more procrastination! /
¡Sin más dilación!

< Line 12 > 이젠 내릴지 말지, 끝을 내보자고! 반복되는 시소 게임, 이젠 그만 해!

Whether getting off or not / Va a irse o no

Now at last, let's decide whether getting off, or not! /
Ahora por fin, ¡decidamos is bajar o no!

This repeated seesaw game, stop it now! /
Este repetitive juego de balancín. ¡Paremos ya!

< Line 20 > (Hol' up, Hol' up) 네가 없는 이 시소 위를 걸어, 네가 없던 처음의 그 때처럼. 네가 없는 이 시소 위를 걸어. 네가 없는 이 시소에서 내려.

I walk by myself on this seesaw like at that time when I didn't know you. /
Camino solo en este balancín como en los tiempos originales en que no te conocía.

I walk by myself on this seesaw. /
Camino solo en este balancín.

I get out of the seesaw that you have already left. /
Me bajo del balancín que ya te has ido.

4. Singularity

Artist: V of BTS
Lyric Writers: Charlie J. Perry, RM

< Line 1 > 무언가 깨지는 소리(에), 난 문득 잠에서 깨.

무엇인가 = **무언가** = 뭔가 = 무엇 (what, something, qué, algo) + 인가 [marker for uncertain subject]

● «이다 (be, ser)» is the only marker that conjugates. «인가» is a noun form of «이다» for uncertainty. «무엇인가» indicates someone who is uncertain or undesignated.

무언가(가) = something that is undesignated / something uncertain /
algo que no está designado / algo incierto

깨다 = [infinitive of verb] break / crack / romper / fracturar

깨지다 = [infinitive of verb] be broken / be cracked / se romper / ser fracturado

깨지는 = present adjective form of 깨지다 = that is being cracked / que se rompe /
siendo fracturado

깨진 = past adjective form of 깨지다 = that was broken / que está roto /
que está rompido [fracturado]

소리(에) = 소리 (sound, noise, sonido) + 에 (at, by, to, por, a)

무언가 깨지는 소리(에) = To the sound that something is being broken /
Al sonido de que algo se rompe

난 = 나는 = 나 (I, yo) + 는 [marker for subject]

문득 = [pronunication] 문득 = [adverb] abruptly / suddenly / unexpectedly /
abruptamente / de repente

● In principle, '문득' is the correct pronunciation, because 'ㄷ' is located between

two voiced sounds 'ㄴ' and 'ㅡ'. However, for an emphasis, the word can be pronounced

as [문뜩].

잠에서 = [pronunciation] 자메서 = 잠 (sleep, nap, slumber, sueño) + 에서 (from, out of,
de, desde)

깨다 = [infinitive of verb] wake / awaken / sober up / get sober / despertarse

깨 = familiar or poetic ending of 깨다.

난 문득 잠에서 깨. = I wake up abruptly out of sleep. /
Me despierto abruptamente del sueño.

< Line 2 > 낯설음 가득한 소리. 귀를 막아보지만, 잠에 들지 못해.

낯설다 = [pronunciation] 낟썰다 = [infinitive of verb] = be unfarmiliar / be strange /
be unknown / ser extraño / ser desconocido
낯설음 = [pronunciation] 낟써름 = noun form of 낯설다 = unfamiliarity / strangeness /
discomfort / extrañeza / desconocimiento

가득하다 = [pronunciation] 가드카다 = [infinitive of adjective] be full of / be filled with /
be fully packed / estar lleno de
가득한 = [pronunciation] 가드칸 = present tense of 가득하다 = full of / filled with /
fully packed / lleno de

● When 'ㅎ' combines with a consonant, the consonant becomes aspirated.
[ㄱ + ㅎ → ㅋ] [ㄷ + ㅎ → ㅌ] [ㅂ + ㅎ → ㅍ] [ㅈ + ㅎ → ㅊ]

소리 = [noun] sound / noise / sonido

낯설음 가득한 소리. = [pronunciation] 낟써름 가드칸 소리
A sound that is full of unfamiliarity / Un sonido que está lleno de desconocimiento

귀를 = 귀 (ear, oreja) + 를 [marker for object]
막다 = [infinitive of verb] block / prevent / cover / stop / cerrar / cubrir / tapar
(해)보다 = [infinitive of verb] have a try / give a shot / attempt at / carry out / venture to /
probar / tratar / intentar / llevar a cabo / atreverse
막아 보다 = try to shut / attempt at clogging / tratar de cerrar / intentar tapar
막아 보지만 = try to shut, but / even though attempt at clogging / in spite of covering-up /
a pesar de cerrar, pero / aunque se tapar

귀를 막아 보지만 = although I cover my ears / aunque me tapo las orejas

잠에 = 잠 (sleep, nap, slumber, sueño) + 에 (in, into, en)

잠에 들다 = [verb phrase] fall into sleep / fall asleep / doze into slumber / quedarse dormido

잠에 들지 = a noun-type conjugation of 잠에 들다

하다 = [infinitive of verb] do / act / make / hacer / realizar

못하다 = [pronunciation] 몯하다 → 모타다 = [infinitive of verb] cannot do / fail to do / not succeed doing / no poder hacer

못해 = [pronunciation] 몯해 → 모태 = familiar or poetic ending of 못하다

잠에 들지 못해. = (I) cannot fall asleep. / No puedo quedarme dormido.

< Line 3 > 목이 자꾸 아파 와(서), 감싸보려 하지만, 나에겐 목소리가 없어.

목이 = 목 (neck, throat, cuello, garganta) + 이 [marker for subject]

자꾸 = [adverb] again and again / more and more / repeatedly / a menudo / cada vez más

아프다 = [infinitive of adjective] hurt / be ill [sick, painful, sore, hurting] / torment / doler / ser doloroso / estar enfermo [dolorido, herido] / atormentar

오다 = [infinitive of verb] come / come to / approach / arrive / venir / venir a / acercarse / llegar (a)

아파 오다 = [verb phrase] become painful / get to be sick / volverse doloroso / enfermarse

아파 와(서) = becoming painful, so / because getting sick, / volviéndose doloroso, entonces / porque enfermando,

목이 자꾸 아파 와(서), = The neck is getting more and more painful, thus / El cuello se vuelve cada vez más doloroso, así

감싸다 = [infinitive of verb] wrap / hold around / cover up / envolver

(해)보다 = [infinitive of verb] have a try / give a shot / attempt to / carry out / venture to / probar / tratar / intentar / llevar a cabo / atreverse

감싸보려 하다 = [verb phrase] attempt to wrap / try to carry out covering / intentar envolver

감싸보려 하지만, = (I) attempt to wrap, but / Although (I) try to carry out covering / Intento envolver, pero / A pesar de que estoy tratando de envolver

나에겐 = 나 + 에게는 = 나 (I, yo) + 에게는 (to, for) = to me / for me / para mí

목소리가 = 목소리 (voice, voz) + 가 [marker for subject]

없다 = [pronunciation] 업다 → 업따 = [infintive of adjective] there is no / not exist / be absent / be without / no hay / no existir / estar ausente / estar sin

없어 = [pronunciation] 업써 = familiar ending of 없다

나에겐 목소리가 없어.

There is no voice to me. / I lost my voice. / No hay voz para mí. / Yo perdí la voz.

< Line 4 > 오늘도 그 소릴 들어.

오늘도 = 오늘 (today, hoy) + 도 [marker for repetition] (also, as well, too, también, tampoco, y además)

그 = [determiner] the / that / those / ese / esos / tal

소릴 = 소리 + 를 = 소리 (sound, sonido) + 를 [marker for object]

듣다 = [pronunciation] 듣따 = [infinitive of verb] hear / listen to / oír / escuchar

들어 = fam or poetic ending of 듣다

오늘도 그 소릴 들어. = Today also, I hear the sound. / Hoy también, escucho el sonido.

< Line 5 > 또 울리고 있어, 그 소리가.

또 = [adverb] again / still / even now / moreover / otra vez / todavía / incluso ahora / de nuevo

울리다 = [infinitive of verb] (re)sound / resonate / ring / reverberate / (re)sonar / reververar

울리고 = an adverb-type conjugation of 울리다

● an adverb-type conjugation combines with an intransitive verb to imply a simultaneous action or the object of an action.

있다 = [pronunciation] 읻다 → 읻따 = [infinitive of verb] there is / be / exist / stay / remain / stand / hay / estar / existir / quedarse / permanecer / pararse

울리고 있다 = [simultaneous action] be reverberating / be ringing / be being heard / estar reverberando / estar sonando / ser escuchado

● The simultaneous action with the verb «있다» can be also the present progressive tense.

울리고 있어 = [pronunciation] 울리고 이써 = familiar ending of 울리고 있다 = is reverberating / is ringing / is being heard / está reverberando / está sonando / es escuchado

그 = [determiner] the / that / those / ese / esos / tal

소리가 = 소리 (sound, sonido) + 가 [marker for subject]

또 울리고 있어, 그 소리가. = (Now) again reverberating, the sound is. / Incluso ahora, está resonando, ese sonido.

< Line 6 > 이 얼어붙은 호수에 또 금이 가.

이 = [determiner] this / these / este / estos

얼다 = [pronunciation] 얼다 = [infinitive of verb] freeze / congelarse

● All the vowels and four consonants (ㄴ, ㄹ, ㅁ, ㅇ) are voiced sounds, which are soft. A consonant that is between any two of them becomes soft as well. The abovee ㄷ of '다' is located between two soft sounds which are ㄹ and ㅏ. So, this ㄷ becomes soft. Because of that, the word is pronounced as «얼다», not «얼따».

얼어붙다 = [pronunciation] 어러붇따 = stronger expression than 얼다

얼어붙은 = [pronunciation] 어러부튼 = past adjective form of 얼어붙다 = that was frozen / frozen / que estaba congelado / congelado

호수에 = 호수 (lake, lago) + 에 (on, at, sobre, en) = on the lake / en el lago

또 = [adverb] again / still / even now / moreover / otra vez / todavía / incluso ahora / de nuevo

금이 = 금 (crack, cleavage, grieta) + 이 [marker for subject]

금이 가다 = crack is formed / crack appears / crack turns out / se forma una grieta / aparecer una grieta

가 = familiar or poetic ending of 가다

이 얼어붙은 호수에 또 금이 가. = On this frozen lake another crack has appeared. / En este lago helado ha aparecido otra grieta.

< Line 7 > 그 호수에 내가 날 버렸잖아!

그 = [determiner] the / that / those / ese / esos / tal

호수에 = 호수 (lake, lago) + 에 (on, into, en) = into the lake / en el lago

내가 = 나 + 이가 = 나 (I, yo) + 이가 [marker for subject]

날 = 나를 = 나 (I, yo) + 를 [marker for object] = me

버리다 = [infinitive of verb] abandon / throw away / dump / discard / abandonar / descartar / lanzar

버렸다 = [pronunciation] 버렫다 → 버렫따 = past tense of 버리다 = abandoned / threw away / dumped / discarded / abandoné / descarté / lancé

버렸지 = [pronunciation] 버렫찌 = a noun-type conjugation of 버렸다

하다 = [infinitive of verb] do / act / make / hacer / realizar

아니 하다 = 안 하다 = 않다 = [pronunciation] 안타 = not do / no hacer

않아? = [pronunciation] 안아 → 아나? = familiar ending of 않다 = I did, didn't I ? / hice, ¿no?

버렸지 않아? = **버렸잖아!** = [pronunciation] 버렫짜나! = [tag questioning] You see, I (already) abandoned [dumped], didn't I? / Verás, ya abandoné [descarté, lancé], ¿no?

그 호수에 내가 날 버렸잖아!.
You see, in fact I (already) abandoned myself in the lake, didn't I? /
Verás, de hecho yo (ya) me abandoné en el lago, ¿no?

● This is an emphasis rather than a question. So, there is no need to raise the tone at the end.

< Line 8 > 내 목소릴 널 위해 묻었잖아!

내 = 나의 = 나 (I, yo) + 의 [marker for possession] = of me / my / mi

목소릴 = 목소리를 = 목소리 (voice, voz) + 를 [marker for object]

널 = 너를 = 너 (you, tú) + 를 [marker for object] = you / te

위하다 = [infinitive of verb] do for the good of / do in behalf of / care for / hacer por el bien de / hacer parar / cuidar de
위하여 = **위해** = adverb form of 위하다 = for / for the benefit of / para / para el beneficio de

묻다 = [pronunciation] 묻따 = [infinitive of verb] bury / hide / inter / enterrar

묻었다 = [pronunciation] 무덛따 = past tense of 묻다 = buried / hid / interred / entierro

묻었지 = [pronunciation] 무덛찌 = a noun-type conjugation of 묻었다
● «noun form» can be regarded as a noun, «adverb-form» can be regarded as an adverb, while «a noun-type conjuation» or «an adverb-type conjugation» is regarded as a verb.

하다 = [infinitive of verb] do / act / make / hacer / realizar

아니 하다 = 안 하다 = 않다 = [pronunciation] 안타 = not do / no hacer

않아? = [pronunciation] 안아 → 아나? = familiar ending of 않다 = I did, didn't I ? / hice, ¿no?

묻었지 않아? = **묻었잖아!** = [pronunciation] 무덛짜나! = [tag questioning] You see, I (already) buried, didn't I? / Verás, ya enterré, ¿no?

내 목소릴 널 위해 묻었잖아!
You see, in fact I (already) buried my voice for you, didn't I? /

Verás, de hecho (ya) enterré mi voz por ti, ¿no? /

● This is an emphasis rather than a question. So, there is no need to raise the tone at the end.

< Line 9 > 날 버린 겨울 호수 위로 두꺼운 얼음이 얼었네.

날 = 나를 = 나 (I, yo) + 를 [marker for object] = me

버리다 = [infinitive of verb] abandon / throw away / dump / discard / abandonar / descartar

버렸다 = [pronunciation] 버렫다 → 버럳따= past tense of 버리다 = abandoned / threw away / dumped / discarded / abandoné / descarté

버리는 = present adjective form of 버리다 = abandoning / throwing away / abandonando / que descarta

버린 = past adjective form of 버리다 = that have abandoned / that have dumped / that have discarded / que he abandonado / que he descartado

겨울 = [noun] winter / winter season / invierno

호수 = [noun] lake / lago

위로 – 위 (the top, the upper side, la cima, la parte superior) + 로 (on, above, sober)

두껍다 = [infinitive of adjective] be thick / be bulky / be massive

두꺼운 = present form of 두껍다 = thick / bulky / massive / espesco / grueso

얼음이 = 얼음 (ice) + 이 [marker for subject] = thick ice / hielo grueso

얼다 = [infinitive of verb] freeze / congelarse

얼었다 = [pronunciation] 어럳따 = past tense of 얼다 = froze / has frozen / se congeló

얼었네 = [pronunciation] 어런네 = poetic ending of 얼었다

날 버린 겨울 호수 위로 두꺼운 얼음이 얼었네.
A thick ice was formed on the lake in which I abandoned myself. /
Se formó un hielo espeso en el lago en el que me abandoné.

< Line 10 > 잠시 들어간 꿈 속에도 나를 괴롭히는 환상통은 여전해.

잠시 = [noun, also used as adverb] moment / instant / for a short while / temporarily / momento / instante/ por un rato / momentáneamente

들어가다 = [infinitive of verb] go into / go inside / enter (into) / entrar

들어가는 = present adjective form of 들어가다 = that go into / that (I) enter / que entro

들어간 = [pronunciation] 드러간 = past adjective form of 들어가다 = that went into / that (I) entered / que entré

꿈 = [noun] dream / vision / illusion / sueño / ilusión

속에도 = 속 (the inside, el interior, dentro) + 에 (in, en, a) + 도 [marker for emphasis] (even, as well, but also, not even, incluso, también, así como, ni siquiera)

잠시 들어간 꿈 속에도 = Even inside the dream in which (I) entered for a short while / Incluso dentro del sueño en el que (yo) entré por un rato

나를 = 나 (I, yo) + 를 [marker for object] = me

괴롭히다 = [pronunciation] 괴로피다 = [infinitive of verb] torment / torture / oppress / cause pain / atormentar

괴롭히는 = [pronunciation] 괴로피는 = ajective form of 괴롭히다 = tormenting / torturing / agonizing / atormentando

● When 'ㅎ' combines with a consonsant, the consonant becomes aspirated.

[ㄱ + ㅎ → ㅋ] [ㄷ + ㅎ → ㅌ] [ㅂ + ㅎ → ㅍ] [ㅈ + ㅎ → ㅊ]

환상통은 = 환상 (fantasy, phantom, delusion, fantasía) + 통 (pain, symptom, agony, agonía, dolor) + 은 [marker for subject]

여전하다 = [infinitive of verb] be as usual / remain / unchange / have not diminished / the same as it was / no ha cambiado / no ha disminuido / lo mismo que era

여전해 = familiar ending of 여전하다

나를 괴롭히는 환상통은 여전해 = The phantom agony tormenting me has not diminished. / La agonía fantasma que me atormenta no ha disminuido.

< Line 11 > 나는 날 잃은 걸까? 아님, 널 얻은 걸까?

나는 = 나 (I, yo) + 는 [marker for subject]

날 = 나를 = 나 (I, yo) + 를 [marker for object] = me

잃다 = [pronunciation] 일타 = [infinitive of verb] lose / stray / miss / perder

잃은 = [pronunciation] 일은 → 이른 = past adjective form of 잃은 = lost / perdí

것이다 = 것 (the thing that ~, the fact that ~, el hecho que ~, lo que ~) + 이다 (be, ser)

걸까? = 것 + 일까? = soliloquy questioning form of 것이다 = Is it the thing that ~? / Is it that ~? / I wonder if ~ / ¿Es el hecho que ~? / ¿Es que ~? / Me pregunto si ~

나는 날 잃은 것 = the fact that I lost myself / el hecho de que me perdí

나는 날 잃은 걸까? = Is it (the fact) that I lost myself? / Did I lose myself? / ¿Es el hecho de que me perdí? / ¿Es que me perdí? / ¿Me perdí?

아니다 = [infinitive of adjective] be not / be no / be not correct / no ser / no ser correcto

아님, = 아니면 = adverb form of 아니다 = if not, / si no,

널 = 너를 = 너 (you, tú) + 를 [marker for object]

얻다 = [pronunciation] 얻따 = [infinitive of verb] gain / acquire / ganar / adquirir

얻은 = [pronunciation] 어든 = past adjctive form of 얻다 = that gained / that acquired / que gané / que adquirí

얻는 = [pronunciation] 언는 = present adjective form of 얻다 = gaining / that acquires / ganando / que adquiero

얻을 = [pronunciation] 어들 = (future) adjective form of 얻다 = that will acquire / que adquiriré

것이다 = 것 (the thing that ~, the fact that ~, el hecho que ~, lo que ~) + 이다 (be, ser)

걸까? = 것 + 일까? = soliloquy questioning form of 것이다 = Is it the thing that ~? / Is it that ~? / I wonder if ~ / ¿Es el hecho que ~? / ¿Es que ~? / Me pregunto si ~

아님, 널 얻은 걸까? = If not, is it that I gained you? / If not, did I gain you? / Si no, ¿es que te adquirí?

< Line 12 > 난 문득 호수로 달려가.

난 = 나는 = 나 (I, yo) + 는 [marker for subject]

문득 = [adverb] abruptly / suddenly / unexpectedly /abruptamente / de repente

● In principle, «문득» is the correct pronunciation, because 'ㄷ' is located between two soft sounds [or voiced sounds] 'ㄴ' and '—'. However, for an emphasis, one can pronounce it as 'ㄸ'. [문뜩]

호수로 = 호수 (the lake, the algo) + 로 (to, a) = to the lake, al lago

달려가다 = [infinitive of verb] run / dash / rush / corer / apresurarse

달려가 = familiar or poetic ending of 달려가다

난 문득 호수로 달려가. = I abruptly rush to the lake. / De repente me apresuro al lago.

< Line 13 > 오! 그 속에 내 얼굴 있어.

오! = [interjection] Oh!

그 = [determiner] the / that / those / ese / esos / tal

그 속에 = [pronunciation] 그 소게 = 그 + 속 (the inside, el interior) + 에 (in, en)
= in the inside / in it / there / en el interior / en el / ahí

내 = 나의 = 나 (I, yo) + 의 [marker for possession] = of me / my / mi

얼굴 = [noun] face / features / rostro / cara

있다 = [pronunciation] 읻다 → 읻따 = [infinitive of verb] there is / be / exist / stay / remain / stand / hay / estar / existir / quedarse / permanecer / pararse

있어 = [pronunciation] 이써 = familiar ending of 있다.

오! 그 속에 내 얼굴 있어 = Oh! There is my face in it. / ¡Oh! Ahí está mi cara.

< Line 14 > 부탁해. 아무 말도 하지 마!

부탁하다 = [pronunciation] 부타카다 = [infinitive of verb] request / make a request / ask / pedir / rogar
부탁해 = [pronunciation] 부타캐 = familiar ending of 부탁하다 = I request you. / I ask you. / Te pido. / Te ruego.

아무 = [determiner] (not) any / alguno / ningún

말도 = 말 (words, comment, saying, palabras) + 도 [marker for emphasis] (even, as well, but also, not even, incluso, también, así como, ni siquiera)

● «아무 말도» is not negative, but one can expect that a negative expression would come along.

하다 = [infinitive of verb] do / act / make / hacer / realizar
말다 = [verb] quit doing / refrain from doing / not do any longer / dejar de hacer / no hacer

● All the vowels and four consonants (ㄴ, ㄹ, ㅁ, ㅇ) are voiced sounds, which are soft. A consonant that is between any two of them becomes soft as well. The above ㄷ is located between two soft sounds which are ㄹ and ㅏ. So, this ㄷ becomes soft. Because of that, the word is pronounced as «말다», not «말따».

하지 마! = [familiar ending for imperative] Don't do it! / Quit doing! / ¡No lo hagas!

아무 말도 하지 마! = Don't even say a word! / ¡Ni siguiera digas una palabra!

< Line 15 > 입을 막으려 손을 뻗어 보지만 …

입을 = [pronunciation] 이블 = 입 (mouth, lips, boca, labios) + 을 [marker for object]

막다 = [pronunciation] 막따 = [infinitive of verb] block / prevent / cover up / stop /
cerrar / cubrir / tapar

막으려 = [pronunciation] 마그려 = in order to block / in order to prevent / for covering up /
para cubrir / para tapar

손을 = 손 (hand, mano) + 을 [marker for object]

뻗다 = [pronunciation] 뻗따 = [infinitive of verb] stretch / extend / reach out / extender

(해)보다 = [infinitive of verb] have a try / give a shot / attempt to / carry out / venture to /
probar / tratar / intentar / llevar a cabo / atreverse

뻗어 보다 = [pronunciation] 뻐더 보다 = [verb phrase] try to extend / attempt to extend /
intentar extender

뻗어 보지만 … = try to stretch, but … / although extend (in vain) … /
intentar extender, pero … / aunque extender (en vano) …

입을 막으로 손을 뻗어 보지만 …
Although (I) extend my hand in vain to prevent talking … /
Aunque extiendo la mano en vano para evitar hablar …

< Line 16 > 결국엔 언젠가 봄이 와(서), 얼음들은 녹아내려 흘러가 …

결국엔 = [pronunciation] 결구겐 = 결국에는 = 결국 (the end, fin) + 에는 (in, at) =
in the end / eventually / al final / por fin

언제 = [pronoun, also used as adverb] what day / someday / some time / when /
qué día / algún día / algún tiempo / cuando

언제인가 = **언젠가** = 언제 + 인가 [adverb for uncertain time] = (maybe) someday /
(tal vez) algún día

봄이 = [pronunciation] 보미 = 봄 (spring, springtime, primavera) + 이 [marker for subject]

오다 = [infinitive of verb] come / come to / approach / arrive / venir / venir a /
acercarse / llegar (a)

와(서) = come (around), so / arrive, thus / draw near, and / llegará, así / vendrá, entonces

결국엔 언젠가 봄이 와(서), = Eventually, (maybe) someday the spring time will come around,
thus / Al final, (tal vez) algún día llegará la primavera, así

얼음들은 = 얼음 (ice, hielo) + 들 [plural] + 은 [marker for subject]

녹다 =[pronunciation] 녹따 = [infinitive of verb] melt / thaw / derretir / descongelar

녹아내리다 = [pronunciation] 노가내리다 = [verb phrase] melt down / thaw down / derretirse / descongelarse

녹아내려 = melt down, and / thaw down, and / derretirse, y / descongelarse, y

흘러가다 = [infinitive of verb] flow away / pass by / fluir lejos / pasar a distancia

흘러가 ... = familiar or poetic ending of 흘러가다

얼음들은 녹아내려 흘러가 ... = Ices melt down, and flow away ... /
Los hielos se derriten, y fluyen lejos ...

< Line 17 > Tell me! 내 목소리가 가짜라면, 날 버리지 말았어야 했는지.

내 = 나의 = 나 (I, yo) + 의 [marker for possession] = of me / my / mi

목소리가 = 목소리 (voice, voz) + 가 [marker for subject]

가짜 = [noun] fake / bogus / sham / phony / falsedad / imitación

이다 = [infinitive of marker that conjugates] be / ser

가짜(이)다 = is fake / is bogus / is sham / is phony / ser falso

가짜(이)라면 = if (it) is fake / if (it) is sham / if (it) is phony / if (it) is not real / si ser falso

내 목소리가 가짜라면, = If my voice is fake, / Si mi voz es falsa,

날 = 나를 = 나 (I, yo) + 를 [marker for object] = me

버리다 = [infinitive of verb] abandon / throw away / dump / discard / abandonar / descartar

버리지 = a noun-type conjugation of 버리다

말다 = [verb] quit doing / refrain from doing / not do any longer / dejar de hacer / no hacer

버리지 말다 = quit abadoning / refrain from throwing away / not dump / dejar de abandoner / no deber tirar

● By doing a noun-type conjugation the first verb can serve as an object of the second verb.
[버리지 말다 = quit abandoning] Here, «버리지 (abandoning)» is the object of «말다 (quit)».

(해야) 하다 = [infinitive of verb] (should) do / (must) make / (debería) hacer / (deber) hacer

(해야) 하였다 = (해야) 했다 = [pronunciation] (해야) 핻따 = [past tense] should have done / must have made / debería haber hecho

버리지 말아야 한다 [present] = 버리지 (abandon) + 말아야 (not do) + 한다 (should do)
= [pronunciation] 버리지 마라야 한다 = shouldn't abandon / no debo abandoar
버리지 말았어야 했다 = [pronunciation] 버리지 마라써야 핻따 = [past tense] shouldn't
have abandoned / no debería haberse abandonado ...

버리지 말았어야 했는지 ... = [pronunciation] 버리지 마라써야 핸는지 =
whether (I) shouldn't have abandoned ... / si no debería haberse abandonado ...

● '지' was originally an independent word, whose meaning is «uncertainty», «probability» or
«whether». Now it is combined with a verb for making a noun form.

● This '지' does not become hard when it comes after 'ㄴ' instead of 'ㄹ'.
[했는지 = 했는 + 지 → 핸는 + 지 → 핸는지]

날 버리지 말았어야 했는지 ...
(Tell me) whether I shouldn't have abandoned myself ... /
(Dime) si no debería haberme abandonado ...

< Line 18 > Tell me! 고통조차 가짜라면, 그 때 내가 무얼해야 했는지.

고통 = [noun] pain / agony / anguish / suffering / distress / dolor / agonía / sufrimiento
조차 = [marker for emphasis] even / as well / but also / incluso / también / (ni) siquiera
고통조차 = even pain / agony as well / but also suffering / incluso el dolor

가짜(이)다 = is fake / is bogus / is sham / is phony / ser falso
가짜(이)라면 = if (it) is fake / if (it) is phony / if (it) is not real / si es falso / si no es real

고통조차 가짜라면, = If this pain is phony as well, / If even this pain is not real, /
Si este dolor también es falso / Si incluso este dolor no es real,

그 = [determiner] the / that / those / ese / esos / tal
때 = [noun] time / occasion / moment / when / tiempo / ocasión / momento / cuando
그 때 = [noun phrase] at that time / en ese tiempo
내가 = 나 + 이가 = 나 (I, yo) + 이가 [marker for subject]

무얼 = 무엇을 = 무엇 (what, something, qué, algo) + 을 [marker for object]
하다 = [infinitive of verb] do / act / make / hacer / realizar

하여야 한다 = 해야 한다 = present form of 해야 하다 = should do / must do / have to do / debería hacer / deber hacer / tengo que hacer

하여야 하였다 = 해야 했다 = [pronunciation] 해야 핻따 = past tense of 해야 하다 = should have done / had to do / debería haber hecho / tenía que hacer

= 하였어야 하였다 [하여써야 하엳따] = 했어야 했다 [해써야 핻따]

(말해 줘) = Tell me / Dime

했는지 = [pronunciation] 핸는지 → 핸는지 = noun form of 했다

● The second verb is not to be seen here. But actually «Tell me (말해 줘)» is the second verb.

● '지' was originally an independent word, whose meaning is «uncertainty», «probability» or «whether». Now it is combined with a verb for making a noun form.

● This '지' does not become hard when it comes after 'ㄴ' instead of 'ㄹ'.

[했는지 = 했는 + 지 → 핸는 + 지 → 핸는지]

무얼 해야 했는지 (말해 줘) = 무얼 했어야 했는지 (말해 줘) = (Tell me) what I should have done / (Tell me) whether I should have done something else … / (Dime) lo que debería haber hecho / (Dime) si debería haber hecho otra cosa …

● In principle, 했어야 했는지 [핸써야 핸는지] is more correct than 해야 했는지.

그 때 내가 무얼해야 했는지 …
(Tell me) what I should have done at that time … /
(Dime) qué debería haber hecho en ese tiempo …

● Someone interpereted that this song is about Kim Tae-Hyung who abandoned himself to be reborn as V, a renowned singer. And V will eventually return to the lake (= home) and conciliate with KIM Tae-Hyung when he retires, in other words, when spring comes back.

5. Mikrokosmos

Artist: *BTS*

Lyric Writers: *Matty Thomson,*
Max Lynedoch Graham, Marcus McCoan, Ryan Lawrie,
Camilla Anne Stewart, RM, Suga, J-Hope, Jordan "DJ Swivel" Young,
Candace Nicole Sosa, Melanie Fontana, Michel "Lindgren" Schulz

< Line 1 > 반짝이는 별빛들. 깜빡이는 불 켜진 건물.

반짝이다 = [pronunciation] 반짜기다 = [infinitive of verb] sparkle / glitter / twinkle / shine / brillar / resplandecer

반짝이는 = [pronunciation] 반짜기는 = present adjective form of 반짝이다 = sparkling / glittering / twinkling / brillante / resplandeciendo / iridiscente

별빛들 = [pronunciation] 별삗뜰 = 별 (star, estrella) + 빛 (light, luz) +들 [plural] = starlights / luces de estrellas

● 《별빛》 is a combination of two independent words which are '별 (star)' and '빛 (light)'. In this case, the first consonant of the second word becomes hard. Therefore, the pronunciation becomes 《별삗》 instead of 《별빋》.

반짝이는 별빛들 = Sparkling starlights / Luces de estrellas brillantes

깜빡이다 = [pronunciation] 깜빠기다 = [infinitive of verb] flicker / blink / parpadear / rutilar / titilar

깜빡이는 = [pronunciation] 깜빠기는 = adjective form of 깜빡이다 = flickering / blinking / parpadeando / rutilando

불 = [noun] light / fire / luz

켜다 = [infinitive of verb] turn on / light up with / switch on / put on / iluminar / alumbrar

켜지다 = be turned up / be lighted up / be switched on / ser iluminado / ser alumbrado

켜진 = adjective form of 켜지다 = turned up / lit up / switched up / iluminado / alumbrado / que está iluminado [alumbrado]

건물 = [noun] building / structure / tower / skyscraper / edificio

깜빡이는 불 켜진 건물 = Buildings that are lit up with flickering lights / Edificios (que están) iluminados con luces parpadeantes

67

< Line 2 > 우린 빛나고 있네. 각자의 방, 각자의 별에서.

우린 = 우리 [pronoun] + 는 = 우리 (we, nosotros) + 는 [marker for subject]

빛나다 = [pronunciation] 빋나다 → 빈나다 = [infinitive of verb] shine / glow / be bright / gleam / lucir / resplandecer

빛나고 = [pronunciation] 빋나고 → 빈나고 = an adverb-type conjugation of 빛나다

있다 = [pronunciation] 읻다 → 읻따 = [infinitive of verb] there is / be / exist / stay / remain / stand / hay / estar / existir / quedarse / permanecer / pararse

빛나고 있다 = [simultaneous action] be shining [glowing, bright] / estar luciendo [resplandeciendo]

● The simultaneous action with the verb «있다» can be also the present progressive tense.

빛나고 있네 = [pronunciation] 빋나고 읻네 → 빈나고 인네 = poetic ending of 빛나고 있다 = is shining [glowing, bright] / está luciendo [resplandeciendo]

우린 빛나고 있네. = [present progressive] We are shining. / Nosotras estamos luciendo.

각자의 = [pronunciation] 각짜에 = 각자 [noun] (each one, cada uno) + 의 [marker for possession] (of, de) = 각자+ 의= of each one / de cada uno

● «의 [marker for possession]» is pronounced as «에». However, in case that it is a part of an independent word, it is pronounced as «의».

[정의 (justice)] [의미 (meaning)] [거의 (almost)]

방 = [noun] room / chamber / habitación

별 = [noun] star / estrella

에서 = [marker for place] at / from / out of / de

각자의 방, 각자의 별에서 = [pronunciation] 각짜에 방, 각짜에 벼레서
from each one's room, and each one's star /
de la habitación de cada uno, y de la estrella de cada uno

< Line 3 > 어떤 빛은 야망, 어떤 빛은 방황.

어떠하다 = [infinitive of adjective] how it is / be such / be like / cómo es / ser así / ser como

어떠한 = **어떤** = present tense of 어떠하다 = a certain / some (kind of) / any (kind of) /

what type of / un cierto / algún (tipo de) / cualquier (tipo de) / qué clase de

빛은 = [pronunciation] 비츤 = 빛 (light, luz) + 은 [marker for subject]

야망 = [noun] ambition / aspiration / ambición

방황 = [noun] wandering / roaming / roving / vagabondage / vagabundeo

어떤 빛은 야망, 어떤 빛은 방황 = A certain light (is) ambition, another (is) vagabondage / Alguna luz (es) ambición, otra (es) vagabundeo

< Line 4 > 사람들의 불빛들. 모두 소중한 하나!

사람들의 = [pronunication] 사람들에 → 사람드레 = 사람 (person, human, persona, ser humano) + 들 [plural] + 의 (of, de) = of people / de la gente

불빛들 = [pronunciation] 불삘뜰 = 불 (fire, fuego) + 빛 (light, luz) + 들 [plural] = lights / luces

● When two independent words combine, the first consonant of the second word becomes strong. [불빛 = 불 + 빛 = 불빋 → 불삘]

● All the vowels and four consonants (ㄴ, ㄹ, ㅁ, ㅇ) are voiced sounds, which are soft. A consonant that is between any two of them becomes soft as well. [사람들 → 사람들] However, a consonant that is not between any two of them becomes hard (or fortis). [빛들 → 빋들 → 빋뜰]

사람들의 불빛들 = [pronunciation] 사람들에 불삘뜰
Lights of people / Luces de la gente

모두 = [adverb] all / the whole / all of us / all of them / every / todo(s) / cada

소중하다 = [infinitive of adjective] be precious / be valuable / be cherished / ser percioso

소중한 = present form of 소중하다 = precious / valuable / cherished / precioso

하나 = [noun] one(s) / uno(s)

모두 소중한 하나! = All of them (are) precious ones! / ¡Cada uno de ellas (es) preciosa!

< Line 5 > 어두운 밤! 외로워 마! 별처럼 다 우린 빛나!

어둡다 = [pronunciation] 어둡따 = [infinitive of adjective] be dark / be dim / be murky / ser oscuro

어두운 = present tense of 어둡다 = dark / dim / murky / oscuro

밤 = [noun] night / night-time / noche

어두운 밤! = Dark night! / ¡Noche oscura!

외롭다 = [pronunciation] 외롭따 = [infinitive of adjective] be lonely / be lonesome / be solitary / ser solitario / sentir solo

외로워 = a noun-type conjugation of 외롭다

(하다) = do / act / make / hacer / realizar

말다 = [verb] quit doing / refrain from doing / not do any longer / dejar de hacer / no hacer

(하지) 마! = familiar ending for imperative mode of 말다 = Don't do! / Quit (doing)! / ¡No (lo) hagas!

외로워 (하지) **마!** = Don't be lonely! / Don't feel lonesome! / ¡No te sientas solo!

별처럼 = 별 (star) + 처럼 (like, such as, como) = like stars / como estrellas

다 = [adverb] all / everything / everyone / totally / completely / todo(s) / totalmente / completamente

우린 = 우리 [pronoun] + 는 = 우리 (we, nosotros) + 는 [marker for subject]

빛나다 = [pronunciation] 빈나다 → 빈나다 = [infinitive of verb] shine / glow / be bright / gleam / brillar / lucir / resplandecer

빛나! = [pronunciation] 빈나! = familiar or poetic ending of 빛나다

별처럼 다 우린 빛나! = Like stars we all shine! / ¡Como estrellas todos brillamos!

< Line 6 > 사라지지 마! 큰 존재니까! Let us shine!

사라지다 = [infinitive of verb] disappear / vanish / go away / be gone / irse / desaparecerse

사라지지 = a noun-type conjugation of 사라지다

● Here, «사라지지» has nothing to do with the original noun '지' for «uncertainty», «probability» or «whether». [cf. 사라질지 (whether ~) = 사라질 + 지 → 사라질찌]

말다 = [verb] quit doing / refrain from doing / not do any longer / dejar de hacer / no hacer

마! = [familiar ending for imperative mode] Don't do! / Quit (doing)! / ¡No (lo) hagas!

사라지지 마! = Don't disappear! / Don't vanish! / Don't be gone! / ¡No desaparezcas! / ¡No te desvanezcas! / ¡No te vayas!

크다 = [infinitive of adjective] be big / be great / be grand / be important / ser grande / ser importante

큰 = present form of 크다 = big / great / grand / important / grande / importante

존재 = [noun] being / existence / figure / existencia / el ser

이다 = [infinitive of marker that conjugates] be / ser

이니까! = 니까! = because you are! / you see, it is! / ¡porque tú eres! / ¡ya ves, tú eres!

큰 존재니까! = Because (you) are an important figure! /
¡Porque eres una existencia importante!

< Line 7 > 어쩜 이 밤의 표정이 이토록 또 아름다운 건 ... 저 별들도 불빛도 아닌 우리 때문일 거야.

어쩜 = 어쩌면 = 어찌하면 = [adverb] maybe / perhaps / probably / quizá / tal vez / probablemente

이 = [determiner] this / these / este / estos

밤의 = [pronunciation] 밤에 → 바메 = 밤 (night, noche) + 의 [marker for possession] = of the night / de la noche

● «의 [marker for possession]» is pronounced as «에». However, in case that it is a part of an independent word, it is pronounced as «의».

[정의 (justice)] [의미 (meaning)] [거의 (almost)]

표정 = [noun] look / expression / feature / countenance / expresión facial / semblante / vista

표정이 = 표정 (look, vista) + 이 [marker for subject]

이토록 = [adverb] like this / this much / tan

또 = [adverb for emphasis] so / so much / even more / mucho más

아름답다 = [pronunciation] 아름답따 = [infinitive of adjective] be beautiful / be pretty / be lovely / ser bello / ser hermoso

아름답던 = [pronunciation] 아름답떤 = past form of 아름답다 = was beautiful / that was pretty / fue bello / que era hermoso

아름다운 = present form of 아름답다 = beautiful / that is pretty / lovely / bello / que es hermoso

아름다울 = (future) adjective form of 아름답다 = that will be beautiful / que será bello [hermoso]

건 = 것은 = 것 (the thing that ~, the fact that ~, la cosa que ~, el hecho que ~, lo que ~)
+ 은 [marker for subject]

아름다운 건 = 아름다운 것은 [아름다운 거슨]
the fact that is is this beautiful /the reason why it is beautiful /
el echo de que es tan hermoso / la razón por la que es hermoso

어쩜 이 밤의 표정이 또 이토록 아름다운 건 …
Maybe the reason why the look of this night is beautiful like this (is) … /
Quizás la razón por la que la vista de esta noche es tan hermosa (es) …

저 = [determiner] that / those / over there / aquel / allí

도 = [marker] (in positive) even, as well, also, too, incluso, también, tampoco, y además /
(in negative) neither, not even, ni, ni siquiera

별들도 = [pronunciation] 별들도 = 별 (star, estrella) + 들 [plural] + 도 [marker] (neither, ni)

● In Korean, the pronunciation of the first consonant just after 'ㄹ' tends to become hard. However, this does not apply to «들 [suffix for plural forms] » and «markers». That is why the pronunciation is '별들도', not '별뜰또'.

● This tendency that the first consonant just after 'ㄹ' becomes hard is not applicable «within a pure Korean word (not a Sino-Korean word)» including «verb and adjective conjugations».
[말다 (quit), 말고, 말지] [달다 (be sweet), 달고, 달지]

● «들 [suffix for plural forms]» and «Markers» are not regarded as an independent word. So, they are a part of a word. In other words, pronunciation-wise «별들도» is regarded as just one word.

불빛도 = [pronunciation] 불삗또 = 불 (fire, fuego) + 빛 (light, luz) + 도 [marker] (nor, ni)

● «불빛» is a combination of two independent words which are '불 (fire)' and '빛 (light)'. Therefore, the pronunciation of the combined word became «불삗» instead of «불빋».

● Pronunciation-wise, combined words are regarded as two independent pure Korean words. So, the first consonant of the second becomes hard. In case of vowels, a sound-linking (or liaison) is not allowed. [한여름 (mid-summer) → 한녀름, not 하녀름]

• In «불빛도», 'ㄷ' is located between ㅊ [which is prounnced as another hard and voiceless sound ㄷ] and ㅗ. So, the above ㄷ is pronounced hard as ㄸ. [불빛도 → 불삗도 → 불삗또]

아니다 = [infinitive of adjective] be not / be no / be not correct / no ser / no ser correcto

아닌 = an adverb-type conjugation of 아니다 = be not, but / be no, but / no ser, sino

우리 = [pronoun] we / nosotros

때문 = [noun] = cause / because of / owing to / porque / debido a / por

우리 때문 = because of us / owing to us / debido a nosotros / por nosotros

이다 = [infinitive of marker that conjugates] be / ser

일 = adjective form for speculation of 이다 = probably [maybe] be / tal vez [probablemente] es

것이다 = 것 (the thing that ~, the fact that ~, el hecho que ~, lo que ~) + 이다 (be, ser)

것이야 = **거야** = familiar ending of 것이다

일 거야 = [pronunciation] 일 꺼야 = Probably it is that ~ / The fact is that it maybe is ~ / Tal vez es que ~ / Es que probablemente es ~

• In Korean, the pronunciation of the first consonant just after 'ㄹ' tends to become hard. [일 거야 → 일 꺼야]

저 별들도 불빛도 아닌 우리 때문일 거야.
It is not because of those stars or those lights, but probably because of us. /
It's neither by those stars nor by those lights, but perhaps by us.

No es por esas estrellas o por esas luces, sino probablemente por nosotros. /
Es ni por esas estrellas ni por esas luces, pero tal vez por nosotros.

< Line 8 > You got me. 난 너를 보며 꿈을 꿔.

난 = 나는 = 나 (I, yo) + 는 [marker for subject]

너를 = 너 (you, tú) + 를 [marker for object] = you / te

보다 = [infinitive of verb] see / watch / look at / observe / ver / mirar / observar

보며 = [simultaenous] while seeing / while watching / while looking at / mientras veo / mientras miro

꿈을 = 꿈(dream, vision, illusion, sueño, ilusión) + 을 [marker for object]

꾸다 = [infinitive of verb] dream / soñar

꾸어 = **꿔** = familiar ending of 꾸다

난 너를 보며 꿈을 꿔. = I dream a dream while looking at you. /
Sueño un sueño mientras te miro.

< Line 9 > I got you. 칠흑 같던 밤들 속, 서로가 본 서로의 빛

칠흑 = [noun] pitch-black / coal-black / jet-black / tono carbón

같다 = [pronunciation] 갇따 = [adjective] be the same [like, identical] /
ser el mismo [como, idéntico]

같은 = [pronunciation] 가튼 = present tense of 같다 = the same / like / that is identical /
el mismo / que es como [idéntico]

같을 = [pronunciation] 가틀 = (future) adjective form of 같다 = that will be the
same [like, identical] / que sera el mismo [como, idéntico]

같던 = [pronunciation] 갇던 → 갇떤 = past tense of 같다 = that was the
same [like, identical] / que era el mismo [como, idéntico]

밤들 = 밤 (night, noche) + 들 [plural] = nights / noches

속(에) = [noun] 속 (the inside, the bottom, el interior) + 에 (in, at, en)

칠흑 같던 밤들 속 = In the inside of the nights that was like pitch-black /
En el interior de las noches que era como un tono carbón

서로 = [adverb] each other / one another / reciprocally / together / uno al otro /
recíprocamente / juntos

서로가 = 서로 + 가 [marker for subject]

보다 = [infinitive of verb] see / watch / look at / observe / ver / mirar / observar

보는 = present adjective form of 보다 = seeing / watching / observing / viendo /
mirando / observando

본 = past adjective form of 보다 = that saw / that observed / que vio / que miró / que observó

서로 = [adverb] each other / one another / reciprocally / together / uno al otro /
recíprocamente / juntos

서로의 = 서로 + 의 [marker for possession] = each other's / de juntos

빛 = [pronunciation] 빈 = [noun] light / glow / beam / ray / luz / rayo

서로가 본 서로의 빛. = Each other's light that each of us saw /
La luz del otro que cada uno de nosotros vio

74

< Line 10 > 같은 말을 하고 있었던 거야, 우린.

같다 = [pronunciation] 갇따 =[adjective] be the same [like, identical] /
ser el mismo [como, idéntico]

같은 = [pronunciation] 가튼 = present tense of 같다 = the same / like / that is identical /
el mismo / que es como [idéntico]

말을 = 말 (words, comment, saying, palabras) + 을 [marker for object]

하다 = [infinitive of verb] do / act / make / hacer / realizar

말을 하다 = say / talk / decir / hablar

하고 = an adverb-type conjugation of 하다

있다 = [pronunciation] 읻다 → 읻따 = [infinitive of verb] there is / be / exist / stay / remain /
stand / hay / estar / existir / quedarse / permanecer / pararse

하고 있다 = [present progressive] be doing / estar haciendo

하고 있었다 = [pronunciation] 하고 이썯따 = [past progressive] was doing / estaba haciendo

하고 있었던 − [pronunciation] 하고 이썯떤= adjective form of 히고 있었다

것이다 = 것 (the thing that ~, the fact that ~, el hecho que ~, lo que ~) + 이다 (be, ser)

것이야 = **거야** = familiar ending of 것이다

우린 = 우리는 = 우리 (we, nosotros) + 는 [marker for subject]

하고 있었던 거야 = [pronunciation] 하고 이썯떤 거야
It is the fact that we were doing / Es el hecho de que estábamos haciendo

같은 말을 하고 있었던 거야, 우린. = The thing is that we were saying the same things. /
You see, we were on the same page. / El hecho es que nosotros decíamos las mismas cosas. /
Verás, estábamos en la misma página.

< Line 11 > 가장 깊은 밤에 더 빛나는 별빛. [twice / dos veces]

가장 = [adverb] the most / extremely / to the extreme / supremely / el más / el mejor /
al máximo

깊다 = [pronunciation] 깁따 = [infinitive of adjective] be deep [profound] /
ser intenso [profundo]

깊은 = [pronuncation] 기픈 = present form of 깊다 = deep / profound / intenso / profundo

밤에 = [pronunciation] 바메 = 밤 (night, noche) + 에 (in, at) = in the night / en la noche

● Pronunciation-wise, «밤의 (of the night)» and «밤에 (in the night)» are the same. However,
they should be distiguished when they are written.

더 = [adverb] more / further / additionally / más / adicionalmente

빛나다 = [pronunciation] 빋나다 → 빈나다 = [infinitive of verb] shine / glow / be bright / gleam / lucir / resplandecer

빛나는 = [pronunciation] 빈나는 = adjective form of 빛나다 = shining / glwoing / gleaming / luciendo / resplandeciendo

별빛 = [pronunciation] 별삗 = [noun] starlight / luz de estrella

● '별빛' is a combination of two independent words which are '별 (star)' and '빛 (light)'.

Therefore, the pronunciation of the combined word became '별삗' instead of '별빋'.

● Markers are not regarded as an independent word. That is why there is no space in front of them.

가장 깊은 밤에 더 빛나는 별빛 = The starlights that shine brighter in the deepest night / Las luces de las estrellas que brillan más intensamente en la noche más profunda

< Line 12 > 밤이 깊을수록 더 빛나는 별빛.

밤이 = 밤 (night, noche) + 이 [marker for subject]

깊다 = [infinitive of adjective] be deep / be profound / ser intenso / ser profundo

깊을수록 = [pronunciation] 기플쑤록 = the more it gets deep / cuanto más se vuelve profundo

● In Korean, the pronunciation of the first consonant just after 'ㄹ' tends to become hard.
[깊을수록 → 기플수록 → 기플쑤록]

밤이 깊을수록 = as the night gets deeper / a medida que la noche se hace más profunda

더 = [adverb] more / further / additionally / más / adicionalmente

더 빛나는 = [pronunciation] 더 빈나는 = is shining brighter / está brillando más

별빛 = [pronunciation] 별삗 = [noun] starlight / luz de estrella

밤이 깊을 수록 더 빛나는 별빛.
The starlights that are shining brighter as the night gets deeper. /
Las luces de las estrellas que brillan más a medida que la noche se hace más profunda.

< Line 13 > 한 사람에 하나의 역사, 한 사람에 하나의 별.

한 = [numeral] one / un

사람에 = 사람 (person, human, persona, ser humano) + 에 (to, for, in, en)

한 사람에 = in [to, for, by, of] one person / en [para, por, de] una persona

하나의 = [pronunciation] 하나에 = 하나 [noun] + 의 = 하나 (one unit, uno) + 의 = one / un

● «의 [marker for possession]» is pronounced as «에». However, in case that it is a part of

an independent word, it is pronounced as «의».

[정의 (justice)] [의미 (meaning)] [거의 (almost)]

하나의 역사 = [noun phrase] one history / one chronicle / una historia / una crónica

하나의 별 = [noun phrase] one star / una estrella

한 사람에 하나의 역사, 한 사람에 하나의 별
One chronicle for [to] one person, one star for [to] one person.
Una crónica de [a] una persona, una estrella de [a] una persona.

< Line 14 > 70 억 개의 빛으로 빛나는 70 억 가지의 world. 70 억 가지의 삶.

70 = 칠십

70 억 = 칠십억 = 7 billion

십 = [numeral] ten [10] [10]

백 = [numeral] hundred [100] [100]

천 = [numeral] thousand [1000] [1,000]

만 = [numeral] ten thousand [1,0000] [10,000]

억 = [numeral] hundred million [1,0000,0000] [100,000,000]

70 억 = [numeral] seven billion [70,0000,0000] [7,000,000,000]

조 = [numeral] one trillion [1,0000,0000,0000] [1,000,000,000,000]

경 = [numeral] ten quadrillion [1,0000,0000,0000,0000] [10,000,000,000,000,000]

일 (1) / 이 (2) / 삼 (3) / 사 (4) / 오 (5) / 육 (6) / 칠 (7) / 팔 (8) / 구 (9) / 십일 (11) / 십이 (12)

개의 = [pronunciation] 개에 = 개 (units) + 의 [marker for possession] = units of / unidades de

빛으로 = [pronunciation] 비츠로 = 빛 (lights, luces) + 으로 (as, with, por, como, con)

70 억 개의 빛으로 = with 7 billion units of lights = with 7 billion lights / por 7 mil millones

70 억 개의 빛으로 **빛나는** = shining with 7 billion lights / luciendo por 7 mil millones

빛나는 = [pronunciation] 빋나는 → 빈나는

가지의 = 가지 (kinds, sorts, types, styles) + 의 [marker for possession] = clases de / tipos de / estilos de

70 억 가지의 **world** = 70 billion sorts of the world / 70 mil millones clases del mundo

70 억 가지의 **삶** = 70 billion styles of the lives / 70 mil millones estilos de vidas

70 억 개의 빛으로 빛나는 70 억 가지의 world. 70 억 가지의 삶.

70 billion sorts of the world that is shining with 70 billion lights. 70 billion styles of lives.

70 mil millones de clases del mundo que brillan con 70 mil millones de luces.
70 mil millones de estilos de vidas

< Line 15 > 도시의 야경은 어쩌면 또 다른 도시의 밤. 각자 만의 꿈.

도시의 = 도시 (city, ciudad) + 의 [marker for possession] = of a city / de una ciudad

야경은 = 야경 (nightscape, paisaje nocturno) + 은 [marker for subject]

어쩌면 = [adverb] maybe / perhaps / probably / quizá(s) / tal vez / probablemente

또 = [adverb] again / still / even now / moreover / otra vez / todavía / incluso ahora / de nuevo

다르다 = [infinitive of adjective] be different / ser diferente

다른 = present tense of 다르다 = different / diferente

또 다른 = [adverb phrase] another / even more different / unique / otro / más diferente / único

밤 = [noun] night / night-time / noche

도시의 야경은 어쩌면 또 다른 도시의 밤.
The nightscape of a city is perhaps another night (aspect) of the city.
The nightscape of a city is its own unique beauty of the night.

El paisaje nocturno de una ciudad es quizás otro (aspecto de la) noche de la ciudad.
El paisaje nocturno de una ciudad es su propia belleza única de la noche.

각자 = [noun] each person / each one / cada persona / cada uno

만의 = 만 (uniqueness, only, own, alone, propio, único) + 의 [marker for possession]

꿈 = [noun] dream / vision / illusion / sueño / ilusión

각자만의 꿈 = each one's own dream / each one's unique dream /
el sueño único de cada uno

< Line 16 > Let us shine! 넌 누구보다 밝게 빛나.

넌 = 너는 = 너 (you, tú) + 는 [marker for subject]

누구보다 = 누구 (anyone, alguien) + 보다 (than, más que) = than anyone else / más que nadie

(더) = [adverb] more / further / aditionally / más / de nuevo

밝다 = [pronunciation] 박따 = [adjective] be bright / be radiant / ser brillante / ser luminoso

밝은 = [pronunciation] 발근 = present tense of 밝다 = bright / radiant / beaming / brillante / luminoso

밝게 = [pronunication] 발께 = adverb form of 밝다 = brightly / radiantly / beamingly / brillantemente /luminosamente

빛나다 = [pronunciation] 빋나다 → 빈나다 = [infinitive of verb] shine / glow / be bright / gleam / lucir / resplandecer

빛나 = [pronunciation] 빈나 = familiar ending of 빛나다

넌 누구보다 (더) 밝게 빛나. = You shine brighter than anyone else. / Brillas más que nadie.

< Line 7-1 > 어쩜 이 밤의 표정이 이토록 또 아름다운 건 ...
저 어둠도 달빛도 아닌 우리 때문일 거야.

Maybe the reason why the look of this night is beautiful like this (is) …
Quizás la razón por la que la vista de esta noche es tan hermosa (es) …

어둠도 = 어둠 (darkness, oscuridad) + 도 [marker] (neither, ni)

달빛도 = 달빛 (moonlight, luz de la luna) + 도 [marker] (nor, ni)

저 어둠도 달빛도 아닌 우리 때문일 거야.
It is because of neither the darkness nor the moonlights, but probably because of us. /
Es ni por esa oscuridad ni por esa luz de la luna, sino tal vez por nosotros.

< Line 8 > You got me. 난 너를 보며 꿈을 꿔.

I dream a dream while looking at you. / Sueño un sueño mientras te miro.

< Line 9 > I got you. 칠흑 같던 밤들 속, 서로가 본 서로의 빛.

In the inside of the nights that was like pitch-black /
En el interior de las noches que era como un tono carbón

Each other's light that each of us saw / La luz del otro que cada uno de nosotros vio

< Line 10 > 같은 말을 하고 있었던 거야, 우린.

The thing is that we ourselves were saying the same things. /
You see, we were on the same page.

Es que nosotros mismos decíamos las mismas cosas. /
Verás, estábamos en la misma página.

< Line 11 > 가장 깊은 밤에 더 빛나는 별빛. **[twice / dos veces]**

The starlights that shine brighter in the deepest night /
Las luces de las estrellas que brillan más intensamente en la noche más profunda

< Line 12 > 밤이 깊을수록 더 빛나는 별빛.

The starlights that are shining brighter as the night gets deeper. /
Las luces de las estrellas que brillan más a medida que la noche se hace más profunda.

< Line 17 > 도시의 불, 이 도시의 별. 어릴 적 올려 본 밤하늘을 난 떠올려.

도시의 = [pronunciation] 도시에 = 도시 (city, ciudad) + 의 [marker for possession]
= of a city / de una ciudad
불 = [noun] light / fire / luz
도시의 불 = [noun phrase] the lights of a city / las luces de una ciudad

이 = [determiner] this / these / este / estos
별 = [noun] star / estrella
이 도시의 별 = the lights of this city / las luces de esta ciudad

어리다 = [infinitive of adjective] be young [little] / ser joven [niño, pequeño]
어렸다 = [pronunciation] 어런따 = past tense of 어리다 = was young [little] /
era joven [niño, pequeño]
어렸을 = [pronunciation] 어려쓸 = **어릴** = [past adjective form] that was young [little] /
que era joven [niño, pequeño]
적 = [noun] time / occasion / case / when / vez / ocasión, / caso / cuando
어릴 적 = [pronunciation] 어릴 쩍

● In Korean, the pronunciation of the first consonant just after 'ㄹ' tends to become hard.
[어릴 적 → 어릴 쩍]

● In priniciple, «어렸을 적 [어려쓸 쩍]» is correct. However, many Koreans habitually use the expression «어릴 적» instead of «어렸을 적».

어릴 적 = when (I) was young / when (I) was a kid / when (I) was little / in (my) younger days / cuando yo era niño [pequeño] / en mi juventud

보다 = [infinitive of verb] see / watch / look at / observe / ver / mirar / observar
올려(다) 보다 = [verb phrase] look up (to) / raise one's eyes toward / turn one's face up toward / mirar hacia arriba / levantar la mirada hacia
올려(다) **본** = [past adjective form] that looked up (to) / that I raised my eyes toward / que miré hacia arriba / que levanté hacia

밤하늘을 = 밤 (night, noche) + 하늘 (sky, cielo) + 을 [marker for object]

난 = 나는 = 나 (I, yo) + 는 [marker for subject]
떠올리다 = [infinitive of verb] recollect / remind / recall / remember / reminisce about / recordar
떠올려 = familiar ending of 떠올리다

어릴 적 올려본 밤하늘을 난 떠올려.
I remember the night sky that I used to look up in my younger days.
Recuerdo el cielo nocturno que solía mirar hacia arriba en mi juventud.

< Line 18 > 사람이란 불, 사람이란 별로 가득한 바로 이곳에서 We shinin'

사람 = [noun] person / human / persona / ser humano
이다 = [infinitive of marker that conjugates] be / ser
이라는 = **이란** = that is called (as) / so-called / that is named as / being known as / that they call / que se llama (como) / así se llama / que se conoce como / que la gente llama / tal como
불 = [noun] light / fire / luz
별로 = 별 (star / estrella) + 로 (with, de, como)

가득하다 = [pronunciation] 가드카다 = [infinitive of adjective] be full of / be filled with / be fully packed / estar lleno de / estar completamente lleno
가득한 = [pronunciation] 가드칸 = present form of 가득하다 = full of / filled with / fully packed / lleno de

바로 = [adverb] just / right / exactly / precisely / justo / exactamente / precisamente

이곳 = [pronunciation] 이곧 = [pronoun] this place / this point / this spot / este lugar / este punto

이곳에서 = [pronunciation] 이고세서 = 이곳 + 에서 (at, on, in, en) = here / aquí

사람이란 불, 사람이란 별로 바로 가득한 바로 이곳에서 **We shinin'**
We are shining right at this place that is full of the lights that are called humans and full of the stars that are called humans. /

Estamos brillando justo en este lugar que es lleno de luces que se llaman humanos y lleno de estrellas que se llaman humanos.

< Line 19 > You got me. 난 너를 보며 숨을 쉬어.

난 = 나는 = 나 (I, yo) + 는 [marker for subject]

너를 = 너 (you, tú) + 를 [marker for object]

보다 = [infinitive of verb] see / watch / look at / observe / ver / mirar / observar

보며 = [simulatenous action] while seeing / look at, and / mientras observo / miro, y

숨을 = 숨 (breath, breathing, respiro, respiración) + 을 [marker for object]

쉬다 = [infinitive of verb] breathe / respire / respirar

쉬어 = familiar ending of 쉬다

난 너를 보며 숨을 쉬어. = I take a breath while looking at you. /
Tomo un respiro mientras te miro.

< Line 9 > I got you. 칠흑 같던 밤들 속에

칠흑 = [noun] pitch-black / coal-black / jet-black / tono carbón

같다 = [pronunciation] 갇다 → 갇따 = be the same / be identical / ser el mismo / ser idéntico

같은 = [pronunciation] 가튼 = present adjective form of 같다 = same / identical / mismo / idéntico

같던 = [pronunciation] 갇떤 = past adjective form of 같다 = that was like / that was identical / que era el mismo / que era idéntico

밤들 = 밤 (night, noche) + 들 [plural] = nights / noches

속에 = [noun] 속 (the inside, the bottom, el interior) + 에 (in, at, en)

칠흑 같던 밤들 속에 = In the inside of the nights that was like pitch-black /
En el interior de las noches que era como un tono carbón

< Line 20 > **Shine, dream, smile. Oh, let us light up the night. 우린 우리대로 빛나.**

우린 = 우리는 = 우리 (we, nosotros) + 는 [marker for subject]

대로 = [marker for individualizatio] in one's own way / in one's own method / a su manera / con su propio método

빛나다 = [pronunciation] 빋나다 → 빈나다 = [infinitive of verb] shine / glow / be bright / gleam / lucir / resplandecer

빛나 = [pronunciation] 빋나 → 빈나 = familiar ending of 빛나다

우린 우리대로 빛나. = We shine in our own way. / Each of us shine in one's own method. / Brillamos a nuestra manera. / Cada uno de nosotros brilla con su propio método.

< Line 21 > **Shine, dream, smile. Oh, let us light up the night.**
우린 그 자체로 빛나! Tonight.

우린 = 우리는 = 우리 (we, nosotros) + 는 [marker for subject]

그 = [determiner] the / that / those / ese / esos / tal

자체 = [noun] itself / oneself / its own / per se / sí mismo / uno mismo / lo propio

로 = [marker for qualification] as / by / como / por

그 자체로 = as it is / as oneself is / as we are / como es / como uno mismo es / como somos

빛나다 = [pronunciation] 빋나다 → 빈나다 = [infinitive of verb] shine / glow / be bright / gleam / lucir / resplandecer

빛나 = [pronuncication] 빋나 → 빈나 = familiar ending of 빛나다

우린 그 자체로 빛나! = We shine as we are! / ¡Brillamos como somos!

6. Life Goes On

Artist: BTS

Lyric Writers: RM, Suga, J-Hope, Pdogg, Ruuth, Chris James, Antonia Armato

< Line 1 > 어느 날 세상이 멈췄어. 아무런 예고도 하나 없이 ...

어느 = [determiner] a / any / some / a certain / which / uno / un cierto / cualquier / alguno / cuál

날 = [noun] day / daylight / día

어느 날 = [noun phrase] a certain day / one day / un día

세상 = [noun] the world / the earth / our era / el mundo / la tierra / nuestra era

세상이 = 세상 + 이 [marker for subject]

멈추다 = [pronunciation] 멈추다 = [infinitive of verb] stop / halt / bring to a stop [halt] / stand still / detenerse / pararse

멈추었다 = [pronunciation] 멈추얻따 = past tense of 멈추다 = stopped / brought to a stop / stood still / se detuvo / se paró

멈추었어 = **멈췄어** = [pronunciation] 멈춰써 = familiar ending of 멈추었다

아무러하다 = [infinitive of adjective] be at random / be not caring / ser al azar / ser indiferente

아무러한 = **아무런** = present tense of 아무러하다 = not any / nothing / no / no cualquiera / ningún / nada

예고 = [noun] forewarning / warning / notice / herald / aviso previo / aviso / heraldo

예고도 = 예고 + 도 [marker] (neither, not even, ni , ni siquiera)

● In principle, «도» itself is not negative. But here, one can expect that a negative expression would come along.

하나 = [noun] one thing / one unit / one / una cosa / una unidad / uno

없이 = [pronunciation] 업씨 = [adverb] without / not having / sin / no teniendo

어느 날 세상이 멈췄어. 아무런 예고도 하나 없이.
One day the world brought itself to a halt, without any forewarning at all. /
Un día el mundo se paró, sin ningún aviso previo.

< Line 2 > 봄은 기다림을 몰라서 눈치없이 와 버렸어.

봄은 = [pronunciation] 보믄 = 봄 (spring / springtime, primvera) + 은 [marker for subject]

기다리다 = [infinitive of verb] wait (for) / await / hold on / expect / esperar / aguardar / retrasarse

기다림 = noun form of 기다리다 = waiting / standy / espera / aguardada / lo retrasarse

● «noun form» can be regarded as a noun, «adverb-form» can be regarded as an adverb, while «a noun-type conjuation» or «an adverb-type conjugation» is regarded as a verb.

기다림을 = [pronunciation] 기다리믈 = 기다림 + 을 [marker for object]

모르다 = [infinitive of verb] not know [aware, realize, notice, understand, learned] / no saber [aprendí] / desconocer / no darse cuenta

몰라서 = don't know, so / did not learn, thus / no sé, entonces / no aprendí, por lo tanto

눈치 = [noun] quick wit / quick sense / smart sense / ingenio rápido / sentido inteligente / agudeza

없이 = [pronunciation] 업씨 = [adverb] without / not having / sin / no teniendo

오다 = [infinitive of verb] come / come to / approach / arrive / venir / venir a / acercarse / llegar (a)

와버리다 = stronger expression than 오다 = it comes, nevertheless / venir sin embargo

와버렸다 = [pronunciation] 와버련따 = [past tense] has come, nevertheless / have arrived / ha venido sin embargo / ha llegado sin embargo

와버렸어 = [pronunciation] 와버려써 = familiar ending of 와버렸다

봄은 기다림을 몰라서 눈치없이 와 버렸어.
Spring did not learn how to hold on. Thus, it has come, nevertheless, without smart sense. / La primavera no aprendió a retrasarse. Así, ha llegado, sin embargo, a tiempo sin agudeza.

< Line 3 > 발자국이 지워진 거리. 여기 넘어져 있는 나 ...

발자국이 = [pronunciation] 발짜구기 = 발자국 (footprints, pasos, huellas) + 이 [marker for subject]

● When two independent words combine, the first consonant of the second word becomes hard. strong. [발 (foot) + 자국 (print, marks) = 발자국→ 발짜국]

지우다 = [infinitive of verb] erase / rub out / efface / eliminate / forget / borrar / eliminar / olvidar

지워지다 = passive form of 지우다 = be erased / be effaced / estar borrado / estar eliminado

지워진 = past form of 지워지다 = erased / removed / that is effaced / borrado / que está eliminado

지워지는 = present form of 지워지다 = being erased / that is being effaced / que se borra

거리 = [noun] street / road / calle / camino

발자국이 지워진 거리.
The street that is erased of footprints / La calle que se borró de pasos

여기 = [pronoun, also used as adverb] this spot [place] / here / over the spot / este lugar / aquí / sobre donde

넘어지다 = [pronunciation] 너머지다 = [infinitive of verb] fall / tumble / tip / collapse / caer / volcar

있다 = [pronunciation] 읻다 → 읻따 = [infinitive of verb] there is / be / exist / stay / remain / stand / hay / estar / existir / quedarse / permanecer / pararse

넘어져 있다 = [pronunciation] 너머져 읻따 = stay fallen / lie tumbled / remain collapsed / permanecer caído / estar tumbado / quedar tirado

넘어져 있는 = [pronunciation] 너머져 인는 = present form of 넘어져 있다 = staying fallen / who is lying tumbled / that is remaining collapsed / quien permanezco caído / quien está tumbado / quien quedo tirado

나 = [pronoun] I / yo

여기 넘어져 있는 나. = Over the spot, it is me who stay fallen. / Sobre donde, soy yo quien me quedo tirado.

< Line 4 > 혼자 가네 시간이. "미안해." 말도 없이 …

혼자 = [adverb] alone / by oneself / solo / por sí mismo

가다 = [infinitive of verb] go (away) / move away / ride / ir / irse / marchar / alejarse / llevarse

가네 = poetic ending of 가다

시간이 = 시간 (time, tiempo, horas) + 이 [marker for subject]

미안하다 = [infinitive of verb] feel sorry / apologize / sentirlo / disculparse

"미안해." = familiar ending of 미안하다 = I am sorry / I feel sorry / lo siento / disculpe

말도 = 말 (words, comment, saying, palabras) + 도 [makrer] (neither, not even, ni, ni siquiera)

● In principle, «도» itself is not negative. But here, one can expect that a negative expression would come along.

없이 = [pronunciation] 업씨 = [adverb] without / not having / sin / no teniendo

혼자 가네, 시간이. "미안해" 말도 없이.
Time goes away alone, even without saying "Sorry." /
El tiempo se va solo, incluso sin decir « Lo siento ».

< Line 5 > 오늘도 비가 내릴 것 같아. 흠뻑 젖어버렸네. 아직도 멈추질 않아.

오늘도 = 오늘 (today, hoy) + 도 [marker for repetition] (as well, also, too, también, tampoco, y además)

비가 = 비 (rain, llueva) + 가 [marker for subject]

내리다 = [infinitive of verb] fall down / come down / drop / caer / bajar

비가 내리다 = It rains. / Llueve.

눈이 내리다 = It snows. / Nieva.

비가 내리는 = present adjective form of 내리다 = raining / lloviendo

비가 내릴 = (future) adjective form of 내리다 = will rain / be going to rain / yendo a llover

것 = [pronunciation] 걷 = [noun] the thing that ~ / the fact that ~ / la cosa que ~ /
el hecho que ~ / el caso que ~ / lo que ~

비가 내릴 것 = [pronunciation] 비가 내릴 껃 = the thing that it will rains /
the fact that it is about to rain / lo que va a llover

● In Korean, the pronunciation of the first consonant just after '르' tends to become hard.
[내릴 것 → 내릴 걷 → 내릴 껃]

같다 = [pronunciation] 갇따 = [infinitive of verb] It looks like / It seems that / Parece que

같아 = familiar ending of 같다

비가 내릴 것 같아 = It looks like (the thing) that it will rain. / Parece (lo) que va a llover.

오늘도 비가 내릴 것 같아. = Today again, it looks like that it will rain. /
Hoy también, parece que va a llover.

흠뻑 = [mimetic adverb] completely (soaking) / (wet to) the bone /
completamente (empapado) / (mojado) hasta los huesos

젖다 = [pronunciation] 젇다 → 젇따 = get wet / be drenched / mojarse / empaparse /
estar calado

젖어버리다 = [pronunciation] 저저버리다 = a word stronger than 젖다

젖어버렸다 = [pronunciation] 저저버렫다 → 저저버렫따 = past tense of 젖어버리다

젖어버렸네 = [pronunciation] 저저버렫네 → 저저버련네 = poetic ending of 젖어버렸다

흠뻑 젖어버렸네. = I've got completely wet. / I am drenched to the bone.
Me mojé completamente empapado. / Estoy calado hasta los huesos.

아직 = [adverb] still / yet / so far / todavía / hasta ahora + 도 [emphasis]

아직도 = [adverb] stronger expression than 아직 = even now / even util this moment /
incluso hasta ahora / ni siquiera todavía

멈추다 = [infinitive of verb] stop / halt / bring to a stop [halt] / stand still / detenerse / pararse

멈추지 = a noun-type cojugation of 멈추다

멈추질 = 멈추지를 = 멈추지 [noun form of 멈추다] + 를 [marker for object]

아니 하다 = 안 하다 = 않다 = [pronunciation] 안타 = not do / no hacer

않아 = [pronunciation] 안아 → 아나 = familiar ending of 않다

아직도 멈추질 않아. = It won't stop even now. / It never stops. /
No se detendrá ni siquiera todavía. / Nunca se detiene.

< Line 6 > 저 먹구름보다 빨리 달려가. 그럼, 될 줄 알았는데 ...

저 = [determiner] that / those / over there / aquel / ese / allí

먹 = [noun] black ink stick / black ink / barra de tinta de carbón / tinta de carbón

먹구름 = [pronunciation] 먹꾸름 = [noun] dark clouds / nubes oscuras

● When two independent words combine, the first consonant of the second word becomes hard.
[먹 (black ink) + 구름 (clouds) → 먹꾸름]

보다 = [marker] than / more than / más que

저 먹구름보다 = more than those dark clouds / más que esas nubes oscuras

빨리 = [adverb] fast / quickly / rapidly / rápidamente

달리다 = [infinitive of verb] run / rush / dash / spurt / correr

달려가다 = stronger word than 달리다 = run with one's strength / correr duro

달려가 = familiar or poetic ending of 달려가다

저 먹구름보다 빨리 달려가. = Running faster than those dark clouds. /
Corriendo más rápido que esas nubes oscuras.

그러하다 = [infinitive of adjective] be (like) such / be like that / ser así / ser como tal

그러하면 = 그러면 = **그럼** = adverb form of 그러하다 = if so / if it is such / if it is like that / then / si es así / si ser / ser así / entonces

되다 = [infinitive of verb] become fine / goes well / be good / se convierten en todo bien / va bien / llegar a estar bien / estar bien hecho

될 = (future) adjective form of 되다 = that will be good / that will be okay / que estará bien

줄 = [noun] possible [promising, plausible, good] way [method] / buena manera / método posible

알다 = [infinitive of verb] know / be aware of / recognize / notice / think / saber / conocer / notar / pensar

될 줄 알다 = [pronunciation] 될 쭐 알다 = [adverb phrase] foresee that (it) is possibly a good way / think that (it) will be okay / prever que posiblemente sea una buena manera / piensa que etaría bien

• In Korean, the pronunciation of the first consonant just after 'ㄹ' tends to become hard. This rule applies only between two independent pure Korean words. [될 줄 → 될 쭐].

• All the vowels and four consonants (ㄴ, ㄹ, ㅁ, ㅇ) are voiced sounds, which are soft. A consonant that is between any two of them become soft as well. The above ㄷ of '다' is located between two voiced (or soft) sounds which are ㄹ and ㅏ. So, this ㄷ becomes soft. Because of that, the word is pronounced as «알다», not «알따».

될 줄 알았다 = [pronunciation] 될 쭐 아랃따 = past tense of 될 줄 알다 = thought that (it) would be okay / pensé que etaría bien

될 줄 알았는데... = [ending for disappointment] thought (wrongly) that (it) would be okay... / pensé (en vano) que todo irá bien ...

그럼, 될 줄 알았는데 ... = Then, everything would be okay, I (wrongly) thought. / Entonces, todo irá bien, pensé (en vano).

< Line 7 > 난 겨우 사람인가 봐.

난 = 나는 = 나 (I, yo) + 는 [marker for subject]

겨우 = [adverb] not more than / nothing but / at most / merely / just / only / solamente / simplemente

사람 = [noun] person / human / persona / ser humano

이다 = [infinitive of marker that conjugates] be / ser

인가 = an adverb-type conjugation of 이다 for uncertainty

보다 = [infinitive of verb] seem to be [do] / it looks like that / perece que / se ve así

(겨우) 인가 보다 = [verb phrase] it seems that ~ , after all / parece que ~ , después de todo

인가 봐 = familiar ending of 인가 보다.

난 겨우 사람인가 봐. = It seems that I am nothing more than a human, after all. / Parece que, después de todo, no soy más que un ser humano.

< Line 8 > 몹시 아프네.

몹시 = [adverb] very badly / terribly / seriously / excessively / exceedingly / immensely / muy

아프다 = [infinitive of adjective] hurt / be ill [sick, painful, sore, hurting] / torment / doler / ser doloroso / estar enfermo [dolorido, herido] / atormentar

아프네 = poetic ending of 아프다

몹시 아프네. = (I) am terribly sick. / Estoy muy enfermo

< Line 9 > 세상이란 놈이 준 감기. 덕분에 눌러보는, 먼지 쌓인 되감기 ...

세상 = [noun] the world / the earth / our era / our times / el mundo / la tierra / nuestra era

이다 = [infinitive of marker that conjugates] be / ser

이라는 = **이란** = that is called (as) / so-called / that is named as / being known as / that they call / que se llama (como) / así se llama / que se conoce como / que la gente llama / tal como

놈이 = 놈 (bloke, fellow, dude, chap, compañero , el tipo) + 이 [marker for subject]

주다 = [infinitive of verb] give / bestow / provide / supply / present / dar / conceder / otorgar / ofrecer / presentar

● The original meaning of «주다» is «give» or «bestow». But if it is used together with another verb, its meaning changes into «kindly do», «do as a favour» or «willing to do». It can also carry the meaning of «Please / Por favor».

주는 = present adjective form of 주다 = giving / that provides / presenting / dando / que proporciona

준 = past adjective form of 주다 = gave / that was given [provided] by / que dio / que es dado por

줄 = (future) adjective form of 주다 = that will give / que dará

감기 = [noun] cold / flu / gripe / resfriado

세상이란 놈이 준 감기 = The flu that a chap called 'the World' gave me / The flu that was given by a bloke called 'Our Times.'

La gripe que me dio un tipo que se llama 'el Mundo'. / El resfriado que me dio un compañero que se conoce como 'Nuestra Era'.

덕분 = [noun] thanks / cause / due / owing / gracias / causa / debido

(그) **덕분에** = thanks to it / because of that / owing to that / by using this opportunity / gracias a lo / causa de lo / debido a lo / al provechar esta oportunidad

누르다 = [infinitive of verb] press / push / click / hit / precionar / hacer clic

(해)보다 = [infinitive of verb] have a try / give a shot / attempt to / carry out / venture to / probar / tratar / intentar / llevar a cabo / atreverse

눌러보다 = [verb phase] press in trial / carry out pressing / hit tentatively / presionar tentativamente

눌러보는, = adjective form of 눌러보다 = pushing tentatively / presionando tentativamente

먼지 = [noun] dust / dirt / polvo

쌓다 = [pronunciation] 싸타 = [verb] stack / pile / accumulate / apilar / amontonar / acumular

쌓인 = [pronunciation] 싸인 = adjective form of 쌓다 = stacked / piled / accumulated / covered / apilado / acumulado / cubierto

먼지 쌓인 = dust-covered / dust-built / cubierto de polvo

되감기 = [noun] rewind (button) / el botón de 'rebobinar'

덕분에 눌러보는, 먼지 쌓인 되감기
The dust-covered 'rewind' button that (I) push tentatively by taking this opportunity /

El botón de 'rebobinar' cubierto de polvo que presiono tentativamente al provechar esta oportunidad

● comma (,) is necessary in the Korean line to clarify that 눌러보는 (pressing) is an ajective for 되감기 (rewind button), not for 먼지 (dust).

< Line 10 > 넘어진 채 청하는 엇박자의 춤 ...

넘어지다 = [infinitive of verb] fall / tumble / tip / collapse / caer / volcar

넘어진 = adject form of 넘어지다 = being fallen [tumbled, collapsed] / estoy caído [tumbado, tirado, volcando]

채 = [noun, also used as adverb] state / condition / status / situation / in the state of / just as it is / while / el estado / condición / situación / en el estado de / tal como es / mientras

넘어진 채(로) = while staying fallen / in the state of lying tumbled / as remaining collapsed / mientras está caído / en el estado que permanezco tumbado / quedo tirado / en la situación de estar volcando

청하다 = [infinitive of verb] invite to do / request to do / ask to do / try to do / invitar a hacer / solicitar hacer / pedir hacer / intentar hacer

청하는 = adjective form of 청하다 = inviting / requesting / asking / trying (to) / invitando / solicitando / pediendo / intentando (hacer)

엇박자 = [pronunciation] 얻빡짜 = [noun] awkwardness / shifted rhythm / un-matching tempo / staggered beat / clumsiness / torpeza / ritmo cambiado / tempo no coincidente / brecha de tempo

엇박자의 = [pronunciation] 얻빡짜에 = 엇박자 + 의 [marker for possession] = [ajective form] off-tempo / out of tempo / un-matching / incómodo / fuera de tempo / fuera de ritmo

● «의 [marker for possession]» is pronounced as «에». However, in case that it is a part of an independent word, it is pronounced as «의».

[정의 (justice)] [의미 (meaning)] [거의 (almost)]

춤 = [noun] dance / dacing / danza / baile

넘어진 채 청하는 엇박자의 춤
(My) awkward off-tempo dance trying while I am staying fallen /
(My) awkward out-of-temp dance being done while I remain tumbled down

(Mi) incómodo baile fuera de ritmo tratando en el estado que permaezco caído. /
(Mi) incómodo baile fuera de compás que se hace mientras me quedo tirado.

< Line 11 > 겨울이 오면 내쉬자, 더 뜨거운 숨.

겨울이 = 겨울 (winter, winter season, invierno) + 이 [marker for sujbect]

오다 = [infinitive of verb] come / come to / approach / arrive / venir / venir a / acercarse / llegar (a)

오면 = when it comes [arrives] / if it gets near / cuando llega / si se acerca

내쉬다 = [infinitive of verb] exhale / breathe out / exhalar / respirar / resollar

내쉬자 = Let's exhale! / Let me exhale. / I will breath out. / ¡Exhalemos! / Respiré.

더 = [adverb] more / further / additionally / más / adicionalmente

뜨겁다 = [infinitive of adjective] be hot / be heated / be passionate / ser caliente / ser apacionado

뜨거운 = present form of 뜨겁다 = hot / heated / passionate / caliente / apacionado

숨 = [noun] breath / breathing / respiration / respiración

겨울이 오면 내쉬자, 더 뜨거운 숨.
When winter comes, I will breathe (out) more passionate breaths. /
Cuando llegue el invierno, exhalaré respiraciones más apacionadas.

< Line 12 > 끝이 보이지 않아. 출구가 있긴 할까?

끝이 = [pronunciation] 끝이 → 끈치 = 끝 (the end, closing, el final) + 이 [marker for subject]

보다 = [infinitive of verb] see / watch / look at / observe / ver / mirar / observar

보이다 = [passive form] be seen / look / look like / be found / verse / encontrarse / mirarse

보이지 = a noun-type conjugation of 보이다

아니 하다 = 안 하다 = [pronunciation] 안타 = not do / no hacer

않아 = [pronunciation] 안아 → 아나 = familiar ending of 않다

보이지 않아 = It does not being seen. / It does not being found / It is not to be seen. /
It is not found. / It cannot be found. / No se ve. / No se encuentra. / No se puede encontrar.

끝이 보이지 않아. = The end is not to be seen. / The end cannot be found. /
El final no se ve. / El final no se puede encontrar.

출구가 = 출구 (exit, way-out, outlet) + 가 [marker for subject]

있다 = [pronunciation] 읻다 → 읻따 = [infinitive of verb] there is / be / exist / stay / remain /
stand / hay / estar / existir / quedarse / permanecer / pararse

있긴 = [pronunciation] 읻낀 = 있기는 = whether there is / whether it exists / si existe / si hay

하다 = [infinitive of verb] do / act / make / hacer / realizar

있긴 할까? = [not optimistic feeling] = I wonder whether there is / Me pregunto si hay

출구가 있긴 할까? = Is there any way-out existing? / I wonder whether there is an exit. /
¿Existe alguna salida? / Me pregunto si hay una salida.

< Line 13 > 발이 떼지질 않아, 않아. Oh ...

발이 = 발 (footstep, walk, footfall, paso, pisada) + 이 [marker for subject]

떼다 = [infinitive of verb] detach / tear [take] off / seperate / start / despegar / separarse / romperse / empezar / quitar

발이 떼지다 = passive voice of 발을 떼다 = be separated from the soil / a step is taken / start to walk / separarse del suelo / se da un paseo / empezar a caminar

발이 **떼지지** = [pronunciation] 바리 떼지지 = a noun-type conjugation of 발이 떼지다

아니 하다 = 안 하다 = 않다 = [pronunciation] 안타 = not do / no hacer

않아 = [pronunciation] 안아 → 아나 = familiar ending of 않다

발이 떼지지 않아.
My feet refuse to walk. / I cannot start walking. / I cannot move forward. /
Mi pies se niegan a caminar. / No puedo empezar a caminar. / No puedo seguir adelante.

< Line 14 > 잠시 두 눈을 감아. 여기 내 손을 잡아. 저 미래로 달아나자!.

잠시 = [adverb] for a moment / for a short while / temporarily / por un rato / momentáneamente

두 = [numeric] two / dos

눈을 = 눈 (eyes / ojos) + 을 [marker for object]

감다 = [pronunciation] 감따 = [infinitive of verb] close / shut / cerrar

● All the vowels and four consonants (ㄴ, ㄹ, ㅁ, ㅇ) are voiced sounds, which are soft. A consonant that is not between any two of them becomes hard (or fortis), if it is applicable like [ㄱ → ㄲ] [ㄷ → ㄸ] [ㅂ → ㅃ] [ㅅ → ㅆ] [ㅈ → ㅉ].
However, 'ㅁ' is flexible to the parts of speech.

- Verbs (Hard): [감다 (close, shut) → 감따] [감고 → 감꼬] [감지 → 감찌]
  [삼다 (make, let) → 삼따] [삼고 → 삼꼬] [삼지 → 삼찌]
- Nouns (Soft): [사람들 (people)] [곰돌이 (teddy bear)] [담배 (cigarette)]
  [담비 (marten)] [김장 (kimchi-making)] [두 섬지기 (two stretches of rice-field)]
- Adverbs (Soft): [쉬엄쉬엄 (with frequent rests)] [주섬주섬 (piece by piece)]

감아! = [pronunciation] 가마 = [familiar ending for imperative mode] Do close! / Do shut! / ¡Cierra!

잠시 두 눈을 감아. = Close (your) two eyes for a moment. / Cierra los ojos por un momento.

여기 = [pronoun, also used as adverb] this spot / this place / here / now / esto / este lugar / aquí / ahora

내 = 나의 = 나 (I) + 의 (marker for possession) = my / of me / of mine / mi

손을 = 손 (hand, mano) + 을 (marker for object)

잡다 = [pronunciation] 잡따 = [infinitive of verb] hold / take hold of / grab / tomar / agarrar / coger

잡아! = [pronunciation] 자바! = [familiar ending for imperative mode] Do hold! / Do take hold of! / ¡Toma!

여기 내 손을 잡아. = Here, hold my hand. / Aquí, toma mi mano.

저 = [determiner] that / those / over there / aquel / ese / allí

미래로 = 미래 (the future, el futuro) + 로 (to, into, towards, a)

달아나다 = [pronunciation] 다라나다 = [infinitive of verb] run away / flee / escape / run off to / elope / huir / escaper / fugarse

달아나자! = [pronunciation] 다라나자! = [familiar ending for proposition] Let's run away. / Let's elope. / Huyamos. / Fugémonos.

저 미래로 달아나자! = Let's elope to the future over there. / Huyamos al futuro de allí.

< Line 15 > Like an echo in the forest, 하루가 돌아오겠지. 아무 일도 없단 듯이 ...

하루 = [noun] a day / another day / daily routine / un día / otro día / rutina diaria

하루가 = 하루 + 가 [marker for subject]

돌아오다 = [infinitive of verb] come back / return / come in turn / volverse / venir por turno

돌아오겠지 = [familiar ending for speculation] (maybe) it would come in turn. / (quizá) vendría a su vez.

하루가 돌아오겠지. = Another day would come in turn. / Otro día vendría a su vez.

아무 = [determiner] not any / no / ningún

일 = [noun] work / affair / incident / event / case / thing / trabajo / asunto / incidente / suceso / caso / cosa / aventura

아무 일 = [noun phrase] nothing / no incident / nada / ninguno asunto

아무 일도 = 아무 일 + 도 [marker] (neither, not even, ni, ni siquiera)

● In principle, «도» itself is not negative. But here, one can expect that a negative expression would come along.

없다 = [pronunciation] 업다 → 업따 = [infintive of adjective] there is no / not exist / be absent / be without / no hay / no existir / estar ausente / estar sin

없는 = [pronunciastion] 업는 → 엄는 = present tense of 없다 = not existing / absent / no estando

없단 = [pronunciation] 업딴 = 없었단 [업썰딴] = 없었다는 [업썰따는] = past adjective tense of 없다 = that have not happened / that was absent / que no estaba / que no pasaba

● In principle, here, «없었단» or «없었다는» is correct . «없단» or «없다는» is for present tense.

듯이 … = [pronunciation] 드시 = [adverb] like / as if / as / como

아무 일도 없(었)단 듯이 = as if nothing had happened / como si nada hubiera pasado

< Line 16 > Yeah, life goes on. Like an arrow in the blue sky, 또 하루 더 날아가지. On my pillow, on my table. Yeah, life goes on like this again.

또 = [adverb] again / still / even now / moreover / otra vez / todavía / incluso ahora / de nuevo

하루(가) = 하루 (a day, another day, un día, otro día) + 가 [marker for subject]

더 = [adverb] more / further / additionally / más / adicionalmente

날아가다 = [infinitive of verb] fly away / be gone / be blown off / volar lejos / irse / ser volado

날아가지 = [pronunciation] 나라가지 = familiar or poetic ending of 날아가다.

또 하루 더 날아가지. = Another day flies away again. / One more day shall be gone. Otro día vuelva de nuevo. / Un día más se habrá ido.

< Line 17 > 이 음악을 빌려 너에게 나 전할께. 사람들은 말해. 세상이 다 변했대.

이 = [determiner] this / these / este / estos

음악을 = [pronunciation] 음아글 = 음악 (music, canción,música) + 을 [marker for object]

빌리다 = [infinitive of verb] borrow / rent / take advantage of / pedir prestado / aprovechar

빌려 = borrowing ~, and / taking advantage of ~, thus / pidiendo prestado, y / aprovechando ~, así

이 음악을 빌려 = through borrowing this music, and / taking advantage of this music, thus / tomando prestada esta música, y / aprovechando esta canción, así

너에게 = 너 (you, tú) + 에게 (marker for direction / to) = to you / te

나 = 날 = 나 (me) + 를 [marker for object] = my feelings / my thought / my heart / mi corazón

전하다 = [infinitive of verb] transfer / send / forward to / pass on to / transmit / entregar / transmitir / pasar

전할께 = familiar ending for commitment of 전하다 = (I) promise to transfer / (I) will pass on (to) / Prometeo pasar / Transmitiré.

이 음악을 빌려 너에게 나 전할께.
Taking advantage of this song I will pass on my feelings to you. /
Aprovechando esta cancion te transmitiré mi corazón.

사람들은 = 사람 (person, human, persona, ser humano) + 들 [plural] + 은 [marker for subject] = people / persons / la gente / personas

말하다 = [infinitive of verb] say / tell / talk / speak / state / decir / hablar / referir

말해 = familiar ending of 말하다.

세상 = [noun] the world / the earth / our era / our times / el mundo / la tierra / nuestra era

세상**이** = 세상 + 이 [marker for subject]

다 = [adverb] all / everything / everyone / totally / completely / todo(s) / totalmente / completamente

변하다 = [infinitive of verb] change / turn into / shift / transform / be different / cambiarse

변하였다 = 변했다 = [pronunciation] 변핻따 = past tense of 변하다 = changed / turned into / transformed / se cambió

변했대 = [pronunciation] 변핻때 = familiar ending for message of 변하다 =
They say that it has changed. / I heard that it is different now. /
La gente dice que ha cambiado. / Escuché que ahora es diferente.

사람들은 말해. 세상이 다 변했대.
People say that the world has changed completely. /
I heard that now is the totally different epoch.

La gente dice que el mundo ha cambiado por completo. /
Escuché que ahora es una época totalmente diferente.

< Line 18 > 다행히도 우리 사이는 아직 여태 안 변했네.

다행 = [noun] luck / good fortune / happiness / buena suerte / buena fortuna

다행히 = adverb form of 다행 = luckily / fortunately / by good luck / afortunadamente / por suerte / felizmente

다행히도 = stronger expression than 다행히 = luckily enough / por suerte suficiente

우리 = [pronoun] we / our / nosotros / nuestro

사이 = [noun] relations / relationship / interval / distance / relación / intervalo / distancia

사이는 = 사이 + 는 [marker for subject]

아직 = 여태 = [adverb] still / yet / so far / till now / up to now / todavía / ni hasta ahora / aún

아니 = **안** = [adverb] not / no

변하다 = [infinitive of verb] change / turn into / shift / transform / be different / cambiarse

변하였다 = past tense of 변하다 = 변했다 [변핻따] changed / turned into / transformed / se cambió

변했네 = [pronunciation] 변핻네 → 변핸네 = poetic ending of 변했다.

다행히도 우리 사이는 아직 여태 안 변했네.
Fortunately (enough), out relationship has not changed until now. /
Por suerte (suficiente), nuestra relación no ha cambiado hasta ahora.

< Line 19 > 늘 하던 시작과 끝, "안녕"이란 말로 오늘과 내일을 또 함께 이어보자고.

늘 = [adverb] always / as always / all the time / as usual / habitually / siempre / todo el tiempo

하다 = [infinitive of verb] do / act / make / hacer / realizar

하는 = present adjective form of 하다 = doing / haciendo

하던 = past adjective form of 하다 = did / used to do / hicimos / que solíamos hacer

시작 = [noun] the beginning / the start / the motive / comienzo / inicio

과 = [marker] and / y

끝, = [noun] the end / closing / el final

안녕 = [interjection] hi and bye / hello and ciao / hola y adios

이다 = [infinitive of marker that conjugates] be / ser

이라는 = **이란** = that is called (as) / so-called / that is named as / being known as / that they call / que se llama (como) / así se llama / que se conoce como / que la gente llama / tal como

말로 = 말 (words, comment, saying, palabras) + 로 (by, with, por, con)

"안녕"이란 말로 = With the words that is known as "An-nyeong" /
Con las palabras que se conoce como «An-nyeong »

늘 하던 시작과 끝 "안녕"이란 말로,
With the words "An-nyeong" that (we) habitually used for the beginning and ending, /
Con las palabras de «An-nyeong» que usamos habitualmente para el principio y el final,

오늘과 내일을 = 오늘 (today, hoy) + 과 (and, y) + 내일 (tomorrow, mañana) + 을 [object marker]
또 = [adverb] again / still / even now / moreover / otra vez / todavía / incluso ahora / de nuevo
함께 = [adverb] together / jointly / juntos

잇다 = [pronunication] 읻다 → 읻따 = [infinitive of verb] connect / thread / piece together / conectar / enhebrar / juntar
(해)보다 = [infinitive of verb] have a try / give a shot / attempt to / carry out / venture to / probar / tratar / intentar / llevar a cabo / atreverse
이어보다 = try to connect [thread] / attempt to piece together / intentar conectarnos
이어보자! = Let's try to connect [thread] / Let's piece together / Intentemos conectarnos
이어보자고! = stronger expression than 이어보자!

오늘과 내일을 또 함께 이어보자고!
Let's try to connect today and tomorrow together! /
¡Intentemos conectarnos hoy y mañana juntos!

< Line 20 > 멈춰 있지만, 어둠에 숨지 마! 빛은 또 떠오르니깐.

멈추다 = [infinitive of verb] stop / halt / bring to a stop (halt) / stand still / quit moving / pararse / detener / dejar de moverse
멈추어 = an adverb-type of conjugation
있다 = [pronunciation] 읻다 → 읻따 = [infinitive of verb] there is / be / exist / stay / remain / stand / hay / estar / existir / quedarse / permanecer / pararse
멈추어 있다 = [present progressive] be standing still / came to a halt / stop moving / está parandose / quedarse / detenerse / dejar de moverse
멈추어 있지만 = **멈춰 있지만** = [pronunciation] 멈춰 읻찌만 = Even though the World stood still, / We brought ourselves to a halt, but / Aunque el mundo se detuvo, /
Nos detuvimos, pero …

어둠에 = 어둠 (darkness, shadow, oscuridad) + 에 (in, under, en)
숨다 = [verb] hide / conceal oneself / lurk in / take refuge / disappear / esconderse / ocultarse

말다 = [verb] quit doing / refrain from doing / not do any longer / dejar de hacer / no hacer

(하지) 마! = [familiar ending for imperative mood] Don't do! / Quit (doing)! / ¡No (lo) hagas!

숨지 마! = Don't hide! / Don't conceal yourself! /Don't lurk in! / ¡No te escondas! /
¡No te oculta!

멈춰있지만, 어둠에 숨지 마!
Even though the World stood still, do not lurk in the shadow! /
Aunque el mundo se detuvo, ¡no te escondas en la oscuridad!

빛은 = [pronunciation] 비츤 = 빛 (light, sunbeam, luz, rayo) + 은 [marker for subject]

또 = [adverb] again / still / even now / moreover / otra vez / todavía / incluso ahora / de nuevo

떠오르다 = [verb] rise / emerge / come up / surface / elevarse / emerger / subir / amanecer

떠오르니까 = because rise / because come up / for (it) is supposed to surface / porque elevarse

떠오르니깐 = stronger expression than 떠오르니까.

You see, because surely rise to the sky / You see, for (it) is destined to surface /
Verás, porque seguro que sube al cielo / Verás, porque está destinado a emerger

빛은 또 떠오르니깐 = You see, because the sunbeam is destined to surface again /
Verás, porque el rayo de sol está destinado a emerger de nuevo

< Line 12 > 끝이 보이지 않아. 출구가 있긴 할까?

The end is not to be seen. / The end cannot be found. /
Is there any way-out existing? / I wonder whether there is an exit.

El final no se ve. / El final no se puede encontrar. /
¿Existe alguna salida? / Me pregunto si hay una salida.

< Line 13 > 발이 떼지질 않아, 않아. Oh

I cannot start walking. / I cannot move forward. / My feet refuse to walk. /
No puedo empezar a caminar. / No puedo seguir adelante. / Mi pies se niegan a caminar.

< Line 14 > 잠시 두 눈을 감아. 여기 내 손을 잡아. 저 미래로 달아나자.

Close (your) two eyes for a moment. / Cierra los ojos por un momento.

Here, hold my hand. / Aquí, toma mi mano.

Let's elope to the future over there. / Fugémonos al futuro de allí.

< Line 15 > Like an echo in the forest, 하루가 돌아오겠지. 아무 일도 없단 듯이 ...

Another day would come in turn as if nothing had happened ... /
Otro día vendría a su vez como si nada hubiera pasado ...

< Line 16 > Yeah, life goes on. Like an arrow in the blue sky, 또 하루 더 날아가지.

Another day flies away again. / One more day shall be gone.

Otro día vuelva de nuevo. / Un día más se habrá ido.

**< Line 17 > On my pillow, on my table. Yeah, life goes on like this again.
I remember, I rember, I remember, I remember ...**

7. Magic Shop

Artist: BTS
Lyric Writers: JK, Hiss Noise, RM, Jordan "DJ Swivel" Young,
Candace Nicole Sosa, ADORA, J-Hope, Suga

< Line 1 > 망설인다는 걸 알아.

망설이다 = [infinitive of verb] hesitate / vacillate / hang back / hesitar / vacilar /
dudar / titubear
있다 = [pronunciation] 읻다 → 읻따 = [infinitive of verb] there is / be / exist / stay / remain /
stand / hay / estar / existir / quedarse / permanecer / pararse
망설이고 있다 = 망설인다 = [present progressive] be hesitating / be vacillating /
be hanging back / estar dudando / estar vacilando / estar titubeando
망설이고 있다는 = **망설인다는** = [adjective form of present progressive] that are hesitating
[vacillating, hanging back, baulking] / que estás hesitando [vacilando, dudando, titubeando]

걸 = 것을 = [pronunciation] 거슬 = 것 (the thing that ~, the fact that ~, el hecho que ~,
lo que ~) + 을 [marker for object]
망설인다는 걸 = the fact that you are hesitating / el echo de que estés dudando

알다 = [infinitive of verb] know / be aware of / recognize / notice / saber / conocer / notar
알아 = familiar ending of 알다 = I know that ~ / I notice that ~ / (yo) sé que ~

망설인다는 것을 알아. = I know that (you) are hesitating. / Sé lo que estés dudando.

< Line 2 > 진심을 말해줘도, 결국 다 흉터들로 돌아오니까.

진심 = [noun] true heart / earnestness / sincerity / wholeheartedness /
verdadero corazón / franqueza
진심을 = [pronunciation] 진시믈 = 진심 + 을 [marker for object]
말하다 = [infinitive of verb] say / tell / talk / speak / state / decir / hablar / referir
주다 = [infinitive of verb] kindly do / give as a favour / willing to do / please, /
amablemente hacer / dar con gusto / dispuesto a hacer / por favor,
말해 주다 = kindly do telling / kindly give telling / kindly tell / honestly confide to others /
decir con gusto / honestamente confiar a los demás

말해 주어도 = **말해 줘도** = even if kindly tell, / even though you honestly confide to others, /
incluso si dices angelicamente, / aunque honestamente confías a los demás,

● All the vowels and four consonants (ㄴ, ㄹ, ㅁ, ㅇ) are voiced sounds, which are soft. A consonant that is between any two of them becomes soft as well. The above 'ㄷ' is located between two vowels ㅓ and ㅗ. Therefore, it becomes soft. [줘도 → 줘도]

결국 = [pronunciation] 결국 = [noun, also used as adverb] eventually / finally / at last / in the end / al final / por fin

다 = [adverb] all / everything / everyone / totally / completely / todo(s) / totalmente / completamente

흉터들로 = 흉터 (scar, wound, cicatriz, herida) + 들 [plural] + 로 (as, como)

돌아오다 = [pronunciation] 도라오다 = [infinitive of verb] come back / return / come around / volver / regresar / devolverse

돌아오니까 = [pronunciation] 도라오니까 = because it comes back / it is supposed to retrun / porque vuelve / se supone que regresará

진심을 말해줘도, 결국 다 흉터들로 돌아오니까.
Even if you kindly confide your heart, it will come around as a scar (to you) in the end. / Incluso si confías honestamente, todo volverá (a ti) como una cicatriz al final.

< Line 3 > "힘을 내!"란 뻔한 말은 하지 않을 거야.

힘을 = 힘 (power, force, strength, energy, fuerza, poder, energía) + 을 [marker for object]

내다 = [infinitive of verb] exert / gather / muster / manifest / display / ejercitar / juntar / mostrar

"힘을 내!" = Do your best! / More strength! / ¡Haz tu major esfuerzo! / ¡ Más fuerza!

(이)라는 = (이)란 = **란** = that is called [named] as / so-called / being known as / that they call / que se llama (como) / así se llama / que se conoce como / que la gente llama / tal como

뻔하다 = [infinitive of adjective] be obvious / be banal [commonplace, hackneyed, insipid, corny] / ser obvio / ser banal [común, trillado, insípido]

뻔한 = present form of 뻔하다 = obvious / banal / obvio / insípido

말은 = 말 (words, comment, saying, palabras) + 은 [marker for object]

● Please note that, here, «은» is a marker for object. It can replace «을 [marker for object]».
In that case, «은» is stronger than «을» as a marker for object.

- 그 말**을** 하지 않을 거야 = I would not say those words.

- 그 말**은** 하지 않을 거야 = I would never say those words.

하다 = [infinitive of verb] do / act / make / hacer / realizar

말을 하다 = [verb phrase] tell / say / speak / talk / decir / hablar

아니 하다 = 안 하다 = 않다 = [pronunciation] 안타 = not do / no hacer

말을 아니 하다 = not tell / not say / not speak / no talk / no decir / no hablar

말을 아니 하다 = 말을 안 하다 = 말을 하지 않다 = [pronunciation] 마를 하지 안타

말을 하지 않다 = not tell / not say / not speak / no talk / no decir / no hablar

말은 하지 않다 = never tell / never say / never talk / nunca decir / nunca hablar

않을 = [pronunciation] 안을 → 아늘 = (future) adjective form of 않다

것이다 = 것 (the thing that ~, the fact that ~, el hecho que ~, lo que ~) + 이다 (be, ser)

것이야 = 거야 = familiar ending of 것이다

말을 하지 않을 거야 = (The fact is that) I would not say it / (El hecho es que) yo no lo diría.

말은 하지 않을 거야 = (The fact is that) I would never say it /
(El hecho es que) yo nunca lo diría.

않을 거야 = [pronunciation] 안을 거야 → 아늘 꺼야

● In Korean, the pronunciation of the first consonant just after '르' tends to become hard.

"힘을 내!"란 뻔한 말은 하지 않을 거야.
I would never do the thing that I tell you those hackneyed words such as "Do your best!" /
I would never tell you those hackneyed words such as "Do your best!"

Nunca haría lo que te digo con esas palabras tal trilladas como « ¡Haz tu major esfuerzo! » /
Nunca te diría esas palabras tal trilladas como « ¡Haz tu major esfuerzo! »

< Line 4 > 난 내 얘길 들려줄께, 들려줄께.

난 = 나는 = 나 (I, yo) + 는 [marker for subject]

내 = 나의 = 나 (I, yo) + 의 [marker for possession] of me / my / mi

얘길 = 얘기를 = 이야기 (story, tale, narration, historia, cuento, narración) + 를 [marker of object]

들려주다 = [infinitive of verb] tell / let hear / narrate / decir / dejar oír / narrar / contar

● Owing to its frequent usage, '들려주다' has become a verb. So, no space between 들려 and 주다.

줄께 = familiar ending for commitment of 주다 = I am willing / I promise / I do with pleasure / Estoy despuesto / Prometo / (Lo) hago con placer

들려줄께 = [familiar ending for commitment] I promise to tell. / I will tell. / I will let you hear. / Prometio contar. / Lo diré. / Te dejaré escuchar.

난 내 얘길 들려줄께. = I will tell you my story. / Te contaré mi historia.

< Line 5 > 내가 뭐랬어? 이길 거랬잖아!

내가 = 나 (I, yo) + 이가 [marker for subject]

뭐라다 = 무엇이라고 하다 = 무엇 (what, qué) + 이라고 하다 (say, decir)

뭐랬어? = [pronunciation] 뭐래써? = 무엇이라고 하였어? = [past familiar ending for questioning] = What did I say? / ¿Qué dije?

내가 뭐랬어? = What did I say? / ¿Qué dije?

● This is an emphasis rather than a question. So, there is no need to raise the tone at the end.

이기다 = [infinitive of verb] win / triumph / overcome / get over / ganar / triunfar / vencer

이길 = (future) adjective form of 이기다 = will win / be going to overcome / come to get over / ganaríamos / vendremos a triunfar / ir a vencer

것 = [noun] the thing that ~ / the fact that ~ / la cosa que ~ / el hecho que ~ / el caso que ~ / lo que ~

이길 것 = [pronunciation] 이길 껏 = the thing that we will win / the fact that we are going to triumph / the fact that we come to get over / lo que ganaríamos / lo que vendremos a trinufar / el hecho que vamos a vencer

이길 것이라고 하다 = [pronunciation] 이길 꺼시라고 하다

이라고 하다 = [verb phrase] say / talk / decir / hablar

이라고 하였다 = [pronunciation] 이라고 하엳따 = [past sense] said / talked / dije / hablé

이라고 하였지 = [pronunciation] 이라고 하엳찌 = a noun-type conjugation of 이라고 하였다

아니 하다 = 안 하다 = 않다 = [pronunciation] 안타 = not do / no hacer

않아? = [pronunciation] 아나? = [tag questioning] I did, didn't I? / hice, ¿no?

이라고 하였지 않아? = [tag questioning] You see, I said so, didn't I? / Verás, ya lo dije, ¿no?

이길 것이라고 하였지 않아? = 이길 거라고 했지 않아! = 이길 거랬지 않아! =
이길 거랬잖아! = [pronunciation] 이길 꺼랜짜나!

이길 거래랬잖아! = You see, I said that we will win, didn't I? /
I said that we are going to triump, didn't I? / Verás, dije que ganaríamos, ¿no? /
Dije que vamos a triunfar, ¿no?

● This is an emphasis rather than a question. So, there is no need to raise the tone at the end.

< Line 6 > 믿지 못했어. (정말) 이길 수 있을까?

믿다 = [pronunciation] 믿따 = [infinitive of verb] believe (in) / trust / confide /
be sure / confiar / creer
믿지 = [pronunciation] 믿찌 = a noun-type conjugation of 믿다

● All the vowels and four consonants (ㄴ, ㄹ, ㅁ, ㅇ) are voiced sounds, which are soft. A
consonant that is not between any two of them becomes hard (or fortis), if applicable like
[ㄱ → ㄲ] [ㄷ→ ㄸ] [ㅂ → ㅃ] [ㅅ → ㅆ] [ㅈ → ㅉ]. [믿지 → 믿찌]

못 = [pronunciation] 몯 = [adverb] not / unable / can't / incapable / won't /
no / no puede / incapaz
하다 = [infinitive of verb] do / act / make / hacer / realizar
하였다 = 했다 = [pronunciation] 핻따 = past tense of 하다 = did / made / hizo / hice
하였어 = **했어** = [pronunciation] 해써 = familiar ending of 하였다 / 했다
믿지 못하였어 = 믿지 못했어 = [pronunciation] 믿찌 몯해써 → 믿찌 모태써 =
familiar ending of 믿지 못하였다 = couldn't believe / couldn't be sure /
was not able to believe / no podía creer / no podía estar seguro

믿지 못했어. = I couldn't be sure. / No podía estar seguro.

정말 = [adverb] really / for real / truly / in reality / verdaderamente / de verdad
이기다 = [infinitive of verb] win / triumph / overcome / get over / ganar / triunfar / vencer
이길 = (future) adjective form of 이기다 = winning / overcoming / getting over / ganando /
triunfando / venciendo
수 = [noun] way / means / resource / possibility / likelihood / medio / recurso / posibilidad /
probabilidad

있다 = [pronunciation] 읻다 → 읻따 = [infinitive of verb] there is / be / exist / stay / remain / stand / hay / estar / existir / quedarse / permanecer / pararse

● All the vowels and four consonants (ㄴ, ㄹ, ㅁ, ㅇ) are voiced sounds, which are soft. A consonant that is not between any two of them becomes hard (or fortis), if applicable like [ㄱ → ㄲ] [ㄷ → ㄸ] [ㅂ → ㅃ] [ㅅ → ㅆ] [ㅈ → ㅉ]. [있다 → 읻다 → 읻따]

이길 수 있다 = [pronunciation] 이길 쑤 읻따 = [verb phrase] can win / can triump / can overcome / can get over

● In Korean, the pronunciation of the first consonant just after 'ㄹ' tends to become hard. This rule applies only between two pure Korean words. [이길 수 → 이길 쑤]

이길 수 **있을까?** = [pronunciation] 이길 쑤 이쓸까? = familiar ending for questioning of 이길 수 있다

이길 수 있을까? = Could (we) win? / Could (we) overcome? / ¿Podríamos ganar? / ¿Podríamos vencer?

< Line 7 > 이 기적이 아닌 기적을 우리가 만든 걸까?

이 = [determiner] this / these / este / estos

기적 = [noun] miracle / marvel / wonder / mystery / milagro / maravilla / misterio

기적이 = [pronunciation] 기저기 = 기적 (miracle, milagro) + 이 [marker for subject]

아니다 = [infinitive of adjective] be not / be no / be different / no ser / ser diferente

아닌 = present tense of 아니다 = that is not / that is no / different / que no ser / diferente

기적을 = [pronunciation] 기저글 = 기적 (miracle) + 을 [marker for object]

우리가 = 우리 (we, nosotros) + 가 [marker for subject]

만들다 = [infinitive of verb] make / produce / create / build / hacer / crear / lograr

만드는 = present adjective form of 만들다 = making / creating / que hacemos / logrando

만든 = past adjective form of 만들다 = that we made / that we created / que hicimos / que logramos

것이다 = 것 (the thing that ~, the fact that ~, el hecho que ~, lo que ~) + 이다 (be, ser)

걸까? = 것 + 일까? = soliloquy questioning form of 것이다 = Is it the thing that ~? / Is it that ~? / I wonder if ~ / ¿Es el hecho que ~? / ¿Es que ~? / Me pregunto si ~

만든 걸까? = Is it the thing that (we) did? / Did (we) make it? / ¿Es lo que hicimos? / ¿Lo logramos?

이 기적이 아닌 기적을 우리가 만든 걸까?

Did we make this miracle (of ours) that is different from other miracles? / ¿Hicimos este milagro (nuestro) que es diferente de otros milagros?

< Line 8 > 난 여기 있었고, 네가 내게 다가와 준 거야. I do believe your Galaxy.

난 = 나는 = 나 (I, yo) + 는 [marker for subject]

여기 = [pronoun, also used as adverb] this spot / this place / here / now / esto / este lugar / aquí / ahora

있다 = [pronunciation] 읻다 → 읻따 = [infinitive of verb] there is / be / exist / stay / remain / stand / hay / estar / existir / quedarse / permanecer / pararse

있었다 = [pronunciation] 이썯따 = past tense of 있다 = there was / was / existed / stayed / había / estaba / existía / quedaba

있었고, = [pronunciation] 이썯고 → 이썯꼬 = there was, and / was, and / remained, and / stayed, and / estaba, y / quedaba, y

네가 = 너 (you, tú) + 이가 [marker for subject]

내게 = 나 (I, yo) + 에게 (to, towards, a) = to me / a mí

다가오다 = [infinitive of verb] come closer / approach / draw [get] near / venir cerca / acercarse

주다 = [infinitive of verb] give as a favour / willing to do / please, / amablemente hacer / dar con gusto / dispuesto a hacer / por favor,

다가와 주다

kindly do approaching / kindly come closer / show the kindness of approaching / amablemente [agradablemente] acercarse / mostrar la amabilidad de acercarse

주는 = present adjective form of 주다 = that do kindly [as a favour] / que das con gusto / que haces amablemente

준 = past adjective form of 주다 = that did did kindly [as a favour] / that diste con gusto / que haciste amablemente

줄 = (future) adjective form of 주다 = that will do kindly / that darás con gusto

것이다 = [pronunciation] 거시다 = 것 (the thing that ~, the fact that ~, el hecho que ~, lo que ~) + 이다 (be, ser)

것이야 = [pronunciation] 거시야 = **거야** = familiar ending of 것이다

다가와 준 **거**야 = [pronunciation] 다가와 준 **거**야 = Here, 'ㄱ' is between ㄴ and ㅓ

다가와 줄 **거**야 = [pronunciation] 다가와 줄 **꺼**야 = The first consonant just after 'ㄹ' tends to become hard. This rule is applicable between two independent words.

난 여기 있었고, 네가 내게 다가와 준 거야.
Here I was, and you kindly approached me. /
I was here, and (the fact is that) it is you who showed the kindness of coming up to me.

Aquí estaba yo, y amablemente te acercaste a mí. /
Estuve aquí, y (es el echo que) fuiste tú quien mostró la bondad de acercarte a mí.

< Line 9 > 듣고 싶어, 너의 멜로디.
너의 은하수의 별들은 너의 하늘을 과연 어떻게 수 놓을지 ...

듣다 = [pronunciation] 듣따 = [infinitive of verb] hear / listen to / oír / escuchar

싶다 = [pronunciation] 십다 → 십따 = [infinitive of verb] feel like / would like to / want to / wish to / desire to / querer / gustar

듣고 싶다 = [pronunciation] 듣꼬 십따 = [verb phrase] feel like listening / want (wish, desire) to hear / tener ganas de escuchar / querer [desear] escuchar

듣고 싶어 = [pronunciation] 듣꼬 시퍼 = familiar ending of 가고 싶다

너의 = 너 (you, tú) + 의 [marker for possession] = of you / your / tu

멜로디 = 곡조 / 선율 = [noun] melody / melodía

듣고 싶어, 너의 멜로디. = I want to hear your melody. / Quiero escuchar tu melodía.

너의 = 너 (you, tú) + 의 [marker for possession] = of you / your / tu

은하수 = [noun] galaxy / milky way / galaxia / vía láctea

은하수의 = 은하수 + 의 [marker for possession] = of the galaxy / de la galaxia

별들은 = 별 (star, estrella) + 들 [plural] + 은 [marker for subject] = stars / estrellas

하늘을 = 하늘 (sky, cielo) + 을 [marker for object]

과연 = [adverb] indeed / sure enough / in reality / en efecto / en realidad

어떻게 = [pronunciation] 어떤케 = [adverb] how / in what way [manner] / cómo / de qué manera

수 = [noun] embroidery / crewelwork / bordado

놓다 = [pronunciation] 노타 = set / put / do / hacer

수(를) 놓다 = 수 (embroidery) + 를 [marker for object] + 놓다 = embroider / decorate / bordar

수(를) 놓을 = (future) adjective form of 수(를) 놓다

수(를) 놓을지 ... = [pronunciation] 수(를) 노을찌 = how will embroider / in which method will decorate / cómo bordará / en qué método decorará

● '지' was originally an independent word, whose meaning is «uncertainty», «probability» or «whether». Now it is combined with a verb for making a noun form.

● In Korean, the pronunciation of the first consonant after '을' tends to become hard.
[놓을지 = 놓을 + 지 → 놓을찌]

너의 은하수의 별들은 너의 하늘을 과연 어떻게 수 놓을지 ...
(I wonder) how the stars of your galaxy will embroider your sky ... /
(I am curious about) in which method the stars of your galaxy will decorate your sky ...

(Me pregunto) cómo las estreallas de tu galaxia bordarán tu cielo ... /
(Tengo curiosidad sobre) en qué método las estrellas de tu galxia decorarán tu cielo ...

< Line 10 > 나의 절망 끝에 결국 내가 널 찾았음을 잊지 마!

나의 = 나 (I, yo) + 의 [marker for possession] = of me / my / mi

절망 = [noun] despair / hopelessness / frustration / desesperanza / desesparación / frustración

끝에 = [pronunciation] 끝테 → 끝체 = 끝 (the end, edge, el final) + 에 (at, a) = at the end / al final

결국 = [pronunciation] 결국 = [noun, also used as adverb] eventually / finally / at last / in the end / al final / por fin

내가 = 나 (I, yo) + 이가 [marker for subject]

널 = 너를 = 너 (you, tú) + 를 [marker for object]

찾다 = [infinitive of verb] find out / discover / detect / encontrar / descubrir

찾았음 = [pronunciation] 차자씀 = noun form of 찾다 = the fact that I discovered it / el echo de que lo descubrí

● «noun form» can be regarded as a noun, «adverb-form» can be regarded as an adverb, while «a noun-type conjuation» or «an adverb-type conjugation» is regarded as a verb.

● In principle, 찾다 = look for / find / buscar vs. 찾아내다 = find out / discover / encontrar / descubrir. In many cases, Korean speakers use 찾다 as 찾아내다 (find out / discover / encontrar / descubrir).

찾았음을 = 찾았음 + 을 [marker for object]

잊다 = [pronunciation] 읻따 = [infinitive of verb] forget / slip one's memory / olvidarse / poner en olvido

잊지 = [pronunciation] 읻찌 = a noun-type conjugation of 잊다

말다 = [verb] quit doing / refrain from doing / not do any longer / dejar de hacer / no hacer

(하지) 마! = [familiar ending for imperative mood] Don't do! / Quit (doing)! / ¡No (lo) hagas!

잊지 마! =Don't forget! / ¡No olvides!

나의 절망 끝에 결국 내가 널 찾았음을 잊지 마!
Don't forget (the fact) that I eventually discovered you at the end of my despair! /
¡No olvides (el hecho) que últimamente te descubrí al final de mi desesparación!

< Line 11 > 넌 절벽 끝에 서 있던 내 마지막 이유야. (Live!)

넌 = 너는 = 너 (you, tú) + 는 [marker for subject]

절벽 = [pronunciation] 절벽 = [noun] cliff / precipice / acantilado / precipicio

끝에 = [pronunciation] 끄테 = 끝 (brink, edge, border, the end, borde, cabo)
+ 에 (on, at, en)

절벽 끝에 = on the brink of a cliff / al borde de un acantilado

서다 = [infinitive of verb] stand / take a stand / erguirse / estar de pie

서 = an adverb-type conjugation of 서다

있다 = [pronunciation] 읻다 → 읻따 = [infinitive of verb] there is / be / exist / stay / remain / stand / hay / estar / existir / quedarse / permanecer / pararse

서 있다 = [pronunciation] 서 읻따 = [present progressive] stand erect / estar erguido

서 있는 = [pronunciation] 서 인는 = present adjective form of 서 있다 = that is standing erect / que está erguido

서 있던 = [pronunciation] 서 읻떤 = past adjective form of 서 있다 = that was stading erect / que estaba erguido

내 = 나의 = 나 (I, yo) + 의 [marker for possession] = of me / my / mi

마지막 = [noun, also used as adjective] the end / closing / last / final / último

이유 = [noun] reason / cause / justification / razón / causa

이다 = [infinitive of marker that conjugates] be / ser

이유이다 = It is the reason / It is the cause / Es la razón / Es la causa

이유야 = familiar ending of 이유이다.

넌 절벽 끝에 서 있던 내 마지막 이유야
You are the last reason (of surviving) for me who stood erect on the brink of a cliff. /
Eres la último razón (de sobrevivir) para mí que estaba erguido al borde de un acantilado.

< Line 12 > 내가 나인 게 싫은 날, 영영 사라지고 싶은 날.

내가 = 나 (I, yo) + 이가 [marker for subject]

나인 게 = 나 (I, yo) + 인 + 것 + 이

인 = adjective form of 이다 [be, ser] = who (I) am / that is (me) / que soy

게 = 것 (the thing that ~, the fact that ~, el hecho que ~, lo que ~) + 이 [marker for subject]

내가 나인 게 = The fact that I am me / El hecho de que yo soy yo

싫다 = [pronunciation] 실타 = [infinitive of verb] dislike / hate / don't want (to) / odiar

싫은 = [pronunciation] 실은 → 시른 = present form of 싫다 = that dislike / when hating /
que odio

싫던 = [pronunciation] 실턴 = past form of 싫다 = that disliked / that hated /
que odié [odiaste]

날 = [noun] day / día

내가 나인 게 싫은 날 = On a day in which I [you] dislike the fact that I am me [you are you]. /
[Korean] On a day when I hate to be myself. =
On a day when you hate to be yourself. [English]

En el día en que no me [te] guste el hecho de ser yo [tú]. /
[Coreano] En el día en que odio ser yo mismo. =
El día en que odias ser tú mismo. [Español]

● Here, one should translate «나/I» as «너/you». One can find that this would be logically correct when reading the next lines of the song.

● English speakers mostly use «you» for generalization. For example, "When you go to Rome, do what Romans do." In case of Korean speakers, they mostly use «나/I» for generalization.

● 내가 로마에 가면, 로마식 대로 해야 하는 거야. If I go to Rome, I should act in

Roman way. / Si voy a Roma, debería actuar de la manera romana.

● The reason why Korean speakers use «나/I» for generalization is because it sounds like ordering or lecturing if «너/you» is used.

● «여기»를 «내 집»처럼 생각하세요! = Please regard «this house» as «my house»! = ¡Mi casa, su casa!
Therefore, «여기 / this house» in Korean = «mi casa» is Spanish, and «내 집 / my house» in Korean = «su casa» in Spanish.
[Korean] ¡This house, my house! = ¡Mi casa, su casa! [Spanish]

영영 = [adverb] forever / for good / eternally / para siempre / perpetuamente
사라지다 = [infinitive of verb] disappear / vanish / go away / be gone / irse / desaparecerse
싶다 = [pronunciation] 십다 → 십따 = [infinitive of verb] feel like / would like to / want to / wish to / desire to / querer / gustar
사라지고 싶다 = [verb phrase] want to disappear / wish to vanish / querar desaparecer
사라지고 싶은 = [pronunciation] 사라지고 시픈 = present form of 사라지고 싶다
사라지고 싶던 = [pronunciation] 사라지고 십떤 = past form of 사라지고 싶다

사라지고 싶은 날 = On a day in which feeling like disappearing /
En el día en que quiera[s] me [te] desaparecer

영영 사라지고 싶은 날 = On a day in which [I, you] feel like disappearing forever /
En el día en que yo [tú] quiera[s] me [te] desaparecer para siempre

● In the next lines, we come to find the correct translation would be you [tú], not I [yo].

< Line 13 > 문을 하나 만들자. 너의 맘 속에다.

문을 = [pronunciation] 무늘 = 문 (gate, door, entrance, entry, portón, puerta) + 을 [marker for object]
하나 = [noun] one / uno
만들다 = [infinitive of verb] make / produce / create / build / crear / componer / construir
만들자 = [familiar ending for propositive mode] let's make / let's build / hagamos / construyamos
너의 = 너 (you, tú) + 의 [marker for possession] = of you / your / tu
맘 = 마음 = [noun] mind / heart / feelings / caring heart / mente / corazón

속에다 = 속 (the inside, el interior) + 에다 (in, at, en)

문을 하나 만들자. 너의 맘 속에다. = (On such a day) let's make a gate in your mind. / (En un día así) hugamos una puerta en tu mente.

< Line 14 > 그 문을 열고 들어가면, 이곳이 (너를) 기다릴 거야.

믿어도 괜찮아. 널 위로해 줄 Magic Shop.

그 = [determiner] the / that / those / ese / esos / tal

문을 = 문 (gate, door, entrance, entry, portón, puerta) + 을 [marker for object]

열다 = [infinitive of verb] open / unlock / uncover / abrir

열고 = open, and / unlock, and / uncover, and / abrir, y

들어가다 = [infinitive of verb] go into / go inside / enter (into) / entrar

들어가면 = if go into / if go inside / when enter into / si entrar / cuando entrar

이곳이 = 이곳 (this spot, this place, here, este lugar, aquí) + 이 [marker for subject]

(너를) = 너 (you, tú) + 를 [marker for object]

기다리다 = [infinitive of verb] wait (for) / await / hold on / expect / esperar / aguardar / esperanzar

기다릴 = (future) adjective form of 기다리다 = will be waiting (for) / estará esperando

것이다 = 것 (the thing that ~, the fact that ~, el hecho que ~, lo que ~) + 이다 (be, ser)

것이야 = **거야** = familiar ending of 것이다

기다릴 거야 = [pronunciation] 기다릴 꺼야

● In Korean, the pronunciation of the first consonant just after ' ㄹ ' tends to become hard.

이곳이 너를 기다릴 거야 = There is a fact that this spot will be waiting for you. / This spot will be waiting for you. / This place will be awaiting you.

Es un hecho que este lugar te estará esperando. / Este lugar estará esperando para ti. / Este lugar te estará esperando.

그 문을 열고 들어가면, 이곳이 너를 기다릴 거야.

If you open and enter the gate, this spot will be waiting for you. /
Si abres y entras por la puerta, este lugar te estará esperando.

믿다 = [pronunciation] 믿따 = [infinitive of verb] believe (in) / trust / confide / be sure /
confiar / creer

믿어도 = [pronunciation] 미더도 = [tone of concession] even in the case of believing /
even if you trust (that place) / incluso si creas / aunque confías (en el lugar)

괜찮다 = [pronunciation] 괜찬타 = [infinitive of verb] be okay [all right, no problem] /
estar bien

괜찮아 = [pronunciation] 괜차나 = familiar ending of 괜찮다

믿어도 괜찮아. = It is okay to trust (this place) / I assure you (of this place) /
Be confident about (this spot) / Está bien confiar (en este lugar). /
Te lo aseguro (de este lugar). / Tén confianza (en este lugar).

널 = 너를 = 너 (you, tú) + 를 [marker for object] = you / te

위로하다 = [infinitive of verb] console / comfort / give comfort to / consolar / aliviar

주다 = [infinitive of verb] kindly do / give as a favour / willing to do / please, /
amablemente hacer / dar con gusto / dispuesto a hacer / por favor,

위로해 주다 = kindly give comfort to / willing to console / dar consuelo con gusto /
amablemente aliviar

위로해 주는 = present adjective form of 위로해 주다 = that kindly comforts / que da consuelo

위로해 준 = past adjective form of 위로해 주다 = that kindly comforted / que diste consuelo

위로해 주던 = past adjective form [repeatedly] = that used to comfort kinldy /
que daba consuelo

위로해 줄 = (future) adjective form of 위로해 주다 = that will kindly comfort /
que dará consuelo

널 위로해 줄 Magic Shop. = (It is the) Magic Shop that will kindly comfort you. /
(Es la) Magic Shop que te dará consuelo con gusto.

< Line 15 > 따뜻한 차 한 잔을 마시며, 저 은하수를 올려다보면, 넌 괜찮을 거야.

Oh, 여긴 Magic Shop. [So, show me. (I'll show you.) X 3] Show you, Show you.

따뜻하다 = [pronunciation] 따뜯하다 → 따뜨타다 = [infinitive of adjective] be warm /

be heartwarming / estar caliente

따뜻한 = [pronunciation] 따뜯한 → 따뜨탄 = present form of 따뜻하다 = warm / heartwarming / caliente

차 = [noun] tea / té

한 = [numerical] a / one / un

잔을 = 잔 (cup, glass, taza, vaso) + 을 [marker for object]

마시다 = [infinitive of verb] drink / have / take / imbibe / beber / inhalar

마시며 = an adverb-type conjugation of 마시다 = [simultaneous action] while drinking / mientras beber / mientras inhalar

저 = [determiner] that / those / over there / aquel / allí

은하수를 = 은하수 (galaxy, milky way, galaxia, vía láctea) + 를 [marker for object]

보다 = [infinitive of verb] see / watch / look at / observe / ver / mirar / observar

올려다 보다 = look up (to) / raise one's eye toward / turn one's face up toward / mirar hacia arriba / levantar la mirada hacia

올려다 보면 = if look up / when turn face up toward / si mirar hacia arriba

넌 = 너는 = 너 (you, tú) + 는 [marker for subject]

괜찮다 = [pronunciation] 괜찬타 = [infinitive of adjective] be okay [all right] / be no problem / está bien

괜찮을 = [pronunciation] 괜찬을 → 괜차늘 = (future) adjective form of 괜찬타 = will be okay / estará bien

것이다 = 것 (the thing that ~, the fact that ~, el hecho que ~, lo que ~) + 이다 (be, ser)

것이야 = **거야** = familiar ending of 것이다

넌 괜찮을 거야 = It will be that you are okay. / You will be okay. / You will become all right. / Será que estás bien. / Estarás bien. / Te pondrás bien.

여기 = [pronoun, also used as adverb] this spot / this place / here / now / esto / este lugar / aquí / ahora

여긴 = 여기 + 는 [marker for subject or emphasis]

따뜻한 차 한 잔을 마시며, 저 은하수를 올려다보면, 넌 괜찮을 거야.

Oh, 여긴 Magic Shop.

If you look up the Galaxy while drinking a heartwarming cup of tea, you will become all right. Oh, this spot is the Magic Shop.

Si miras hacia la Galaxia mientras bebes una caliente taza de té, te pondrás muy bien. Oh, este lugar es la Magic Shop.

< Line 16 > 필 땐 장미꽃처럼, 흩날릴 땐 벚꽃처럼, 질 땐 나팔꽃처럼, 아름다운 그 순간처럼, 항상 최고가 되고 싶(었)어. 그래서 조급했고, 늘 초조했어.

피다 = [infinitive of verb] bloom / blossom / come into flower / florecer / esflorecer

필 = adjective form of 피다 = blooming / blossoming / coming into flower / floreciendo / esfloreciendo

땐 = 때는 = 때 (the time when ~, the moment that ~, el momento en que ~)

+ 는 (at, on, en)

장미꽃 = [pronuncication] 장미꼳 = [noun] rose / rose flower / rosa

처럼 = [adverb] like / as if / as / como

필 땐 장미꽃처럼 = like rose flowers when blooming / como rosas cuando florece

흩어지다 = [pronunciation] 흐터지다 = be scattered [littered / dispersed] / esparcirse

날다 = [infinitive of verb] fly / volarse

흩날리다 = [pronunciation] 흔날리다 = 흩어져 [be scattered, and / ser esparcido, y]

+ 날리다 (be blown off, ser volado, volarse)

흩날리다 = [pronunciation] 흔날리다 = [passive form] be scattered and blown off / flutter / ser esparcido y volado / revolotear

흩날릴 = [pronunciation] 흔날릴 = adjective form of 흩날리다

벚꽃 = [pronunciation] 벋꼳 = [noun] cherry blossoms / flores de cerezo

흩날릴 땐 벚꽃처럼 = like cherry blossoms when fluttering / como flores de cerezo cuando revolotea

지다 = [infinitive of verb] wilt / wither (away) / marchitarse / desflorecer / ponerse mustio / secarse

질 = adjective form of 지다 = withering / wilting / waning / marchitando / menguando / enlaciando

나팔꽃 = [pronunciation] 나팔꼳 = [noun] morning glories / flores de campanilla

질 땐 나팔꽃처럼 = like morning glories when wilting / como flores de campanilla cuando desflorece

항상 = [adverb] always / all the time / the whole time / siempre / todo el tiempo

최고가 = 최고 (the best, the supremacy, the first rank, el mejor) + 가 [marker for subject]

● Here, «최고» is just the subject of verb «되다». It is not the subject of the whole sentence. The subject of the whole sentence «나는 (I, yo)» is omitted.

되다 = [infinitive of verb] become / turn into / volverse / convertirse / resultar / terminarse / hacerse / ser

되고 = a noun-type conjugation of 되다 = to become / to be / convertirse

나는 최고가 되고 싶다 = 나는 (I, yo) + 최고가 (the best, el major) + 되고 (to become, to be, convertirse, ser) + 싶다 (want, quiero) = I want to become [be] the best. / Quiero convertirme [ser] el mejor

싶다 = [pronunciation] 십다 → 십따 = [infinitive of adjective] feel like / would like / want / wish / desire / querer / gustar

● 싶다 is a status of mind rather than an action. Thus, it is an adjective.

되고 싶다 = [adjective phrase] feel like becoming / would like to become / want [wish, desire] to become / tengo ganas de ser / me gustaría volverse / quiero [deseo] convertirse

● By doing a noun-type conjugation the first verb can serve as an object of the second verb. [되고 싶다 = want to become] Here, «되고 (to become)» is the object of «싶다 (want)».

되고 싶어 = [pronunciation] 되고 시퍼 = familiar ending of 되고 싶다

되고 싶었어 = [pronunciation] 되고 시퍼써 = past tense of 되고 싶어 = wanted to become / wished to be / quise ser / quería convertirse / deseaba convertirse en

● Although the original line is 싶어 [present], it is more correct to use 싶었어 in the context.

항상 최고가 되고 싶(었)어. = I always wanted to be at the first rank. / Siempre quise ser el chico supremo.

그리하다 = [infinitive of verb] do it that way / do it in that manner / lo hacer de esa manera

그리하여서 = **그래서** = adverb form of 그리하다 = accordingly / therefore / that's why / por lo tanto / por eso / por así

조급하다 = [pronunciation] 조그파다 = [infinitive of adjective] be impatient / ser impaciente

조급하였다 = [pronunciation] 조그파옏따 = 조급했다 [조그팬따] = past form of 조급하다 = was impatient / estaba impaciente

조급했고 = [pronunciation] 조급핻꼬 → 조그팬꼬 = was impatient, and / acted by impetuosity, and / estaba impaciente, y / actué por impetuosidad, y

● When 'ㅎ' combines with a consonsant, the consonant becomes aspirated.

[ㄱ + ㅎ → ㅋ] [ㄷ + ㅎ → ㅌ] [ㅂ + ㅎ → ㅍ] [ㅈ + ㅎ → ㅊ]

그래서 조급했고 = accordingly, I was driven by impetuosity, and / por eso, actué por impetuosidad, y

늘 - [adverb] always / all the time / the whole time / siempre / todo el tiempo

초조하다 = [infinitive of adjective] be fretful / be nervous / estar nervioso / estar preocupado

초조하였다 = [pronunciation] 초조하옏따 = 초조했다 [초조핻따] = past tense of 초조하다 = was fretful / estaba inquieto [ansioso, agitado]

초조했어 = [pronunciation] 초조해써 = familiar ending of 초조했다

늘 초조했어. = I was fretful all the time. / Todo el tiempo estaba inquieto.

< Line 17 > 남들과(의) 비교는 일상이 돼 버렸고, 무기였던 내 욕심은 되레 날 옥죄고, 또 목줄이 됐어.

남들과(의) = 남 (stranger, other person, otra persona) + 들 [plural] + 과(의) [with, con] = with others / con los demás / con otros

비교는 = 비교 (comparison, comparación) + 는 [marker for subject]

남들과의 비교는 = The comparison with others / La comparación con los demás

일상이 = 일상 (daily routine, rutina diaria) + 이 [marker for subject]

되다 = [infinitive of verb] become / turn into / volverse / convertirse / resultar / terminarse / hacerse / ser

버리다 = [infinitive of verb] abandon / throw away / dump / discard / abandonar / descartar

돼 버리다 = 되어 버리다 = stronger expression than 되다 = end up becoming /
turn out to be / terminar / terminar convirtiéndose / resultar ser

돼 버렸다 = [pronunciation] 돼 버럳따 = past tense of 돼 버리다 = ended up becoming /
terminó convirtiéndose

돼 버렸고 = [pronunciation] 돼 버럳꼬 = ended up becoming, and /
terminó convirtiéndose, y

남들과의 비교는 일상이 돼 버렸고,
The comparison with others has ended up becoming a daily routine, and
La comparación con otros ha terminado convirtiéndose en una rutina diaria, y

무기 = [noun] arms / weapon / weaponry / arma / armamento

이다 = [infinitive of marker that conjugates] be / ser

이었다 = [pronunciation] 이얻따 = past tense of 이다 = was / has been / fue / ha sido

이었던 = **였던** [엳떤] = adjective form of 이었다 = that was / que fue / que era

내 = 나의 = 나 (I, yo) + 의 [marker for possession] = of me / my / mi

욕심은 = 욕심 (greed, avarice, self-interest, codicia, avaricia, interés propio) + 은 [marker
for subject]

무기였던 내 욕심(은) = the greed that was my weapon / la codicia que era mi arma

되레 = 도리어 = [adverb] on the contrary / rather / instead / ironically / al contraio /
irónicamente / antes bien

날 = 나를 = 나 (I, yo) + 를 [marker for object]

옥죄다 = [verb infinitive] sofocate / tighten / constrict / squeeze / sofocar / asifixiar /
contraer / apretar

옥죄고, = sofocate, and / constrict, and / squeeze, and / sofocar, y / asifixiar,y / apretar, y

또 = [adverb] again / in addition / moreover / otra vez / además / de nuevo

목줄이 = [pronunciation] 목쭐이 → 목쭈리 = 목 (neck, cuello) + 줄 (cord, cuerda) + 이
= 목줄 (leash, tendón de la garganta, collar, correa del cuello) + 이 [marker for subject]

● When two independent words combine, the first consonant of the second word becomes hard.
[목 (neck) + 줄 (cord) = 목줄 → 목쭐]

되다 = [infinitive of verb] become / turn into / volverse / convertirse / resultar / terminarse /
hacerse / ser

되었다 = [pronunciation] 되얻따 = 됐다 [됀따] = past tense of 되다 = became /
has become / turned into / se volvió / se convirtió / resultó

되었어 = [pronunciation] 되어써 = 됐어 [돼써] = familiar ending of 되었다

또 목줄이 되었어 = 또 목줄이 됐어 = moreover (it) turned into the neck leash. / además se convirtió en la correa del cuello.

남들과(의) 비교는 일상이 돼 버렸고, 무기였던 내 욕심은 되레 날 옥죄고,

또 목줄이 됐어.

The comparison with others has ended up becoming a daily routine, and the greed that used to be my weapon ironically came to suffocate me, and moreover turned into the neck leash.

La comparación con otros ha terminado convirtiéndose en una rutina diaria, y la codicia que solía ser mi arma irónicamente llegó a sofocarme, y además se convirtió en la correa del cuello.

< Line 18 > 그런데 말야, 돌이켜 보니 사실은 말야.

나, 최고가 되고 싶었던 것이 아닌 것만 같아.

그런데 = [adverb] by the way / but / however / a propósito / pero / por cierto / pues / mas

말이다 = 말 (words, comment, saying, palabras) + 이다 (be, ser) = say / talk / decir / hablar

말이야 = **말야** = familiar ending of 말이다 = if I say something / si digo algo

그런데 말야 = By the way, if I say something / Por cierto, si digo algo

돌이키다 = turn around [one's head] / get back / dar vuelta / girar la cabeza / volver

보다 = [infinitive of verb] see / watch / look at / observe / ver / mirar / observar

돌이켜 보다 = look around / look back (upon) / retrospect / mirar a mi alrededor / mirar hacia atrás

돌이켜 보니 = adverb form of 돌이켜보다 = looking back / upon reflecting / on my retrospect / mirando [hacia atrás, al reflexionar, sobre mi retrospectiva]

사실 = [noun] fact / reality / truth / hecho / realidad / verdad

사실은 = [adverb form] in fact / in reality / actually / indeed / de hecho / en efecto / realmente

말이다 = 말 (words, comment, saying, palabras) + 이다 (be, ser) = say / talk / decir / hablar

말이야 = **말야** = ending of 말이다 = if I tell the fact / si digo la realidad

사실은 말이야 = 사실은 말야 = [adverb phrase] if I tell the fact / let me tell the truth si digo la realidad / déja me decir la verdad

나, = 나(는) = 나 (I, yo) + (는) [marker for subject]

- Here, comma (,) is used to replace 는 [marker for subject]

최고가 = 최고 (the best person, the top ranker, la prima persona) + 가 [marker for subject]

- Here, the subject of the whole sentence is «나, [= 나는]». In Korean, «최고(the best)가» is the subject of the verb of 되고 (to become). But in English it the complement [to become the best].

나는 최고가 되고 싶다. = 나는 (I, yo) 최고가 (the best, el mejor) 되고 (to become, ser) 싶다 (want, quiero). = I want to become the best. = Yo quiero ser el mejor.

되다 = [infinitive of verb] become / turn into / volverse / convertirse / resultar / terminarse / hacerse / ser
싶다 = [pronunciation] 십다 → 십따 = [infinitive of adjective] feel like / would like / want / wish / desire / querer / gustar

- 싶다 is a status of mind rather than an action. Thus, it is an adjective.

되고 싶다 = [adjective phrase] feel like becoming / would like to become / want [wish, desire] to become / tengo ganas de ser / me gustaría volverse / quiero [deseo] convertirse
되고 싶었다 = [pronunciation] 되고 시펀따 = past tense of 되고 싶다
되고 싶었던 = [pronunciation] 되고 시펀떤 = adjective form of 되고 싶었다
= that wanted to become / que quería convertirse

것이 = 것 (the thing that ~, the fact that ~, el hecho que ~, lo que ~) + 이 [marker for subject]
되고 싶었던 것 = the fact that I wanted to become / el hecho de que quería convertirme
최고가 되고 싶었던 것이 = the fact that I wanted to become the top ranker /
el hecho de que quería convertirme en la prima persona + 이 [marker for subject]

아니다 = [infinitive of adjective] be not / be no / be not correct / no ser / no ser correcto
아닌 = present form of 아니다
것 = [noun] the thing that ~ / the fact that ~ / la cosa que ~ / el hecho que ~ /
el caso que ~ / lo que ~
것만 = [pronunciation] 걷만 → 건만 = 것 + 만 [marker for emphasis]

아닌 것만 = the thing that is not (correct) / el hecho que es no (correcto) + 만 (plainly, claramente)

같다 = [pronunciation] 갇따 = [infinitive of adjective] It looks like / It seems that / Parecer que
같아 = familiar ending of 같다.

● 아닌 것만 같다 is stronger expression than 아닌 것 같다.

아닌 것 같아 = It seems not to be true correct. / Parece que no es correcto.

아닌 것만 같아 = It seems plainly not to be correct. / Claramente parece que no es correcto.

최고가 되고 싶었던 것이 아닌 것만 같아.
The fact that I wanted to become the top ranker seems plainly not to be correct./
Plainly speaking, it seems not correct to say that I wanted to become the top ranker.

El hecho de que quería convertirme la primera persona parece que claramente no es correcto. /
Claramente, no parece correcto decir que quería convertirme en la primera persona.

그런데 말야, 돌이켜 보니 사실은 말야. 나, 최고가 되고 싶었던 것이 아닌 것만 같아.

By the way, upon reflecting, let me tell the truth. I, I seemed not wanting to become the top ranker.

Por cierto, al reflexionar, déja me decir la verdad. Yo, yo parecía no querer convertirme en la primera persona.

< Line 19 > 위로와 감동이 되고 싶었던 나. 그대의 슬픔 · 아픔 거둬 가고 싶어, 나.

위로와 = 위로 (comfort, consolation, consuelo, alivio) + 와 (and, y)

감동이 = 감동 (deep emotion, touching impression, gran emoción) + 이 [marker for subject]

되다 = [infinitive of verb] become / turn into / volverse / convertirse / resultar / terminarse / hacerse / ser
싶다 = [pronunciation] 십다 → 십따 = [infinitive of adjective] feel like / would like / want / wish / desire / querer / gustar

● 싶다 is a status of mind rather than an action. Thus, it is an adjective.

되고 싶다 = [adjective phrase] feel like becoming / would like to become / want [wish, desire] to become / tengo ganas de ser / me gustaría volverse / quiero [deseo] convertirse
되고 싶었다 = [pronunciation] 되고 시펀따 = past tense of 되고 싶다

되고 싶었던 = [pronunciation] 되고 시펀떤 = adjective form of 되고 싶었다
= that wanted to become / que quería convertirse

나 = [pronoun] I / me / yo

위로와 감동이 되고 싶었던 나. = Me who wanted to become comfort and deep emotion / Yo que quería convertirme en el consuelo y en gran emoción

그대 = [pronoun] poetic expression of you, dear, tú, amado, amada

그대의 = 그대 + 의 [marker for possession] = of you / your / tu

슬픔 · 아픔 = 슬픔 (sorrow, sadness, tristeza, aflicción) + 과 (and, y) + 아픔 (pain, dolor, pena)

거두다 = [infinitive of verb] collect / gather / bring together / take in / recoger / reunir

가다 = [infinitive of verb] go (away) / move away / ride / ir / irse / marchar / alejarse / llevarse

거두어 가다 = 거둬 가다 = [verb phrase] to collect and take away / recoger y llevar

싶다 = [pronunciation] 십다 → 십따 = [infinitive of adjective] feel like / would like / want / wish / desire / querer / gustar

가고 싶다 = [verb phrase] feel like going / would like to go away / want to take away / tengo ganas de ir / me gustaría irse / quiero llevar

가고 싶어 = [pronunciation] 가고 십퍼 = familiar ending of 가고 싶다

거두어 가고 싶어, = **거둬 가고 싶어** = (I) want to collect and take away / Quiero recoger y llevar

나(는) = 나 (I, yo) + 는 [marker for subject] = I myself / yo mismo

그대의 슬픔 · 아픔 거둬 가고 싶어, 나.

I want to collect and take away your sorrolw and pain, I myself.
Quiero recoger y llevar tus tristeza y dolor, yo mismo.

< Line 12 > 내가 나인게 싫은 날, 영영 사라지고 싶은 날.

On a day in which I [you] dislike the fact that I am me [you are you]. /
[Korean] On a day when I hate to be myself. =
On a day when you hate to be yourself. [English]

En el día en que no me [te] guste el hecho de ser yo [tú]. /
[Coreano] En el día en que odio ser yo mismo. = El día en que odias ser tú mismo. [Español]

On a day in which I [you] feel like disappearing forever /

En el día en que quiera[s] desaparecer para siempre

< Line 13 > 문을 하나 만들자. 너의 맘 속에다.

(On such a day) let's make a gate in your mind. /
(En un día así) hugamos una puerta en tu mente.

< Line 14 > 그 문을 열고 들어가면, 이곳이 (너를) 기다릴 거야. 믿어도 괜찮아.

널 위로해 줄 Magic Shop.

If you open and enter the gate, this spot will be waiting for you.
Be confident about (this spot)
(It is the) Magic Shop that will kindly comfort you.

Si abres y entras por la puerta, este lugar te estará esperando.
Tén confianza (en este lugar).
(Es la) Magic Shop que te dará consuelo con gusto.

< Line 15 > 따뜻한 차 한 잔을 마시며, 저 은하수를 올려다보면, 넌 괜찮을 거야.

Oh, 여긴 Magic Shop. [So, show me. (I'ill show you.) X 3] Show you, Show you.

If you look up the Galaxy while drinking a heartwarming cup of tea, you will become
all right. Oh, this spot is the Magic Shop.

Si miras hacia la Galaxia mientras bebes una caliente taza de té, te pondrás muy bien.
Oh, este lugar es la Magic Shop.

< Line 20 > 나도 모든 게 다 두려웠다면 믿어 줄래?

나도 = 나 (I, yo) + 도 [marker] (as well, also, too, también, tampoco, y además) = I also /
me, too / yo también

모든 = [determiner] all / every / whole / entire / todo(s) / cada / entero

게 = 것 (things, facts, cases, cosas, hechos, casos) + 이 [marker for subject]

● In Korean, the distinction between «singular» and «plural» is not important.

모든 게 = 모든 것이 = [noun phrase] everything / all things / todas las cosas /
todos los hechos / todo

다 = [adverb] all / everything / everyone / totally / completely / todo(s) / totalmente /
completamente

두렵다 = [pronunciation] 두렵따 = [infinitive of adjective] be afread / be feared / be scared / temer / tener miedo / estar asustado

두려웠다 = [pronunciation] 두려웓따 = past tense of 두렵다 = was afread / was feared / was scared / tenía miedo / estaba asustado

두려웠다면 = 두려웠다고 (말)한다면 = if I say that I was afraid / if I say that I was feared / if I say I was scared / si digo que tuvo miedo / si digo que estaba asustado

믿다 = [pronunciation] 믿따 = [infinitive of verb] believe (in) / trust / confide / be sure / confiar / creer

주다 = [infinitive of verb] kindly do / give as a favour / willing to do / please, / amablemente hacer / dar con gusto / dispuesto a hacer / por favor,

믿어 주다 = [pronunciation] 미더 주다 = kindly believe / be willing to trust / honestly confide / amablemente creer

믿어 줄래? = familiar ending for questioning of 믿어 주다 = can you kindly believe? / can you be willing to trust? / ¿amablemente creerás? / ¿me creerás con gusto?

나도 모든 게 다 두려웠다면 믿어 줄래?

If I say that I also was afread of everything, will you kindly believe me, (please)? / Si digo que yo también le tenía miedo a todo, ¿me amablemente creerás, (por favor)?

< Line 21 > (1) 모든 진심들이, (2) 남은 시간들이, (3) 너의 모든 해답은

(a) 네가 찾아낸 이곳에, (b) 너의 은하수에, (c) 너의 마음 속에 (있어).

● This sentence has three subjects and three complements, respectively. In addition, the verb 있다 (there is, hay) is missing.

모든 = [determiner] all / every / whole / entire / todo(s) / cada / entero

진심 = [noun] true heart / earnestness / sincerity / wholeheartedness / verdadero corazón / franqueza

진심들이 = 진심 + 들 [plural] + 이 [marker for subject]

남다 = [infinitive of verb] be left over / remain / stay behind / quedarse (atrás)

남은 = adjective form of 남다 = being left over / remaining / staying behind / se quedando (atrás)

시간들이 = 시간 (time, tiempo, hora) + 들 [plural] + 이 [marker for subject]

너의 = 너 (you, tú) + 의 [marker for possession] = of you / your / tu

모든 = [determiner] all / every / whole / entire / todo(s) / cada / entero

해답은 = 해답 (answer, solution, respuesta, solución) + 은 [marker for subject]

네가 = 너 + 이가 = 너 (you, tú) + 이가 [marker for subject]

찾아내다 = [infinitive of verb] find out / discover / detect / encontrar / descubrir

찾아내는 = [pronunciation] 차자내는 = present adjective form of 찾아내다 = finding out / that finds out / discovering / that discovers / encontrando / que encontras / descubriendo / que descubres

찾아낸 = [pronunciation] 차자낸 = past form of 찾아내다 = that found out / that discovered / que encontró / que descubrió

이곳 = [pronunciation] 이곧 = [pronoun] this place / this point / this spot / este lugar / este punto

이곳에 = [pronunciation] 이고세 = 이곳 + 에 (at, on, in, en) = here / aquí

너의 = 너 (you, tú) + 의 [marker for possession] = of you / your / tu

은하수에 = 은하수 (galaxy, milky way, galaxia, vía láctea) + 에 (at, on, in, en)

너의 = 너 (you, tú) + 의 [marker for possession] = of you / your / tu

마음 = [noun] mind / heart / feelings / caring heart / mente / corazón

속에 = 속 (the inside, the bottom, el interior) + 에 (in, at, en)

(있다) = [pronunciation] 읻다 → 읻따 = [infinitive of verb] there is / be / exist / stay / remain / stand / hay / estar / existir / quedarse / permanecer / pararse

(있어) = familiar ending of 있다

(1) 모든 진심들이, (2) 남은 시간들이, (3) 너의 모든 해답은

(a) 네가 찾아낸 이곳에, (b) 너의 은하수에, (c) 너의 마음 속에 (있어).

[1] All of your sincerities, [2] your remaining time, and [3] all of your solutions (are existing) [a] at this place that you found, [b] in your galaxy, namely, [c] in your mind.

[1] Todas tus sinceridades, [2] tu tiempo restante, y [3] todas tus solaciones (hay) [a] en este lugar que encontraste, [b] en tu galaxia, es decir, [c] en tu mente.

< Line 22 > You gave me the best of me. So, you'll give you the best of you.

(넌) 날 찾아냈잖아! 날 알아줬잖아!

(넌) = 너는 = 너 (you, tú) + 는 [marker for subject]

날 = 나를 = 나 (I, me) + 를 [marker for object]

찾아내다 = [infinitive of verb] find out / discover / detect / encontrar / descubrir

찾아냈다 = [pronunciation] 차자낻따 = past form of 찾아내다 = found out / encontraste

찾아냈지 = [pronunciation] 차자낻찌 = a noun-type conjugation of 찾아냈다

아니 하다 = 안 하다 = 않다 = [pronunciation] 안타 = not do / no hacer

않아? = [pronunciation] 아나? = [tag questioning] We did, didn't we? / it is right, isn't it? / hicimos, ¿no? / es correcto, ¿no?

찾아냈지 않아? = **찾아냈잖아!** = [pronunciation] 차자낻짜나! = [tag question] You see, you (already) found it out, didn't you? / Verás, (ya) lo descubriste, ¿no?

(넌) 날 찾아냈잖아! = You found me out, didn't you? / Me descubriste, ¿no?
● This is an emphasis rather than a question. So, there is no need to raise the tone at the end.

날 = 나를 = 나 (I, yo) + 를 [marker for object]

알아주다 = [infinitive of verb] acknowledge / empathize with / appreciate / reconocer / compenetrarse / apreciar
● Owing to its frequent usage, '알아주다' has becmo a verb. So, no space between 알아 and 주다.

알아주었다 = 알아줬다 = past tense of 알아주다 = acknowleged / felt for / appreciated / reconociste / apreciabas

알아주었지 = [pronunciation] 아라주얻찌 = a noun-type conjugation of 알아주다

아니 하다 = 안 하다 = 않다 = [pronunciation] 안타 = not do / no hacer

않아?= [pronunciation] 아나? = [tag questioning] You did, didn't you? / it is right, isn't it? / hiciste, ¿no? / es correcto, ¿no?

알아주었잖아? = **알아줬잖아!** = [pronunciation] 아라줟짜나! = [tag questioning] You acknowledged me, didn't you? / Apreciabas, ¿no? / Apreciaste, ¿no?

(넌) 날 알아줬잖아! = You acknowledged me, didn't you? / Me apreciabas, ¿no?

● This can be an appreciation of BTS towards ARMY.

< Line 23 > > You gave me the best of me. So, you'll give you the best of you.
넌 찾아낼거야, 네 안에 있는 Galaxy.
[So, show me. (I'ill show you.) X 3] Show you, Show you.

넌 = 너는 = 너 (you, tú) + 는 [marker for subject]

찾아내다 = [infinitive of verb] find out / discover / detect / encontrar / descubrir

찾아낼 = (future) adjective form of 찾아내다 = will find out / will discover / encontrarás / descubrirás

것이다 = 것 (the thing that ~, the fact that ~, el hecho que ~, lo que ~) + 이다 (be, ser)

것이야 = **거야** = familiar ending of 것이다

찾아낼 거야 = [pronunciation] 차자낼 꺼야 = will find out / descubrirás

네 = 너의 = 너 (you, tú) + 의 [marker for possession] = of you / your / tu

안에 = [pronunciation] 아네 = 안 (the interior, mind, el interior, mente) + 에 (in, at, en)
= inside / dentro

● Many Korean speakers including pronounce «네 안에» as «니 안에». That is not correct.

있다 = [pronunciation] 읻다 → 읻따 = [infinitive of verb] there is / be / exist / stay / remain / stand / hay / estar / existir / quedarse / permanecer / pararse

있는 = [pronunciation] 읻는 → 인는 = adjective form of 있다 [verb] = existing / that exists / estando / que está

Galaxy = [in Korean] 은하수 = literally means 'silver river water' / literalmente significa 'agua de río plateado'

넌 찾아낼 거야, 네 안에 있는 Galaxy.

(It is the fact that) you will find out the Galaxy that exists in your mind. /
You will find out the Galaxy that exists in your mind.

(Es el hecho que) descubrirás la Galaxia que está en tu mente. /
Descubrirás la Galaxia que está en tu mente.

8. Only then (그 때 헤어지면 돼)

Artist: Roy Kim
Lyric Writer: Roy Kim

< Line 1 > 나를 사랑하는 법은 어렵지 않아요.

나를 = 나 (I, yo) + 를 [marker for object]

사랑하다 = [infinitive of verb] love / have an affection for / amar / querer / tener cariño por

사랑하는 = adjective form of 사랑하다 = loving / to love / queriendo / para amar

법은 = [pronunciation] 버븐 = 법 (method, way, método, manera) + 은 [marker for subject]

어렵다 = [pronunciation] 어렵따 = [infinitive of adjective] be difficult / be hard / ser difícil / ser complejo

어렵지 = [pronunciation] 어렵찌 = an adverb-type conjugation of 어렵다

아니하다 = 않다 = [pronunciation] 안타 = [infinitive of adjective] not be / no ser / no estar

● Here, «아니하다» or «않다» is not a verb, but an adjective, because it does not mean an action.

어렵지 않다 = [verb phrase] be not difficult [hard] / no ser difícil [complejo]

어렵지 않아요 = [pronunciation] 어렵찌 아나요 = polite ending of 어렵지 않다

나를 사랑하는 법은 어렵지 않아요. = The method to love me is not difficult. / El método para amarme no es difícil.

< Line 2 > 지금 모습 그대로(의) 나를 꼭 안아 주세요.

지금 = [noun] now / the present / the current moment / ahora / el presente / el momento actual

모습 = [noun] looks / figure / features / aparencia / figura / aspecto

그대로 = [adverb] as it is / as I am / in the same way as before / como estoy / de la misma manera

(의) = [marker for possession] of / de

130

그대로(의) 나 = me (of) as I am / me who is as I am / yo (de) como estoy /
yo qui soy como soy

나를 = 나 (I, yo) + 를 [marker for object]

꼭 = [adverb] firmly / tightly / closely / firmemente / con fuerza

안다 = [pronunciation] 안따 = hug / embrace / cuddle / abrazar

주다 = [infinitive of verb] kindly do / give as a favour / willing to do / please, / amablemente
hacer / dar con gusto / dispuesto a hacer / por favor,

안아 주다 = [verb phrase] warmly cuddle / abrazar amablemente [cálidamente]

안아 주세요 = polite ending for imperative mood of 안아 주다 = Please, hug /
Por favor, abrázame

지금 모습 그대로(의) 나를 꼭 안아 주세요. = Please, hug me tightly as I am. /
Por favor, abrázame fuerte como estoy.

< Line 3 > 우린 나중에는 어떻게 될진 몰라도, 정해지지 않아서 그게 나는 좋아요.

우린 = 우리 [pronoun] + 는 = 우리 (we, nosotros) + 는 [marker for subject] = we /
our relationship / nosotros / nuesta relación

나중 = [adverb, also used as noun] days to come / future / días por venir / futuro + 에는
(in, en)

나중에는 = stronger expression than 나중에 = in the days to come / in the future /
en los días por venir / en el futuro

어떻게 = [pronunciation] 어떠케 = [adverb] how / in what way [manner] / cómo /
en qué manera

● When 'ㅎ' combines with a consonsant, the consonant becomes aspirated.
[ㄱ + ㅎ → ㅋ] [ㄷ + ㅎ → ㅌ] [ㅂ + ㅎ → ㅍ] [ㅈ + ㅎ → ㅊ]

되다 = [infinitive of verb] become / turn into / volverse / convertirse / resultar / terminarse /
hacerse / ser

될 = (future) adjective form of 되다

어떻게 될지 = [pronunciation] 어떠게 될찌 = a noun-type conjugation of 되다 =
how we turn into / whether we become like this or like that / cómo nos volvemos /
si nos convertimos en así u otro

● '지' was originally an independent word, whose meaning is «uncertainty», «probability» or «whether». Now it is combined with a verb for making a noun form.

● In Korean, the pronunciation of the first consonant after '

ㄹ' tends to become hard.
[될지 = 될 + 지 → 될찌]

모르다 = [infinitive of verb] not know [aware, realize, notice, understand, learned] /
no saber [aprendí] / desconocer / no darse cuenta
될지 모르다 = do not know how we becomes / not be aware how we turns into [ends up] /
no sé cómo nos hacemos / no sé cómo nos volvemos / no sé cómo nos terminaremos

몰라도 = [tone of concession] although do not know / be not aware, but / aunque no sé /
no podemos suponer, pero
될진 몰라도 = 될지는 몰라도 = stronger expression than 될지 몰라도

● When «는» or «은» is combined with an adverb, it becomes an emphasizing form or
a stronger expression. [될지 → 될지는]

우린 나중에는 어떻게 될진 몰라도, = [pronunciation] 우린 나중에는 어떠케 될찐 몰라도
Although we do not know how we will become in the future, /
Although we are not aware what our relationship brings us later, /
Regardless of knowing how our relationship may end up in the future,

Aunque no sepamos cómo seremos en el futuro, /
Aunque no seamos conscientes de lo que nos trae nuestra relación después, /
Independientemente de saber cómo terminará nuestra relación en el futuro,

정하다 = [infinitive of verb] decide / determine / set / fix / decidir / determinar

정해지다 = be decided / be determined / be set / be fixed / ser decidido / ser determinado

아니 하다 = 안 하다 = 않다 = [pronunciation] 안타 = not do / no hacer

정해지지 않다 = has not been determined / has not been set / The fate has not decided yet /
no se ha determinado / no se fijó / El destino aún no ha decidido
정해지지 않아서 = because it has not been determined / porque no se ha determinado

그게 = 그것이 = 그것 (it, the thing, the fact, eso, la cosa, el hecho) + 이 [marker for subject]
나는 = 나에게는 = 나 (I, yo) + 에게는 (to, for, a, para)

좋다 = [pronunciation] 조타 = [infinitive of verb] be good [satisfactory, be likable] / querer / ser bueno [satisfactorio, agradable]

좋아요 = [pronunciation] 조아요 = polite ending for 좋다

정해지지 않아서 그게 나는 좋아요.

It is good to me because things have not been determined. /
Eso me quiere porque las cosas no se han determinado.

< Line 4 > 남들이 뭐라는 게 뭐가 중요해요?

남들이 = 남 (stranger, other person, otra persona) + 들 [plural] + 이 [marker for subject] = others / other people / otros / los demás / la gente

무엇이라고 하는 것이 = 뭐라고 하는 게 = 뭐라는 게

뭐라는 게 = 무엇이라고 하는 것이 = 무엇 (what, something, qué, algo) + 이라고 하는 (say, decir) + 것 (the thing that ~, the fact that ~, el hecho que ~, lo que ~) + 이 [marker for subject] = what others say / the thing that people say / lo que otros dicen / lo que la gente dice

뭐가 = 무엇이 = 무엇 (what, something, qué, algo) + 이 [marker for subject] = why / for what / por qué / para qué

중요하다 = [infinitive of verb] be important [signicant] / do matter / ser importante [significativo]

중요해요? = polite questioning of 중요하다

뭐가 중요해요? = Why is it important? / Why does it matter? /
¿Por qué es importante? / ¿Por qué eso importa?

● 그게 (it, that, eso) 뭐가 중요해요? = What is important for that? / Why is it important? /
¿Qué es importante para eso? / ¿Por qué es eso importante? / ¿Para qué eso importa?

남들이 뭐라는 게 뭐가 중요해요? = What does it matter what others say? /
¿Para qué importa lo que digan los demás ?

< Line 5 > 서로가 없음 죽겠는데 뭘 고민해요?

서로 = [adverb] each other / one another / reciprocally / together / uno al otro / recíprocamente / juntos

서로가 = 서로 + 가 [marker for subject]

없음 = [pronunciation] 업씀 = 없으면 [업쓰면] = if (one) is absent / if (one) disappears / if (one) is missing / si no está ausente / si uno desaparece / si falt uno

죽다 = [infinitive of verb] die / die out / be dead / morir / estar muerto

죽을 것 같다 = 죽을 (to die, morir) + 것 (the fact, the thing, el echo) + 같다 (it looks like, it seems that ~, parecer que ~) = 죽겠다 [죽껟따] = feel like dying / feel likely to die / cannot survive / sentirse como morir / sentirse propenso a morir / no puede sobrevivir / parecer que muera

죽겠는데 = [pronunciation] 죽겥는데 → 죽껜는데 = present progressive form of 죽겠다 = feel like dying / being in the situation of feeling likely to die / Tenemos ganas de morir / estando en la situación de sentirse propenso a morir

뭐를 = 무엇을 [무어슬] = 무엇 (what, something, qué, algo) + 을 [marker of object]

고민하다 = [infinitive of verb] be in agony / suffer from anguish / distress oneself / concern / estar en agonía / sufrir angustia / angustiarse / preocuparse

고민해요? = polite questioning form of 고민하다

서로가 없음 죽겠는데 뭐를 고민해요?

Between us, if one is missing, the other is likely to die. So, is there anything that will distresses us? /
Between us, if one is missing, the other feels likely to die. So, is there any other thing for us to concern?

Entre nosotros, si falta uno, es probable que el otro muera. Entonces, ¿hay algo que nos angustiará? /
Entre nosotros, si uno falta, el otro se siente propenso a morir. Entonces, ¿hay alguna otra cosa que nos preocupe?

< Line 6 > 우리 함께 더 사랑해도 되잖아요?

우리 = [pronoun] we / nosotros

함께 = [adverb] together / jointly / each other / juntos / el uno al otro

더 = [adverb] more / further / additionally / más / adicionalmente

사랑하다 = [infinitive of verb] love / have an affection for / amar / querer / tener cariño por

사랑해도 = [tone of concession] even if we love each other / even though we have an affection for / incluso si nos amamos / auque nos queramos / incluso si tengamos cariño por

되다 = [infinitive of verb] become fine / goes well / be good / se convierten en todo bien / va bien / llegar a estar bien / estar bien hecho

되지 = an adverb-type conjugation of 되다

아니하다 = 않다 = [pronunciation] 안타 = [infinitive of adjective] not be / no ser / no estar

되지 않아? = 되잖아? = [pronunciation] 되자나? = [tag questioning] wouldn't we? / ¿no?

되지 않아요? = **되잖아요?** = [pronuciation] 되자나요? = polite ending of 되지 않아?

사랑해도 되잖아요?

We would go well by loving each other, wouldn't we? /
Nos volveríamos bien amándonos el uno al otro, ¿no?

우리 함께 더 사랑해도 되잖아요?

We would go well by loving each other more affectionately, wouldn't we? /
We would be okay to love each other more affectionately, wouldn't we? /
It would be okay even if we love each other more affectionately, wouldn't it?

Nos volveríamos bien amándonos más afectuosamente, ¿ no es así?
Podemos amarnos el uno al otro más afectuosamente, ¿no? /
Estaría bien incluso si nos amamos más cariñosamente, ¿no es así?

● This is more an emphasis rather than a question. Therefore, it is not necessary to raise the tone at the end.

< Line 7 > 네가 다른 사람이 좋아지면, 내가 너 없는 게 익숙해지면,

그 때가 오면, 그 때가 되면, 그 때 헤어지면 돼.

네가 다른 사람이 좋아지면, = If someone else becomes likable to you,

● «네가 (you, tú)» is the formal subject, but it can be actually regarded as an adverb phrase [to you, for you, a ti, para ti]. Therefore, the actual subject is «다른 사람이 (someone else)».

네가 = 너 (you, tú) + 이가 [marker for subject] = to you / for you / a ti / para ti

● Many Korean speakers including Roy Kim pronounce «네가» as «니가». That is not correct.

다르다 = [infinitive of adjective] be different / ser diferente

다른 = present tense of 다르다 = different / diferente

사람이 = 사람 (person, human, persona, ser humano) + 이 [marker for subject]

다른 사람 = [noun phrase] someone else / another guy / alguien más / otro tipo / otro chico

좋아하다 = [pronunciation] 조아하다 = [infinitive of verb] like / be fond of / enjoy / care for / gustar / querer / agradar / encariñar

좋아지다 = [pronunciation] 조아지다 = [infinitive of verb] become likable / develop a liking / aficionarse de / volverse agradable / llegar a ser simpático

좋아지면 = [pronunciation] 조아지면 = if become to be likable / if develop liking / si aficionarse / si volverse agradable / si llegar a ser agradable

네가 다른 사람이 좋아지면, = To you, if someone else becomes likable / If you develop a liking for another guy / If you come to like another guy /

Para ti, si alguien más se vuelve agradable [simpático] /
Si desarrollas un gusto por otro tipo [chico] / Si te llega a querer otro chio

내가 너 없는 게 익숙해지면, = If the fact that you are not with me gets familiar with me

● «내가 (I, yo)» is the formal subject, but it can be actually regarded as an adverb phrase [to me, for me, a para mí]. Therefore, actual subject is «너 없는 게 (the fact that you are not with me)».

내가 = 나 (I, yo) + 이가 [marker for subject] = to you / for you / a ti / para ti

너 = [pronoun] you / tú

없다 = [pronunciation] 업다 → 업따 = [infintive of adjective] there is no / not exist / be absent / be without / no hay / no existir / estar ausente / estar sin

없는 = [pronunciation] 업는 = present tense of 없다

게 = 것 (the thing that ~, the fact that ~, el hecho que ~, lo que ~) + 이 [marker for subject]

너 없는 게 = 너 없는 것이 = the fact that you are not with me /
el hecho de que no estas conmigo

익숙하다 = [infinitive of verb] be used to / be accustomed to / estar acostumbrado a

익숙해지다 = get used to / get accustomed to / acostumbrarse a

익숙해지면 = if it becomes get used to me / si se acostumbrará a mí

내가 너 없는 게 익숙해지면, = If the fact that you are not with me gets familiar with me / If I get used to the fact that you are not with me,

Si el hecho de que no estés conmigo se familiariza conmigo /
Si me acostumbro al hecho de que no estás conmigo,

그 때가 오면, 그 때가 되면,

그 = [determiner] the / that / those / ese / esos / tal

때 = [noun] time / occasion / moment / when / tiempo / ocasión / momento / cuando

그 때 = [noun phrase, but used as adverb phrase] at that time / at the occasion / only then / en ese momento / en la ocasión / solo entonces

그 때가 = 그 때 + 가 [marker for subject]

오다 = [infinitive of verb] come / come to / approach / arrive / venir / venir a / acercarse / llegar (a)

오면, = if it comes / if it comes near / if it arrives / si venir / si acercarse

되다 = [infintive of verb with time or situation] become / get near / reach / happen / ser / llegar / pasar

되면, = if it becomes / if it get near / if it reaches / si ser / si llegar a

그 때가 오면, 그 때가 되면, = If the moment comes, and if that occasion happens, / Si venga el momento, y si pase esa ocasión,

그 때 헤어지면 돼.

그 때 = [noun phrase, but used as adverb phrase] at that time / at the occasion / only then / en ese momento / en la ocasión / solo entonces

헤어지다 = [infinitive of verb] break up / separate / part / split up / separarse / despedirse

헤어지면 = if break up / if separate / if part / if split up / si separarse / si despedirse

되다 = [infinitive of verb] become fine / goes well / be good / se convierten en todo bien / va bien / llegar a estar bien / estar bien hecho

되어 = **돼** = familiar ending of 되다

헤어지면 돼 = It will be okay to break up [be parted] / Estará bien separarnos / Podremos separarnos

그 때 헤어지면 돼. = Only then, it will be okay to break up. / Only then, we can be parted. / Solo entonces, estará bien separarnos. / Solo entonces, podremos separarnos.

< Line 8 > 너를 사랑하는 법도 어렵지 않아요.

너를 = 너 (you, tú) + 를 [marker for object]

사랑하다 = [infinitive of verb] love / have an affection for / amar / querer / tener cariño por

사랑하는 = adjective form of 사랑하다 = loving / to love / amando / queriendo

법도 = [pronunciation] 법또 = 법 (method, way, método, manera) + 도 [marker] (as well, also, too, también, tampoco, y además)

어렵다 = [pronunciation] 어렵따 = [infinitive of adjective] be difficult / be hard / ser difícil / ser complejo

어렵지 = [pronunciation] 어렵찌 = an adverb-type conjugation of 어렵다

아니하다 = 않다 = [pronunciation] 안타 = [infinitive of adjective] not be / no ser / no estar

● Here, «아니하다» or «않다» is not a verb, but an adjective, because it does not mean an action.

어렵지 않다 = [verb phrase] be not difficult [hard] / no ser difícil [complejo]

어렵지 않아요 = [pronunciation] 어렵찌 아나요 = polite ending of 어렵지 않다

너를 사랑하는 법도 어렵지 않아요. = The method to love me is not difficult, too. / El método para amarte tampoco no es difícil.

< Line 9 > 한 번 더 웃어 주고, 조금 더 아껴 주면 ...

한 = [numeral] one / un

번 = [noun] time / vez

한 번 = one time / once / una vez

더 = [adverb] more / further / additionally / más / adicionalmente

138

웃다 = [pronunciation] 욷다 → 욷따 = [infinitive of verb] laugh / grin / smile / reír / sonreír

주다 = [infinitive of verb] kindly do / give as a favour / willing to do / please, / amablemente hacer / dar con gusto / dispuesto a hacer / por favor,

웃어 주다 = [pronunciation] 우서 주다 = [verb phrase] kindly laugh / warmly smile / reír amablemente / sonreír calurosamente

웃어 주고 = kindly laugh, and / warmly smile, and / reír amablemente, y / sonreír calurosamente, y

조금 = [adverv] a little (bit) / slight / a short while / pequeño / un poco / gota / ligero / breve / rato

더 = [adverb] more / further / additionally / más / adicionalmente

아끼다 = [infinitive of verb] esteem / cherish / show affection / estimar / apreciar / mostrar cariño

주다 = [infinitive of verb] kindly do / give as a favour / willing to do / please, / amablemente hacer / dar con gusto / dispuesto a hacer / por favor,

아끼어 주다 = 아껴 주다 = [verb phrase] kindly cherish / show warm affection / apreciar mucho / mostrar cálido cariño

아끼어 주면 = **아껴 주면** = if kindly cherish / if show warm affection / si apreciar mucho / si mostrar cálido cariño

한 번 더 웃어 주고, 조금 더 아껴 주면 …
If I smile once (more) and show a little bit warmer affection … (it will be good)
Si sonrío una vez (más) y muestro un poco más de cariño … (será bueno)

< Line 10 > 우리(를) 사랑하는 법도 어렵지 않아요.

우리(를) = 우리 (we, nosotros) + 를 [marker for object]

사랑하다 = [infinitive of verb] love / have an affection for / amar / querer / tener cariño por

사랑하는 = adjective form of 사랑하다 = loving / to love / amando / queriendo

법도 = [pronunciation] 법또 = 법 (method, way, método, manera) + 도 [marker] (as well, also, too, también, tampoco, además)

● All the vowels and four consonants (ㄴ, ㄹ, ㅁ, ㅇ) are voiced sounds, which are soft. Any consonant that is not between any two of them become hard (or fortis). [법도 → 법또]

어렵다 = [pronunciation] 어렵따 = [infinitive of adjective] be difficult / be hard / ser difícil / ser complejo

어렵지 = [pronunciation] 어렵찌 = an adverb-type conjugation of 어렵다

아니하다 = 않다 = [pronunciation] 안타 = [infinitive of adjective] not be / no ser / no estar

어렵지 않다 = [verb phrase] be not difficult [hard] / no ser difícil [complejo]

어렵지 않아요 = [pronunciation] 어렵찌 아나요 = polite ending of 어렵지 않다

너를 사랑하는 법도 어렵지 않아요. = The method to love us is not difficult, too. / El método para amarnos tampoco no es difícil.

< Line 11 > 매일 처음 만난 눈빛으로 서로를 바라봐 주면 ...

매일 = [noun, also used as adverb] every day / each day / day by day / todos los días / cada día / día a día

처음 = [noun, also used as adverb] for the first time / in the beginng / por primera vez / al principio

만나다 = [infinitive of verb] meet / encounter / come across / run into / hallar / encontrarse

만나는 = present adjective form of 만나다 = meeting / encountering / hallando / se encontrando

만난 = past adjective form of 만나다 = that met / that encountered / que se encontró / que halló

눈빛 = [pronunciation] 눈삩 = [noun] 눈 (eyes, ojos) + 빛 (light, luz) = gaze / look / sight / straring / glittering look / mirada / vista / mirada brillante

● When two independent words combine, the first consonant of the second word becomes strong. [눈빛 → 눈빋 →눈삩]

눈빛으로 = [pronunciation] 눈삐츠로 = 눈빛 + 으로 (with, con)

서로 = [adverb] each other / one another / reciprocally / we together / uno al otro / recíprocamente / juntos

서로를 = 서로 (each other / we / el un del otro / nosotros) + 를 [marker for object]

바라보다 = look at / stare / see / view / watch / mirar / ver / observar

주다 = [infinitive of verb] kindly do / give as a favour / willing to do / please, / amablemente hacer / dar con gusto / dispuesto a hacer / por favor,

바라보아 주다 = 바라봐 주다 = kindly look at / warmly stare / mirar amablemente / ver cálidamente

바라봐 주면 … = if kindly look at / if warmly stare / si mirar amablemente / si ver cálidamente

매일 처음 만난 눈빛으로 서로를 바라봐 주면 …

Day by day, if warmly staring each other with a glittering look that came across for the first time … /

Día a día, si viéndose cálidamente el uno al otro con una mirada brillante que se encontró por prima vez …

< Line 4 > 남들이 뭐라는 게 뭐가 중요해요?

Why does it matter what others say? /
¿Por qué importa lo que digan los demás ?

< Line 5 > 서로가 없음 죽겠는데 뭐를 고민해요?

Between us, if one is missing, the other is likely to die. So, is there anything that will distresses us? /
Between us, if one is missing, the other feels likely to die. So, is there any other thing for us to concern?

Entre nosotros, si falta uno, es probable que el otro muera. Entonces, ¿hay algo que nos angustiará? /
Entre nosotros, si uno falta, el otro se siente propenso a morir. Entonces, ¿hay alguna otra cosa que nos preocupe?

< Line 6 > 우리 함께 더 사랑해도 되잖아요?

It would be okay even if we love each other more affectionately, wouldn't it? /
Eastaría bien incluso si nos amáramos más afectuosamente, ¿no?

< Line 7 > 네가 다른 사람이 좋아지면, 내가 너 없는 게 익숙해지면,

그 때가 오면, 그 때가 되면, 그 때 , 그 때, 그 때 …

네가 다른 사람이 좋아지면, = To you, if someone else becomes likable /
If you develop a liking for another guy / If you come to like another guy

Para ti, si alguien más se vuelve agradable [simpático] /
Si desarrollas un gusto por otro tipo [chico] / Si te llega a querer otro chio

내가 너 없는 게 익숙해지면,

If the fact that you are not with me gets familiar with me /
If I get used to the fact that you are not with me,

Si el hecho de que no estés conmigo se familiariza conmigo /
Si me acostumbro al hecho de que no estás conmigo,

그 때가 오면, 그 때가 되면, = If the moment comes, and if that occasion happens, /
Si venga el momento, y si pase esa ocasión,

그 때 , 그 때, 그 때 … = Only then, only then, only then … /
Sólo entonces, sólo entonces, sólo entonces

< Line 12 > 네가 원하든 말든 널 잡을 거고 …
내가 더 이상 지쳐 걷지 못할 때,

네가 = 너 (you, tú) + 이가 [marker for subject]

원하다 = [infinitive of verb] = want / desire / wish / querer / desear

말다 = [verb] quit doing / refrain from doing / not do any longer / dejar de hacer / no hacer

네가 원하든 말든 = regardless of your wish / regardless of the fact that you want it or not /
independientemente de tu deseo / independientemente del hecho de que lo desees o no

널 = 너를 = 너 (you, tú) + 를 [marker for object]

(붙)잡다 = [pronunication] 붇짭다 = [infinitive of verb] hold tight / take hold of / keep /
abrazar fuerte / tomar / mantener

잡는 = present adjective form of 잡다 = holding tight / keeping / tomando / manteniendo

잡을 = (future) adjective form of 잡다 = will hod tight / will keep / tomaré / mantendré

것이다 = 것 (the thing that ~, the fact that ~, el hecho que ~, lo que ~) + 이다 (be, ser)

널 잡을 것이다 = there will a fact that I hold you tight / I will hold you tight / habrá un hecho de que te habrazo fuerte / te habrazaré fuerte

널 잡을 것이고 … = **널 잡을 거고** = I will hold you tight, and … / te habrazaré fuerte, y …

네가 원하든 말든 널 (붙)잡을 거고 …

Regardless of your wish, I will hold you tight, and … / independientemente de tu deseo, te habrazaré fuerte

내가 = 나 (I, yo) + 이가 [marker for subject]

더 이상 = [adverb phrase] no more / no further / no aditionally / no más / no adicionalmente

● The words '더 이상' itself is not negative. But one can expect that a negative expression will come along.

지치다 = [infinitve of verb] get tired / become exhausted / be fatigued / estar cansado / estar exhausto

지쳐(서) = get tired, thus / because becoming exhausted / as having been fatigued / cansarme, por lo tanto / porque esté cansado / como he sido fatigado

걷다 = [pronunciation] 걷따 = [infinitive of verb] walk / tread / tramp / hike / caminar / pisar / vagar

하다 = [infinitive of verb] do / act / make / hacer / realizar

아니 하다 = 안 하다 = [verb phrase] = not do / no hacer

못하다 = [pronunciation] 몯하다 → 몯타다 = [infinitive of verb] cannot do / no poder hacer

못할 = [pronunciation] 몯할 → 모탈 = [adjective form] that cannot do / que no puedo hacer

● When 'ㅎ' combines with a consonsant, the consonant becomes aspirated.

[ㄱ + ㅎ → ㅋ] [ㄷ + ㅎ → ㅌ] [ㅂ + ㅎ → ㅍ] [ㅈ + ㅎ → ㅊ]

때 = [noun, also used as adverb] time / in the occasion / at the moment / when / tiempo / en la ocasión / en el momento / cuando

걷지 못할 때 = when I cannot walk / in the occasion that I cannnot walk / cuadno no puedo caminar

내가 더 이상 지쳐 걷지 못할 때,

In the occasion that I cannot walk any further because I get tired, /

When I cannot walk any further owing to exhaustion,

En la ocasión en que no puedo caminar más porque me canso, /
Cuando no puedo caminar más debido al cansancio,

< Line 7-1 > 그 때가 오면, 그 때가 되면, 그 때 헤어지면 돼.

그 때 헤어지면 돼.

If the moment comes, and if that occasion happens,
Si venga el momento, y si pase esa ocasión,

Only then, only then, only then …
Sólo entonces, sólo entonces, sólo entonces

Only then, it will be okay to break up. / Only then, we can be parted.
Sólo entonces, estará bien separarnos. / Sólo entonces, podremos separarnos.

9. Spring Day (봄날)

Artist: BTS

Lyric Writers: Pdogg, ADORA, 방시혁,

Arlissa Ruppert, Peter Ibsen, RM

< Line 1 > "보고 싶다!" 이렇게 말하니까 더 보고 싶다.

보다 = [infinitive of verb] see / watch / look at / observe / ver / mirar / observar

보고 = a noun-type conjugation of 보다 = to see / to look at / ver / observar

싶다 = [pronunciation] 십다 → 십따 = [infinitive of verb] feel like / would like / want / wish / desire / querer / gustar

보고 싶다 = [verb phrase] feel like seeing / want [wish, desire] to see / can't wait to meet / tener ganas de ver /querer [desear] mirar / extrañar = I miss you! / ¡Te extraño!

이러하다 = [infinitive of adjective] be like this [this way, as follows] / ser así [éste, la siguiente]

이러하게 = **이렇게** = [pronunciation] 이런케 = adverb form of 이러하다= so / like this / like such / como éste / como tal

말하다 = [infinitive of verb] say / tell / talk / speak / state / decir / hablar / referir

이렇게 말하니까 = by saying so [like this, like such as] / when saying so [like this, like such as] / al decirlo / al hablar así

더 = [adverb] more / further / additionally / más / adicionalmente

보고 싶다 = [verb phrase] feel like seeing / want [wish, desire] to see / can't wait to meet / tener ganas de ver / querer [desear] mirar / extrañar

"보고 싶다!" 이렇게 말하니까 더 보고 싶다.

"I miss you!" By saying so, I can't wait to see you even more. /
« ¡Te extraño! » Al decirlo, No puedo esperar a verte aún más.

< Line 2 > 너희(의) 사진을 보고 있어도 보고 싶다.

너희(의) = [pronoun] you guys / you all / vosotros / ustedes chicos + 의 [marker for possession] = of you guys / de vostros chicos

사진을 = [pronunciation] 사지늘 = 사진 (photos, pictures, snapshots, fotos, fotografías) + 을 [marker for objects]

● In Korean, the distinction between «singular» and «plural» is not important.

보다 = [infinitive of verb] see / watch / look at / observe / ver / mirar / observar

있다 = [pronunciation] 읻다 → 읻따 = [infinitive of verb] there is / be / exist / stay / remain / stand / hay / estar / existir / quedarse / permanecer / pararse

보고 있다 = [present progressive] be seeing / be watching / be looing at / estoy viendo / estoy mirando, estoy observando

보고 있어도 = [pronunciation] 보고 이써도 = even though seeing / even when watching / aunque viendo [mirando, observando]

보고 싶다 = [pronunciation] 보고 십따 = [verb phrase] feel like seeing / want [wish, desire] to see / tener ganas de ver / querer [desear] mirar / extrañar

너희 사진을 보고 있어도 보고 싶다.
I miss you so much even when I am looking at the photos of you guys. /
Los extreño mucho incluso cuando veo las fotos de vosotros chicos.

< Line 3 > 너무 야속한 시간! 나는 우리가 밉다.

너무 = [adverb] too much [many] / excessively / quite / demasiado / excessivamente / tanto bien / hasta no más

야속하다 = [pronunciation] 야소카다 = [infinitive of adjective] be unkind [heartless, unfeeling] / ser insensible [frío, seco]

야속한 = [pronunciation] 야소칸 = present tense of 야속하다 = unkind / heartless / unfeeling / insensible / frío / seco

시간 = [noun] time / tiempo / hora

너무 야속한 시간! = Time. How insensible you are! / Tiempo, ¡Cuánto eres insensible!

나는 = 나 (I, yo) + 는 [marker for subject]

우리가 = 우리 (we, nosotros) + 가 [marker for subject]

밉다 = [pronunciation] 밉따 = [infinitive of adjective] be hateful / ser odioso

우리가 밉다 = We are hateful. / Nosotros somos odiosos.

나는 우리가 밉다

To me, we are hateful. / I hate us. / Para mí, somos odiosos / Nos odio.

< Line 4 > 이젠 얼굴(을) 한 번 보는 것도 힘들어진 우리가 ... (밉다)

이젠 = 이제는 = 이제 (now, ahora) + 는 [marker for emphasis] = (on the contrary) now / now at last / eventually now / coming to now / (al contrario) ahora / ahora por fin / llegando a ahora

얼굴(을) = 얼굴 (face, features, rostro, cara) + 을 [marker for object]

한 = [numeral] one / un

번 = [noun] time / vez

한 번 = [adverb phrase] one time / once / una vez

보다 = [infinitive of verb] see / watch / look at / observe / ver / mirar / observar

보는 = adjective form of 보다 = seeing / watching / observing / viendo / mirando / observando

얼굴(을) 한 번 보는 **것** = the occurrence (that is) seeing each other's face once / el hecho de vernos la cara una vez

도 = [marker for emphasis] even / as well / but also / not even / incluso / también / así como / ni siquiera

것도 = [pronunciation] 걷또

얼굴(을) 한 번 보는 것도

even the occurrence (that is) seeing each other's face once / incluso el hecho de vernos la cara una vez

힘들다 = [infinitive of verb] be hard / be difficult / be tough / be virtually impossible / ser duro / ser difícil / ser virtualmente imposible

힘들어진 = came to be hard / got to be difficult / became virtually impossible / llegó a ser difícil / se volvió virtualmente imposible

우리가 = 우리 (we, nosotros) + 가 [marker for subject]

(밉다) = [infinitive of adjective] be hateful / does not appeal / ser odioso / no me gustar

이젠 얼굴(을) 한 번 보는 것도 힘들어진 우리가 ... (밉다)

I hate us who, by now, have got difficulties in seeing each other's face even for once. /

Odio a nosotros que por ahora tenemos dificultades para vernos la cara aunque sea por una vez.

< Line 5 > 여긴 온통 겨울뿐이야. 팔월에도 겨울이 와.

여기 = [pronoun, also used as adverb] this spot / this place / here / now / esto / este lugar / aquí / ahora

여긴 = 여기 + 는 [marker for subject or emphasis]

온통 = [adverb] all / wholly / entirely / fully / en mass / todo / totalmente / en masa

겨울 = [noun] winter / winter season / invierno

뿐 = [marker] only / merely / alone / nothing but / solo / meramente / nada más que

이다 = [infinitive of marker that conjugates] be / ser / hay

이야 = familiar ending of 이다

여긴 온통 겨울뿐이야. = In this place, there is nothing but the winter. /
En este lugar, no hay nada más que el invierno.

팔월 = 8 월 = [noun] eighth month / August / agosto

에도 = [marker for emphasis] even in / incluso en

팔월에도 = 8 월에도 = [adverb phrase] even in August / incluso en agosto

겨울이 = 겨울 (winter, invierno) + 이 [marker for subject]

오다 = [infinitive of verb] come / come to / approach / arrive / venir / venir a / acercarse / llegar (a)

와 = familiar ending of 오다

팔월에도 겨울이 와. = Winter is here even in August. /
El invierno está aquí incluso en agosto.

< Line 6 > 마음은 시간을 달려가네. 홀로 남은 설국열차.

마음은 = 마음 (mind, heart, feelings, caring heart, mente, corazón) + 은 [marker for subject]

시간을 = 시간 (time, tiempo, horas) + 을 [marker for object]

(거스르다) = [infinitive of verb] go backwards / go against / ir hacia atrás [en contra]

(거슬러) = adverb form of 거스르다 = backwards / against / hacia atrás / en contra

달려가다 = [infinitive of verb] run / dash / rush / correr

달려가네 = poetic ending of 달려가다

마음은 시간을 달려가네.

● In principle, this sentence does not make sense, because «달려가다 (run, corer) » is an intransitive verb. Accordingly, it cannot have an object. However, here is the object is «시간 (time, hora)». In this case, we need to check out the attitude of the artist towards the time. It seems that he is negative towards the time.

- 너무 야속한 시간! = Time. How unkind you are! / Horas. ¡Qué insensible eres!

● Therefore, we assume that he ran against the time, instead of running along the time. While running against the time, he found a train named as «설국열차 (Snowpiercer)» that has no passengers in it.

마음은 시간을 (거슬러) 달려가네. = My mind ran backwards the time. / Mi mente corrió hacia atrás en el tiempo.

홀로 남은 설국열차.

홀로 = [adverb] alone / single / on one's own / by oneself / solo

남다 = [infintive of verb] remain behind / be left over / linger / quedarse atrás / rezagar

남은 = adjective form of 남다 = that remains behind / being left over / que se queda atrás

설국열차 = 설국 (snow country, país de nieve) + 열차 (train, tren) = Snowpiercer / le Transperceneige

홀로 남은 설국열차 = The Snowpiercer that is left alone / El Snowpiercer que se queda solo.

● The Snowpiercer was our system which was terribly inefficient and unfair. The reason why the Snowpiercer was left alone. It deserted its passengers who happened to be the friends of the artist.

< Line 7 > 네 손(을) 잡고 지구 반대편까지 가(서) 겨울을 끝내고 파.

네 = 너의 = 너 (you, tú) + 의 [marker for possession] = of you / your / tu

손(을) = 손 (hand, mano) + 을 [marker for object]

149

잡다 = [infinitive of verb] hold / take hold of / grab / tomar / agarrar / coger

잡고 = an adverb-type conjuation of 잡다 = while holding / take hold of, and / mientras tomar [agarrar] / tomar [agarrar], y

지구 = [noun] the globe / the earth / the planet / el globo / la tierra / el planeta

반대편 = 반대 (other, opposite, otro, opuesto) + 편 (the side, el lado) [the other side / the opposite side / el otro lado / el lado opuesto]

까지 = [marker] to / up to / till / until / a / aun / hasta

가다 = [infinitive of verb] go (away) / move away / ride / ir / irse / marchar / alejarse / llevarse

가(서) = go, and / go away, and / reach, and / arrive, and / ir, y / irse, y / alcanzar, y / llegar, y

겨울을 = 겨울 (winter, winter season, invierno) + 을 [marker for object]

끝나다 = [pronunciation] 끋나다 → 끈나다 = [infinitive of verb] it ends / it closes / it finishes / acabarse / cerrarse / terminarse

끝내다 = [infinitive of verb] end it / we close / finish off / fainalize / terminate it / make an end of / bring to a close / terminarlo / cerrar / finalizar / hacer un final de / llevar a un final

끝내고 = [pronunciation] 끋내고 → 끈내고 = a noun-type conjugation of 끝내다 = to end / to terminate / to make an end / terminar / finalizar

싶다 = [pronunciation] 십다 → 십따 = [infinitive of adjective] feel like / would like / want / wish / desire / querer / gustar

싶어 = [pronunciation] 십퍼 = present ending of 싶다

파 = poetic ending of 싶어

끝내고 파 = wish to end it / desire to finish off / want to terminate / deseo terminarlo / querer terminar

네 손(을) 잡고 지구 반대편까지 가(서) 겨울을 끝내고 파.
I want to go as far as the other side of the earth holding your hand to terminate this Winter. / Quiero llegar hasta el otro lado de la tierra tomándote de la mano para terminar este invierno.

< Line 8 > 그리움들이 얼마나 눈처럼 내려야 그 봄날이 올까, **Friend?**

그리움들이 = 그리움 (yearning, longing, añoranza, anhelo) + 들 [plural] + 이 [marker for subject]

● In principle, «그리움 (yearning, longing, añoranza, anhelo) » is unaccountable. Thus, there should be no plural form. However, in order to describe the situation that multiple number of people are yearning for multiple number of persons, the singer adopted a plural form here.

얼마나 = [adverb] how much / how many / cuánto / cuántos

눈처럼 = 눈 (snow, nieve) + 처럼 (like, as, como, al igual que)

내리다 = [infinitive of verb] fall down / come down / drop / caer / bajar / nevar [llover]

내려야 = after falling down / have to come down / after dropping / después de caer / tener que bajar

그 = [determiner] the / that / those / ese / esos / tal

봄날 = [noun] spring day / spring days / día de primavera / días primaverales

봄날이 = 봄날 + 이 [marker for subject]

오다 = [infinitive of verb] come / come to / approach / arrive / venir / venir a / acercarse / llegar (a)

올까? = familiar questioning of 오다

그리움들이 얼마나 눈처럼 내려야 그 봄날이 올까?

How many yearnings have to fall like snowflakes to let those spring days come over here? / After how many yearnings have come down like snowflakes, will those spring days arrive here?

¿Cuántas añoranzas tienen que caer como copos de nieve para que lleguen esos días primaverales? /
Después de cuántos anhelos han bajado como copos de nieve, ¿llegarán aquí esos días de primavera?

< Line 9 > 허공을 떠도는 작은 먼지처럼, 작은 먼지처럼
날리는 눈이 나라면 조금 더 빨리 네게 닿을 수 있을 텐데 ...

허공을 = 허공 (empty air, space, midair, cielo vacío, aire) + 을 [marker for object]
떠돌다 = [infinitive of verb] float / drift / waft / flutter / flotar / volarse
떠도는 = adjective form of 떠돌다 = floating / drifting / that wafts / que flota / se volando
작다 = [pronunciation] 작따 = [infinitive of adjective] be small / be little / be tiny / ser pequeño / ser chico

151

작은 = [pronunciation] 자근 = present tense of 작다 = small / little / that is tiny / pequeño / que es chico

먼지처럼 = 먼지 (dust, dirt, mote, polvo, mota) + 처럼 (like, as, como, al igual que)

허공을 떠도는 작은 먼지처럼 = Like a little dust that is floating in the empty air, / Como un poco de polvo que flota en el aire vacío,

날다 = [infinitive of verb] fly / soar / volarse / revolotear

날리다 = [infinitive of verb] be flown / be blown / flutter / volarse / estar revoloteado

날리는 = adjective form of 날리다 = being flown / that is blown / fluttering / se volando / que están revoloteado

눈이 = 눈 (snow, nieve) + 이 [marker for subject]

나다. = 나이다. = 나 (I, yo) + 이다 (be, ser) = It is me. / Soy yo.

나라면 = 나 + 이라면 (if it is, si es) = If it is me. / Si soy yo.

날리는 눈이 나라면 = if the fluttering snow is me, / Si yo es la nieve que se volando,

조금 더 빨리 네게 닿을 수 있을 텐데 ...

조금 = [adverv] a little (bit) / slight / a short while / pequeño / un poco / gota / ligero / breve / rato

더 = [adverb] more / further / additionally / más / adicionalmente

빨리 = [adverb] quickly / fast / rapidly / soon / rápido / pronto / rápidamente

네게 = 너에게 = 너 (you, tú) + 에게 (to, towards, a, hacia)

닿다 = [pronunciation] 닫타 = [infinitive of verb] reach / touch / access / alcanzar / llegar / tocar

닿을 = [pronunciation] 다을 = reaching / arriving / touching / alcanzando / llegando / tocando

수 = [noun] means / resource / possibility / likelihood / medio / recurso / posibilidad / probabilidad

닿을 수 = [pronunciation] 다을 쑤 = can reach / possibly touch / poder alcanzar / posiblemente tocar

있다 = [pronunciation] 읻다 → 읻따 = [infinitive of verb] there is / be / exist / stay / remain / stand / hay / estar / existir / quedarse / permanecer / pararse

● 나에게 연필이 있다 = There is a pencil on me. / I have a pencil. / Hay un lápiz en mí. / Tengo un lápiz.

있을 = adjective form of 있다 = is being / existing / getting / estando / existiendo / consiguiendo

터 = [noun] site / foundation / basis / situaction / sitio / cimiento / base / situación

닿을 수 있을 터 + 이다 (be, ser) = would be able to get the situation that I reach you / será posible conseguir la situación de que podría llegar a ti

닿을 수 있을 터인데 … = 닿을 수 있을 **텐데** … = [familiar ending for discontent]
would be able to get the situation that I reach you, but … /
será posible conseguir la situación de que podría llegar a ti, pero …

(내가) 조금 더 빨리 네게 닿을 수 있을 텐데 …

It will be possible to get the situation that I could reach you a little bit faster, but … /
I would be able to touch you a bit more rapidly …

Será posible conseguir la situación de que podria llegar a ti un poco mas rápido, pero … /
Podría te tocar un poco más rápidamente …

< Line 10 > 눈꽃이 떨어져요. 또 조금씩 멀어져요. [보고 싶다. (보고 싶다) X 2]

눈꽃 = [pronunciation] 눈꼳 = 눈 (snow, nieve) + 꽃 (flower, flor) = snowflakes / copos de nieve

눈꽃이 = [pronunciation] 눈꼬치 = 눈꽃 + 이 [marker for subject]

떨어지다 = [pronunciation] 떠러지다 = [infinitive of verb] fall / come down / drop / caer / bajar

떨어져요 = [pronunciation] 떠러져요 = polite ending of 떨어지다

눈꽃이 떨어져요 = Snowflakes are falling down. / Los pocos de nieve se caen.

또 = [adverb] again / still / moreover / in addition / otra vez / todavía / de nuevo / además

조금씩 = [adverb phrase] 조금 (a little, un poco) + 씩 (together, bundle, juntos, haz) = little by little / bit by bit / gradually / poco a poco / gradualmente

멀어지다 = [infinitive of verb] get distant / drift apart / recede / get away / distanciarse / alejarse

멀어져요 = polite ending of 멀어지다

또 조금씩 멀어져요. = In addition, we are getting distant bit by bit further form each other. /
Además, nos estamos alejando poco a poco más lejos el uno del otro.

보고 싶다 = I desire to see you. / I miss you. / Tengo ganas de ti ver. / Te extraño.

< Line 11 > 얼마나 (오래) 기다려야, 또 몇 밤을 더 새워야 [널 보게 될까? (널 보게 될까?)] [만나게 될까? (만나게 될까?)]

얼마나 = [adverb] how much / how many / cuánto / cuántos

(오래) = [adverb] for long / for a long time / por mucho tiempo

얼마나 (오래) = [adverb phrase] for how long / por cuánto tiempo

기다리다 = [infinitive of verb] wait (for) / await / hold on / expect / esperar / aguardar / esperanzar

기다려야 = have to wait / should await / tengo que esperar / debo aguardar

또 = [adverb] again / and / moreover / in addition / otra vez / y / de nuevo / además

몇 = [pronunciation] 면 = [determiner] uncertain number of / how many / several / de número incierto / unos (cuantos) / cuántos

밤을 = 밤 (nights, noches) + 을 [marker for object]

더 = [adverb] more / further / additionally / más / adicionalmente

새우다 = sit up (all night) / sit out (the night) / keep vigil / trasnocharse / velarse / pernoctarse

새워야 = after sitting up / having to sit out / after keeping vigil / después de trasnocharse / tener que velarse / después de pernoctarse

널 = 너를 = 너 (you, tú) + 를 [marker for object]

보다 = [infinitive of verb] see / watch / look at / observe / ver / mirar / observar

만나다 = [infinitive of verb] meet / encounter / come across / run into / hallar / encontrarse

(하게) 되다 = [infinitive of verb with another verb] come to / get to / venir a / llegar a / volverse

널 보게 되다 = come to see you / get to look at you / venir a verte / llegar a mirarte

만나게 되다 = come to meet you / get to encounter you / venir a hallarte / llegar a encontrarte

널 보게 될까? = future questioning form of 널 보게 되다

만나게 될까? = future questioning form of 만나게 되다

얼마나 (오래) 기다려야, 또 몇 밤을 더 새워야 널 보게 될까? (널 보게 될까?)

만나게 될까? (만나게 될까?)

After how long I should wait, and after how many nights I sit up, can I see you?
When do I come to meet you? /
How long do I have to wait, and how many nights do I have to keep vigil in order to
see you again? When do I come to meet you?

Después de cuánto tiempo debo esperar, y después de cuántas noches me velo, ¿puedo verte?
¿Cuando llego a encontrarte? /
¿Cuánto tiempo tengo que esperar y cuántas noches tengo que velar para poder verte
de nuevo? ¿Cuando llego a encontrarte?

< Line 12 > 추운 겨울 끝을 지나(서), 다시 봄날이 올 때까지, 꽃 피울 때까지 그곳에 좀 더 머물러 줘. 머물러 줘.

춥다 = [infinitive of adjective] be cold / be chilly / feel cold / hacer frío / tener frío / sentir frío

추운 = present form of 춥다 = cold / chilly / frío

겨울 = [noun] winter / winter season / invierno

끝을 = [pronunciation] 끝틀 → 끝츨 = 끝 (the end, edge, el final) + 을 [marker for object]

지나다 = [infinitive of verb] pass through / go by / go past / pasar (por) / marchar / atravesar

지나(서) = pass through, and / go past, and / pasar, y / marchar, y / atravesar, y

추운 겨울 끝을 지나(서), = Passing through the end of the cold winter, /
Pasando por el final del frío invierno,

다시 = [adverb] again / back / even now / moreover / otra vez / todavía / incluso ahora /
de nuevo

봄날 = [noun] spring day / spring days / día de primavera / días primaverales

봄날이 = 봄날 + 이 [marker for subject]

오다 = [infinitive of verb] come / come to / approach / arrive / venir / venir a /
acercarse / llegar (a)

올 = (future) adjective form of 오다 = will come / will arrive / vendrá / vuelvan

때 = [noun] time / occasion / moment / when / tiempo / ocasión / momento / cuando

까지 = [marker] to / up to / till / until / a / aun / hasta

다시 봄날이 올 때까지 = until the spring days will come back /
hasta que vuelvan los días primaverales

꽃(이) = 꽃 (flowers, fores) + 이 [marker for subject]

피다 = [infinitive of verb] bloom / blossom / effloresce / florecer / resplandecer

필 = (future) adjective form of 피다

때 = [noun] time / occasion / moment / when / tiempo / ocasión / momento / cuando

까지 = [marker] up to / till / until / hasta

피우다 = [infinitive of verb] let bloom / make blossom / dejar florecer /
hacer resplandecer

꽃이 필 때까지 = until the flowers will bloom / hasta que florezcan las flores

꽃 피울 때까지 = until the flowers will let bloom / hasta que las flores dejen florecer

● One can find that the second line '꽃 피울 때까지 (until let bloom)' is grammatically incorrect.

그곳에 좀 더 머물러 줘.

이곳 = [pronunciation] 이곧 = [pronoun] this place / this point / this spot / este lugar /
este punto

저곳 = [pronunciation] 저곧 = [pronoun] that place / that point / that spot / aquello lugar /
aquello punto

그곳 = [pronunciation] 그곧 = [pronoun] the place / the point / the spot / ese lugar / ese punto

이곳에 = [pronunciation] 이고세 = here / at this place / aquí / en este lugar

저곳에 = [pronunciation] 저고세 = over there / at that place / allí / en aquello lugar

그곳에 = 그곳 + 에 (at, on, in, en) = there / at the place / ahí / en ese lugar

좀 = 조금 = [adverv] a little (bit) / slight / a short while / pequeño / un poco / gota /
ligero / breve / leve

더 = [adverb] more / further / additionally / más / adicionalmente

머물다 = [infinitive of verb] stay / remain / detenerse / quedarse / alojarse / permanecer

주다 = [infinitive of verb] kindly do / give as a favour / willing to do / please, /

amablemente hacer / dar con gusto / dispuesto a hacer / por favor,

머물러 주다 = kindly stay / willing to stay / amablemente quedar / quedar con gusto

머물러 주어 = **머물러 줘** = familiar ending for imperative modo of 머물러 주다 = Please, stay / Por favor, quedate

그곳에 좀 더 머물러 줘. = Please, stay there a little longer. / Por favor, quedate un poco más ahí.

< Line 13 > 네가 변한 건지? (네가 변한 건지) / 아니면, 내가 변한 건지? (내가 변한 건지)

네가 = 너 + 이가 = 너 (you, tú) + 이가 [marker for subject]

● Many Korean speakers including BTS pronounce «네가» as «니가». That is not correct.

변하다 = [infinitive of verb] change / turn into / shift / transform / be different / cambiarse

변하는 = present adjective form of 변하다 = changing / that transforms / se cambiando

변한 = past adjective form of 변하다 = that has changed / que se has cambiado

것이다 = 것 (the thing that ~, the fact that ~, el hecho que ~, lo que ~) + 이다 (be, ser)

건지? = 것인지? = 것 + 인지? = questioning form of 것이다 = is it the thing that ~? / is it that ~? / I wonder if ~ / ¿Es el hecho que ~? / ¿Es que ~? / Me pregunto si ~

● '건지?' is a soliloquy (= I wonder) rather than a questioning. Therefore, it is not necessary to raise the tone at the end.

네가 변한 건지? (네가 변한 건지) / 아니면, 내가 변한 건지?

Is it that you have changed? If not, is it that I have changed?
Is it you that have changed? Or, is it me that have changed?
I wonder if it is you that have changed, or if it is me that have changed.

¿Es el hecho que has cambiado? Si no, ¿es el hecho que he cambiado?
¿Eres tú el que ha cambiado? ¿O soy yo el que he cambiado?
Me pregunto si eres tú el que has cambiado, o si soy yo el que he cambiado.

< Line 14 > 이 순간 흐르는 시간조차 미워.

이 = [determiner] this / these / este / estos

순간 = [noun] moment / instant / momento / instante

흐르다 = flow / run / stream / go by / pass (by) / fluir / correr / transcurrir / pasar

흐르는 = adjective form of 흐르다 = that flows / that is running / streaming / passing by / fluyendo / corriendo / que transcurre / que estar pasando

시간조차 = 시간 (time, tiempo, horas) + 조차

조차 = [marker for emphasis] even / as well / but also / incluso / también / (ni) siquiera

밉다 = [infinitive of adjective] be hateful / does not appeal / ser odioso / no me gustar

미워 = familiar ending of 밉다

이 순간 흐르는 시간조차 미워. = Even the time that flows at this moment is hateful. / I hate even the time that is still passing by at this moment.

Incluso el tiempo que fluye en este momento es odioso. / Odio incluso el tiempo que todavía está pasando en este momento.

< Line 15 > 우리가 변한 거지, 뭐! 모두가 그런거지, 뭐!

우리가 = 우리 (we, nosotros) + 가 [marker for subject]

변하다 = [infinitive of verb] change / turn into / shift / transform / be different / cambiarse

변한 = past adjective form of 변하다 = that has changed / que se has cambiado

것이다 = 것 (the thing that ~, the fact that ~, el hecho que ~, lo que ~) + 이다 (be, ser)

것이지 = **거지** = soliloquy ending of 것이다

뭐 = [interjection] well / uh! / ¡bueno! / ¡fu!

우리가 변한 거지, 뭐! = (The thing is that) we have changed, well! / Well! It is both of us that have changed. / (El hecho es que) hemos cambiado, ¡fu! / ¡Fu! Somos nosotros los dos que hemos cambiado.

모두 = [adverb] all / the whole / all of us / all of them / every / todo(s) / cada

모두가 = 모두 + 가 [marker for subject]

그렇다 = [pronunciation] 그런타 = 그러하다 = [infinitive of adjective] be such / be like that / be like such and such / ser así / ser como tal y tal

그러한 = 그런 = present form of 그러하다

그러한 것이지 = **그런거지** = the fact is that things are such and such / el hecho es que las cosas son tales y tales

158

뭐 = [interjection] well / uh / bueno / fu

모두가 그런거지, 뭐! = Well! The fact is that everything is such and such. / El hecho es que todo es tal y cual, ¡fu!

< Line 16 > 그래! 밉다, 네가. 넌 떠났지만, 단 하루도 너를 잊은 적이 없었지, 난.

그러하다 = [infinitive of adjective] be (like) such / be like that / ser así / ser como tal

그러해! = **그래!** = familiar edning of 그러하다 = [interjection] Right! / Yes! / ¡Correcto! / ¡Sí!

밉다 = [infinitive of adjective] be hateful / does not appeal / ser odioso / no me gustar

네가 = 너 (you, tú) + 이가 [marker for subject]

그래. 밉다, 네가. = Yes. You're hateful. / Right! I hate you. / Sí, eres odioso. / ¡Correcto! Te odio.

넌 = 너는 = 너 (you, tú) + 는 [marker for subject]

떠나다 = [infinitive of verb] leave / depart / go away / be going / irse / partir / eliminarse

떠났다 = [pronunciation] 떠낟따 = past tense of 떠나다 = left / departed / have gone / te has ido / partiste / te eliminaste

떠났지만 = [pronunciation] 떠낟찌만 = although have left / even though have gone / auque te hayas ido / aunque partiste

넌 떠났지만 = although you have left / even though you have gone / auque te hayas ido / a pesar de que partiste

단 = [determiner] only one / a single / incluso uno / un solo / sólo uno

하루 = [noun] a day / another day / un día / otro día

도 = [marker for emphasis] even / as well / but also / not even / incluso / también / así como / ni siquiera

단 하루도 = not a single day / ni un solo día

● «단 하루도» itself is not negative. But, one can expect that a negative expression would come along.

너를 = 너 (you, tú) + 를 [marker for object]

잊다 = [pronunciation] 읻따 = [infinitive of verb] forget / slip one's memory / olvidarse / poner en olvido

잊은 = past adjective form of 잊다

적이 = 적 (time, occasion, case, when, vez, ocasión, caso, cuando) + 이 [marker for subject]

없다 = [pronunciation] 업다 → 업따 = [infintive of adjective] there is no / not exist / be absent / be without / no hay / no existir / estar ausente / estar sin

없었다 = past tense of 없다 = there has been no / not eixisted / no ha habido / no existió / estaba sin

없었지 = [pronunciation] 업썯찌 = soliloquy ending of 없었다

난 = 나는 = 나 (I, yo) + 는 [marker for subject]

단 하루도 너를 잊은 적이 없었지, 난.

There has not been even a single day that I forgot you. /
Even for a single day I have not forgotten you.

No ha habido ni un solo día en que te olvide. / Ni por un solo día te he olvidado.

< Line 17 > 솔직히 보고 싶은데, 이만 너를 지울께.
그게 너를 원망하기보단 덜 아프니까.

솔직하다 = [pronunciation] 솔찌카다 = [infinitive of adjective] be frank [truthful] / be straightforward [open] / ser franco [sincere, abierto, llano]

솔직히 = [pronunciation] 솔찌키 = [adverb] frankly / to be honest / plainly / candidly / francamente / abiertamente / llanamente
● «솔직히» is an adverb, not an adverb form.

● When 'ㅎ' combines with a consonant, the consonant becomes aspirated.
[ㄱ + ㅎ → ㅋ] [ㄷ + ㅎ → ㅌ] [ㅂ + ㅎ → ㅍ] [ㅈ + ㅎ → ㅊ]
[솔직히 → 솔찍히 → 솔찌키]

보고 싶다 = [verb phrase] feel like seeing / want [wish, desire] to see / tener ganas de ver / querer [desear] mirar / extrañar

보고 싶은데 = although I miss you / I miss you, but / aunque te extraño / te extraño, pero

솔직히 보고 싶은데 = To be honest, I miss you, but / Aunque te extraño francamente,

이만 = [adverb] by this (far) / by this (much) / now / solo hasta este puto / ahora

너를 = 너 (you, tú) + 를 [marker for object]

지우다 = [infinitive of verb] erase / rub out / efface / eliminate / forget / borrar / eliminar / olvidar

지울께 = familiar ending of 지우다 = let me erase / I will efface / déjame borrar / eliminaré

이만 너를 지울께 = I will erase you now. / Déjame te borrar ahora. / Te eliminaré ahora.

그게 = 그것이 = 그것 (it, the thing, the fact, eso, la cosa, el hecho) + 이 [marker for subject]

너를 = 너 (you, tú) + 를 [marker for object]

원망하다 = [infinitive of verb] have a grudge / resent / blame / guardar rencor / resentirse / culpar

원망하기 = noun form of 원망하다

● «noun form» can be regarded as a noun, «adverb-form» can be regarded as an adverb, while «a noun-type conjuation» or «an adverb-type conjugation» is regarded as a verb.

보다 = [marker] than, more than, más que

보단 = 보다는 = 보다 + 는 [marker for emphasis] = rather than / más bien que

더 = [adverb] more / further / additionally / más / adicionalmente

덜 = [adverb] less / little / insufficiently / menos / poco / insuficientemente

아프다 = [infinitive of adjective] hurt / be ill [sick, painful, sore, hurting] / torment / doler / ser doloroso / estar enfermo [dolorido, herido] / atormentar

아프니까 = because it hurts / because it causes pain / porque herir / porque causa dolor

그게 너를 원망하기보단 덜 아프니까. = Because it hurts me less than blaming you. / Because it causes less pain than having a grudge on you.

Porque me duele menos que culparte. / Porque causa menos dolor que guardarte rencor.

< Line 18 > 시린 널 불러내 본다, 연기처럼, 하얀 연기처럼.

시리다 = [infinitive of verb] painfully cold / achingly chilled / be pitiful / be plaintive / penosamente frío / dolorosamente helado / ser lamentable / ser lastimero / estar con el corazón en vilo

시린 = adjective form of 시리다

널 = 너를 = 너 (you, tú) + 를 [marker for object]

시린 너 = you who is pitiful [plaintive] / tú que eres lamentable [lastimero]

● Although «시린» is an adjective, here it woul be better to interpret it as adverb, because «you who are plaintive» actually means that «my heart becomes plaintive when I think of you ».

불러내다 = [infinitive of verb] call (towards me) / summon / llamar (hacia mí) / evocar / convocar

(해)보다 = [infinitive of verb] have a try / give a shot / attempt to / carry out / venture to / probar / tratar / intentar / llevar a cabo / atreverse

불러내 보다 = [infinitive of verb phrase] try to call / attempt to summon / intentar llamar / probar evocar

불러내 본다 = present tense of 불러내 보다

하얗다 = [pronunciation] 하얃타 = [infinitive of adjective] be white / ser blanco

하얀 = present tense of 하얗다 = white / blanco

연기처럼 = 연기 (smoke, fumes, humo) + 처럼 (like, as, como, al igual que)

시린 널 불러내 본다, 연기처럼, 하얀 연기처럼.
I try to call you towards me plaintively, you who are like fumes, white fumes. /

Intento llamarte lastimeramente hacia mí, tú que eres como humo, como humo blanco. Pruebo te evocar con el corazón en vilo, tú que sea como humo, como humo blanco.

< Line 19 > 말로는 지운다 해도, 사실 난 아직 널 보내지 못하는데 ...

말로는 = 말 (words, saying, palabras) + 로는 (by, with, por, con) = by words / con palabras

지우다 = [infinitive of verb] erase / rub out / efface / eliminate / forget / borrar / eliminar / olvidar

하다 = [infinitive of verb] do / act / make / hacer / realizar

하여도 = **해도** = [tone of concession] even if doing / in spite of doing / although doing / incluso si haciendo / a pesar de hacer / aunque haciendo

말로는 지운다(고) 해도 = In spite of my words that I would erase you / Though I said that I would efface you / A pesar de mis palabras que te borraría / Aunque dije que te eliminaría

사실 = [used as adverb] in fact / in reality / actually / indeed / de hecho / en efecto / realmente

난 = 나는 = 나 (I, yo) + 는 [marker for subject]

아직 = [adverb] still / yet / so far / todavía / hasta ahora

널 = 너를 = 너 (you, tú) + 를 [marker for object]

보내다 = [infinitive of verb] send (off) / let go / enviar / despachar / déjate ir / despedirse

하다 = [infinitive of verb] do / act / make / hacer / realizar

못하다 = [pronunciation] 몯하다 → 모타다 = [infinitive of verb] cannot do / not be able to do / not succeed doing / no poder hacer

못하는데 = [pronunciation] 몯하는데 → 모타는데 = cannot do, so .... / no poder hacer, entonces

보내지 못하는데 ... = I cannot send you off, so ... / No puedo te enviar, entonces ...

사실 널 보내지(는) 못하는데 ... = I indeed still cannot send you off, so ... / De hecho, no puedo todavía te enviar, entonces ...

< Line 10 > 눈꽃이 떨어져요. 또 조금씩 멀어져요. [보고 싶다. (보고 싶다) X 2]

Snowflakes are falling down. / Los pocos de nieve se caen.

In addition, (we) are growing distant bit by bit (from each other). / Y además, (nosotros) nos distanciamos poco a poco (el uno del otro).

I desire to see you. / I miss you. / Tengo ganas de ti ver. / Te extraño.

< Line 11 > 얼마나 기다려야, 또 몇 밤을 더 세워야 널 보게 될까? (널 보게 될까?) 만나게 될까? (만나게 될까?)

After how long I (should) wait, and after how many nights I (have to) sit up, do I come to see you? And do I come to meet you?

Después de cuánto tiempo (debería) esperar, y después de cuántas noches (tengo que) velarme, ¿vengo a verte? ¿Y vengo a encontrarte?

< Line 20 > You know it all. You're my best friend. 아침은 다시 올 거야.

아침은 = 아침 (morning, dawn, mañana, alba, amanecer) + 은 [marker for subject]

다시 = [adverb] again / back / even now / moreover / otra vez / todavía / incluso ahora / de nuevo

오다 = [infinitive of verb] come / come to / approach / arrive / venir / venir a /

acercarse / llegar (a)

올 = (future) adjective form of 오다 = will come / will arrive / vendrá / vuelvan

것이다 = 것 (the thing that ~, the fact that ~, el hecho que ~, lo que ~) + 이다 (be, ser)

올 것이야 = **올 거야** = [pronunciation] 올 꺼야 = familiar ending of 것이다

● In Korean, the pronunciation of the first consonant just after ' ㄹ ' tends to become hard.
[올 거야 → 올 꺼야]

아침은 다시 올 거야.
The fact is that morning will come again. / Morning will find us again. /
El caso es que la mañana volverá. / El alba nos encontrará de nuevo.

< Line 21 > 어떤 어둠도, 어떤 계절도 영원할 순 없으니까.

어떠하다 = [infinitive of adjective] how it is / be such / be like / cómo es / ser así / ser como

어떠한 = **어떤** = present tense of 어떠하다 = a certain / some (kind of) / any (kind of) /
what type of / un cierto / algún (tipo de) / cualquier (tipo de) / qué clase de

어둠도, 계절도 = neither darkness, nor season / ni oscuridad, ni temporada /
ni las tinieblas, ni las estaciones

영원하다 = [infinitive of adjective] be eternal / be permanent / be perpetual / ser eterno /
ser perpetuo

영원한 = present adjective form of 영원하다 = eternal / that is permanent / eterno /
que es perpetuo

영원할 = (future) adjective form of 영원하다 = (that) will be eternal / será eterno /
que era perpetuo

수 = [noun] means / resource / possibility / likelihood / medio / recurso / posibilidad /
probabilidad

순 = 수는 = 수 + 는 [marker for subject]

있다 = [pronunciation] 읻다 → 읻따 = [infinitive of verb] there is / be / exist / stay / remain /
stand / hay / estar / existir / quedarse / permanecer / pararse

없다 = [pronunciation] 업다 → 업따 = [infintive of adjective] there is no / not exist /
be absent / be without / no hay / no existir / estar ausente / estar sin

할 수(는) 있다 = [pronunciation] 할 쑤 읻따 = [verb phrase] can do / poder hacer = [action]

할 수(는) 없다 = [pronunciation] 할 쑤 업따 = There is no means to do. /
Hay no forma de hacerlo. = [situation or status]

● In Korean, a 'verb' means an action and an 'adjective' means a situation or status. In case of «없다 (no exist)», it is always an adjective. However, «있다 (be, exist, estar)» can be either a verb or an adjective.

없으니까 = [pronunciation] 업쓰니까 = because there is no / because be without / porque no hay

영원할 순 없으니까. = [pronunciation] 영원할 쑨 업쓰니까

because it cannot be permanent / porque no puede perpetuo

어떤 어둠도, 어떤 계절도 영원할 순 없으니까.

Because neither any darkness nor any season cannot be perpetual. / Porque ni las tinieblas ni las estaciones no pueden ser perpetuas.

< Line 22 > 벚꽃이 피나 봐요. 이 겨울도 끝이 나요. [보고 싶다. (보고 싶다)] X 2

벚꽃 = [pronunciation] 벋꼳 = [noun] cherry blossoms / cherry flowers / flores de cerezo

벚꽃이 = [pronunciation] 벋꼬치 = 벚꽃 + 이 [marker for subject]

피다 = [infinitive of verb] bloom / blossom / effloresce / florecer / resplandecer

보다 = [infinitive of verb] seem to be [do] / it looks like that / perece que / verse así

피나 보다 = [verb phrase] (they) seem to bloom / it looks like that (they) are blooming / parece que florecen / parecer que están floreciendo

피나 봐요 = polite ending of 피나 보다

벚꽃이 피나 봐요 = It looks like that the cherry flowers are blomming. / Cherry flowers seem to be in bloom. / Parece que las flores de cerezo están floreciendo. / Las flores de cerezo parecen estar floreciendo.

보고 싶다. (보고 싶다) X 2

I desire to see you. / I miss you. / Tengo ganas de ti ver. / Te extraño.

< Line 23 > 조금만 기다리면 (기다리면), 며칠 밤만 더 새우면,

만나러 갈께 (만나러 갈께). 데리러 갈께 (데리러 갈께).

조금 = [adverv] a little (bit) / slight / a short while / pequeño / un poco / gota / ligero / breve / rato

조금만 = 조금 + 만 [marker for emphasis] = only for a short while, solamente por un rato

기다리다 = [infinitive of verb] wait (for) / await / hold on / expect / esperar / aguardar / esperanzar

기다리면 = if (you) wait / if await / si (tú) esperas / si aguardar

조금만 기다리면 = I you wait only for a little while, / Si tú eperas solamente por un rato,

며칠 = [noun] several days / several days and nights / varios días / varios días y noches

며칠 밤 = [pronunciation] 며칠 빰 = [noun phrase] several nights / a few nights / varios noches / unas noches

● In Korean, the pronunciation of the first consonant just after ' ㄹ ' tends to become hard.

며칠 밤만 = 며칠 밤 + 만 [marker for emphasis] (only, solamente)

더 = [adverb] more / further / additionally / más / adicionalmente

새우다 = sit up (all night) / sit out (the night) / keep vigil / trasnocharse / velarse / pernoctarse

새우면 = if sit up / if sit out / if keep vigil / si trasnocharse / si velarse / si pernoctarse

며칠 밤만 더 새우면
If we sit up a few more nights, / after a few more nights of vigilance /
Si nos velamos unas cuantas noches más, / después de más noches de vigilancia

만나다 = [infinitive of verb] meet / encounter / come across / run into / hallar / encontrarse

만나러 = in order to see / to meet / for encountering / para hallar / para encontrarse

데리다 = [infinitive of verb] bring back / pick up / take / go to fetch / traer de vuelta / recoger

데리러 = in order to bring back / to pick up / for taking / para traer de vuelta / para recoger

가다 = [infinitive of verb] go (away) / move away / ride / ir / irse / marchar / alejarse / llevarse

만나러 가다 = go in order to meet / go to encounter / ir para hallar / irse a encontrarte

데리러 가다 = go in order to bring back / go to pick up / ir para traer / irse a recogerte

만나러 갈께 = familiar ending for commitment = I will go in order to meet you /
will go to encounter you / iré para hallarte / me acercaré a encontrarte

데리러 갈께 = familiar ending for commitment = I will go in order to bring you back /
I will go to pick you up / iré para traerte de vuelta / me acercaré a recogerte.

166

조금만 기다리면 (기다리면), 며칠 밤만 더 새우면, 만나러 갈께 (만나러 갈께).

데리러 갈께 (데리러 갈께).

If you wait a little bit, after a few nights of vigilance, I will go [come] to see you. I will go [come] to pick you up.

Si esperas por un rato, después de unas noches de vigilancia, vendré a verte. Vendré a recogerte.

● Please note that Korean speakers say, "I will go to you. (네게 갈께)", while Western speakers say, "I will come to you." or «Vendré a ti ».

< Line 12 > 추운 겨울 끝을 지나, 다시 봄날이 올 때까지, 꽃 피울 때까지
그곳에 좀 더 머물러 줘. 머물러 줘.

Passing through the end of the cold winter, / Pasando por el final del frío invierno,

until the spring days will come back, / hasta que vuelvan los días de primavera,

until the flowers will bloom, / hasta que florezcan las flores,

Please, stay there a little longer there. / Por favor, quedate un poco más ahí.

Please, stay (longer there). / Por favor, quédate (más ahí).

10. Serendipity

Artist : Jimin of BTS

Lyric Writers : 방시혁*, Ashton Foster,*

Ray Michael Djan Jr., RM, Slow Rabbit

< Line 1 > 이 모든 건 우연이 아냐. 그냥, 그냥, 나의 느낌으로.

이 = [determiner] this / these / este / estos

모든 = [determiner] all / every / whole / entire / todo(s) / cada / entero

건 = 것은 = 것 (things, facts, cases, cosas, hechos, casos) + 은 [marker for subject]

● In Korean, the distinction between «singular» and «plural» is not important.

우연이 = 우연 (coincidence, chance, coincidencia, casualidad) + 이 [marker for subject]

아니다 = [infinitive of adjective] be not / be no / be not correct / no ser / no ser correcto

아니야 = 아냐 = familiar ending of 아니다

이 모든 건 우연이 아냐.

All these things are not just coincidences. / Nothing has occurred by chance. /
Todas estas cosas no son meras coincidencias. / Nada ha ocurrido por casualidad.

그냥 = [adverb] just / simply / as it is / simplemente / tal como está

나의 = 나 (I, yo) + 의 [marker for possession] = of me / my / mi

느낌 = [noun] feelings / senses / impression / sentimiento / sentido / impresión

으로 = [marker] by / with / through / por / con

그냥, 그냥, 나의 느낌으로.

Just, just, by my feelings / I know it simply through my senses. /
Simplement, simplement, por mis sentimientos. / Lo sé sólo por mis sentidos.

< Line 2 > 온 세상이 어제완 달라. 그냥, 그냥 너의 기쁨으로.

온 = [determiner] all / every / whole / entire / todo(s) / cada / entero

세상이 = 세상 (the world, el mundo) + 이 [marker for subject]

어제완 = 어제와는 = 어제 (yesterday, ayer) + 와는 (from, since, de, desde)

다르다 = [infinitive of adjective] be different / has changed / ser diferente / ha cambiado

달라 = familiar ending of 다르다

온 세상이 어제완 달라.
The whole world has changed (completely) since yesterday. /
El mundo entero ha cambiado (por complete) desde ayer.

그냥 = [adverb] just / simply / as it is / simplemente / tal como está

너의 = 너 (you, tú) + 의 [marker for origin] = from you / desde tú

기쁨 = [noun] joy / delight / pleasure / alegría / deleite / placer

으로 = [marker] by / with / owing to / por / con / debido a

그냥, 그냥 너의 기쁨으로.
Just, just by your delight. / Simply owing to the pleasure from you. /
Sólo, sólo por tus deleites. / Simplemente debido a los placeres desde tú.

< Line 3 > 네가 날 불렀을 때, 나는 너의 꽃으로.

네가 = 너 (you, tú) + 이가 [marker for subject]

날 = 나를 = 나 (I, yo) + 를 [marker for object]

부르다 = [infinitive of verb] call / call one's name / llamar / llamar el nombre de uno

불렀다 = [pronunciation] 불럳다 → 불럳따 = past tense of 부르다

불렀을 = [pronunciation] 불러쓸 = adjective form of 불렀다

때 = [noun] time / occasion / moment / when / tiempo / ocasión / momento / cuando

나는 = 나 (I, yo) + 는 [marker for subject]

너의 = 너 (you, tú) + 의 [marker for possession] = of you / your / tu

꽃 = [pronunciation] 꼳 = [noun] flower / blossom / flor

으로 = [marker] into / en

꽃으로 = [pronunciation] 꼬츠로 = into the flower / en la flor

네가 날 불렀을 때, 나는 너의 꽃으로.

When you called my name, I turned into your blossom. /
Cuando tú llamaste mi nombre, me convertí en tu flor.

< Line 4 > 기다렸던 것처럼, 우린 시리도록 피어.

기다리다 = [infinitive of verb] wait (for) / await / hold on / expect / esperar / aguardar / esperanzar

기다렸다 = [pronunciation] 기다렫다 → 기다렫따 = past tense of 기다리다

기다렸던 = [pronunciation] 기다렫떤 = adjective form of 기다렸다

것처럼 = 것 (the thing that ~, the fact that ~, el hecho que ~, lo que ~) + 처럼 (like, as if, como, como si)

우린 = 우리 (we, nosotros) + 는 [marker for subject]

시리다 = [infinitive of verb] painfully cold / achingly chilled / be pitiful / be plaintive / penosamente frío / dolorosamente helado / ser lamentable / ser lastimero / estar con el corazón en vilo

시리도록 = until (we) become painfully cold / until (we) become pitifully plaintive / hasta que nos volvamos penosamente fríos / hasta que nos volvamos lastimosamente dolorosos

피다 = [infinitive of verb] bloom / blossom / come into flower / florecer / esflorecer

피어 = familiar ending of 피다

기다렸던 것처럼, 우린 시리도록 피어.

As if we have waited for the moment, we bloom (in full) until we become pitifully cold [plaintive].

Como si hubiéramos esperando el momento, florecemos (por completo) hasta que nos volvamos lastimosamente fríos [dolorosos].

< Line 5 > 어쩌면 우주의 섭리? 그냥 그랬던 거야.

어찌하다 = [infinitive of verb] do somehow / manage to do / employ some means to do / hacer de alguna manera / lograr hacer / emplear algunos medios para hacer

어찌하면 = adverb form of 어찌하다 = if (we) do somehow / si lo hacemos / de alguna manera

어쩌면 = [adverb] maybe / perhaps / probably / quizá / tal vez / probablemente

우주의 = [pronunciation] 우주에 = 우주 (universe, cosmos, universe) + 의 [marker for possession]

● «의 [marker for possession]» is pronounced as «에». However, in case that it is a part of an independent word, it is pronounced as «의». [정의 (justice)] [의미 (meaning)] [거의 (almost)]

섭리 = [pronunciation] 섭니 → 섬니 = [noun] providence / dispensation / providencia

어쩌면 우주의 섭리? = Is this maybe the providence of the Universe? /
¿Es éste quizás la providencia del Universo?

그냥 = [adverb] just / simply / as it is / simplemente / tal como está
그러하다 = [infinitive of adjective] be (like) such / be like that / ser así / ser como tal
그러하였다 = [pronunciation] 그러하엳따 = past tense of 그러하다
그러하였던 = **그랬던** = [pronunciation] 그랟떤 = adjective form of 그러하였다
것이다 = 것 (the thing that ~, the fact that ~, el hecho que ~, lo que ~) + 이다 (be, ser)
것이야 = **거야** = familiar ending of 것이다

그냥 그랬던 거야. = The fact is that it just has been like that. /
Just it always has been the providence of the Universe.

El hecho es que simplemente ha sido así. /
Siempre sólo ha sido la providencia del Universo.

< Line 6 > You know, I know, 너는 나, 나는 너.

We both know that you are me, and I am you.
Los dos sabemos que eres yo, y yo soy tú.

< Line 7 > 설레는 만큼 많이 두려워.

설레다 = [infintive of verb] throb / beat fast / palpitate / agitarse / latir rápido / palpitar
설레는 = adjective form of 설레다 = throbbing / that palpitates / se agitando / que late alta

만큼 = [noun] as much / to that extent / equal to / tanto como / en esa medida / igual a

많이 = [pronunciation] 마니 = [adverb] a lot / much / many / aplenty / abundantly / quite / in profusion / mucho(s) / abundantemente / en profusion / tanto

두렵다 = [infinitive of adjective] be afread / be feared / be scared / temer / tener miedo / estar alarmente

두려워 = familiar ending of 두렵다

설레는 만큼 많이 두려워. = I am quite afraid as much as the heart beating this fast / Tengo mucho miedo tanto como el corazón latiendo tan rápido

< Line 8 > 운명이 우릴 자꾸 질투해서, 너 만큼 나도 많이 무서워.

운명이 = 운명 (fate, destiny, hado, destino) + 이 [marker for subject]

우릴 = 우리를 = 우리 (we, nosotros) + 를 [marker for object]

자꾸 = [adverb] repeatedly / again and again / constantly / repetidamente / a menudo / constantemente

질투하다 = [infinitive of verb] be jealous / envy / estar celoso / envidiar

질투해서 = owing to be jealous / because envy / porque estar celoso / debido a que enviar

너 = [pronoun] you / tú

만큼 = [noun] as much / to that extent / equal to / tanto como / en esa medida / igual a

나도 = 나 (I, also) + 도 [marker] (as well, also, too, también, tampoco, y además)

많이 = [pronunciation] 마니 = [adverb] a lot / much / many / aplenty / abundantly / quite / in profusion / mucho(s) / abundantemente / en profusion / tanto

무섭다 = [pronunciation] 무섭따 = [infinitive of adjective] feel dreadful [terrifying, frightful] / sentir temeroso [miedoso, muy mal]

무서워 = familiar ending of 무섭다

운명이 우릴 자꾸 질투해서, 너 만큼 나도 많이 무서워.

Because the fate is constantly jealous of us, I also feel quite dreadful as much as you do. / Debido a que el destino está constantemente celoso de nosotros, también me siento muy mal tanto como tú.

< Line 9 > When you see me, when you touch me, 우주가 우릴 위해 움직였어. 조금의 어긋남조차 없었어.

우주가 = 우주 (universe, cosmos, universe) + 가 [marker for subject]

우릴 = 우리를 = 우리 (we, nosotros) + 를 [marker for object]

위하다 = [infinitive of verb] do for the good of / do in behalf of / care for / hacer por el bien de / hacer parar / cuidar de
위하여 = **위해** = adverb form of 위하다 = for / for the benefit of / para / para el beneficio de

움직이다 = [infinitive of verb] move / work / operate / moverse / operarse / trabajar / funcionar
움직였다 = [pronunciation] 움지겯따 = past tense of 움직이다 = moved / worked / operated / se movió / trababó / funcionaba
움직였어 = [pronunciation] 움지겨써 – familiar ending of 움직였다

우주가 우릴 위해 움직였어. = The Universe worked for us. /
El universe trababó para nosotros.

조금 = [adverv] a little (bit) / slight / a short while / pequeño / un poco / gota / ligero / breve / rato
조금의 = [pronunciation] 조그메 = 조금 + 의 [marker for possession] = adjective form of 조금 = a little bit of / un poco de

● «의 [marker for possession]» is pronounced as «에». However, in case that it is a part of an independent word, it is pronounced as «의».
[정의 (justice)] [의미 (meaning)] [거의 (almost)]

어긋나다 = [pronunciation] 어귿나다 → 어근나다 = [infinitive of verb] deviate from / go wrong [amiss] / desviarse / dislocarse / fallar
어긋남 = [pronunciation] 어귿남 → 어근남 = noun form of 어긋나다 = discrepancy / aberration / mismatch / error / discrepancia / desviación / desjuste

조차 = [marker for emphasis] not even / as well / but also / incluso / ni siquiera

없다 = [pronunciation] 업다 → 업따 = [infintive of adjective] there is no / not exist / be absent / be without / no hay / no existir / estar ausente / estar sin

없었다 = [pronunciation] 업썯따 = past tense of 없다

없었어 = [pronunciation] 업써써 = familiar ending of 없었다

조금의 어긋남조차 없었어. = There was not even a slight error. / Ni siquiera hubo un pequeño error.

< Line 10 > 너와 내 행복은 예정됐던 걸, cause you love, and I love you.

너와 = 너 (you, tú) + 와 (and, y) = your and / tú y

내 = 나의 = 나 (I, yo) + 의 [marker for possession] = of me / my / mi

행복 = [noun] happiness / well-being / bliss / fortune / felicidad / bienestar / dicha / fortuna

너와 내 행복은 = your and my happiness / tu y mi felicidad + 은 [marker for subject]

예정 = [noun] schedule / plan / prearrangement / el programa / el plan / preordinación

예정되다 = [infinitive of verb] be planned / be predetermined / be slated / be expected / ser planificado / ser predeterminado / predeterminar

예정되었다 = [pronunciation] 예정되얻따 = past tense of 예정되다 = 예정됐다

= [pronunciation] 예정됃따 = was predetermined / estaba predeterminado

예정되었던 것이다 [예정되얻떤 거시다] = 예정됐던 것이다 [예정됃떤 거시다]

= [poetic ending] **예정됐던 걸** = [pronunciation] 예정됃떤 걸 =

has been planned [predetermined, slated] / The thing is that it has been predetermined. / se ha planificado [predeterminado, programado] / El hecho es que ha sido predeterminado.

너와 나의 행복은 예정됐던 걸, = Your and my happiness has been slated. / Tu y mi felicidad ha sido planificada.

< Line 11 > 너는 내 푸른 곰팡이. 나를 구원해 준 나의 천사, 나의 세상.

너는 = 너 (you, tú) + 는 [marker for subejct]

174

내 = 나의 = 나 (I, yo) + 의 [marker for possession] = of me / my / mi

푸르다 = [infinitive of adjective] be azure / be greenish blue / ser azul / ser azul verdoso

푸른 = present tense of 푸르다

곰팡이 = [noun] mould / fungus / moho / hongo

푸른 곰팡이 = [noun phrase] green mould / penicillin / moho verde / penicilina

나를 = 나 (I, yo) + 를 [marker for obejct]

구원하다 = [infitive of verb] rescue / save / redeem / rescatar / salvar / redimir

주다 = [infinitive of verb] kindly do / give as a favour / willing to do / please, / amablemente hacer / dar con gusto / dispuesto a hacer / por favor,

구원하여 주다 = 구원해 주다 = kindly rescue / be willing to save / amablemente rescatar / mostrar la bondad de redimir

구원해 준 = past adjective form of 구원해 주다 = who kinldy saved / que amablemente rescató

나의 = 나 (I, yo) + 의 [marker for possession] = of me / my / mi

천사 = [noun] angel / ángel / angelita

세상 = [noun] world / mondo

너는 내 푸른 곰팡이. 나를 구원해 준 나의 천사, 나의 세상.
You are my green mould. My angel, and my world who kindly saved me.
Eres mi moho verde. Mi angelita, y mi mundo que amablemente me salvó.

< Line 12 > 난 네 삼색 고양이, 널 만나러 온. Love me now. Touch me now. Just let me love you. Just let me love you.

난 = 나는 = 나 (I, yo) + 는 [marker for subject]

네 = 너의 = 너 (you, tú) + 의 [marker for possession] = of you / your / tú

삼색 = [noun] tricolor / tres colores

고양이 = [noun] cat / kitty / puss / feline / gato / gatito / felino

삼색 고양이 = [noun phrase] tricolor cat / Calico kitty / gato tricolor / gaitito calicó

널 = 너를 = 너 (you, tú) + 를 [marker for object]

만나다 = [infinitive of verb] meet / encounter / come across / run into / hallar / encontrarse

만나러 = in order to meet / for the purpose of encountering / con el fin [propósito] de encontrar

오다 = [infinitive of verb] come / come to / approach / arrive / venir / venir a / acercarse / llegar (a)

만나러 오다 = come to meet / come to see / venir a encontrar / venir a ver

만나러 **온** = past adjective forme of 만나러 오다 = that came to see / que vino a ver

난 네 삼색 고양이, 널 만나러 온. = I am your Calico kitty that came to see you. / Soy tu gatito calicó que vino a verte.

< Line 13 > 우주가 처음 생겨났을 때부터 모든 건 정해진 거였어.
Just let me love you.

우주가 = 우주 (universe, cosmos, universe) + 가 [marker for subject]

처음 = [noun, also used as adverb] the first time / in the beginng / primera vez / al principio

생겨나다 = [infinitive of verb] come into existence / be born / llegar a exisitr / nacer

생겨났다 = [pronunciation] 생겨낟다 → 생겨낟따 = past tense of 생겨나다

생겨났을 = [pronunciation] 생겨나쓸 = adjective form of 생겨났다

때 = [noun] time / occasion / moment / when / tiempo / ocasión / momento / cuando

부터 = [marker] since / from / desde / de

우주가 처음 생겨났을 때부터
Since the time that the Universe came into existence /
Since the birth of the Universe

Desde el momento en que nació el universo /
Desde el nacimiento del universo

모든 = [determiner] all / every / whole / entire / todo(s) / cada / entero

건 = 것은 = 것 (things, facts, cases, cosas, hechos, casos) + 은 [marker for subject]

정하다 = [infinitive of verb] plan / predetermine / set / planificar / predeterminer / programar

정해지다 = be planned / be predetermined / be set / ser planificado / ser predeterminado

정해진 = past adjective form of 정해지다

것이다 = [pronunciation] 거시다 = 것 (the thing that ~, the fact that ~, el hecho que ~,

lo que ~) + 이다 (be, ser)

것이었다 = past tense of 것이다 = 것 + 이었다 (was, fue) = past tense of 것이다

것이었어 = [pronunciation] 거시어써 = **거였어** [거엳써] = familiar ending of 것이었다

= It was (the fact) that ~ / Fue el hecho que ~

우주가 처음 생겨났을 때부터 모든 건 정해진 거였어.

Since the birth of the Universe all the destinies of ours already have been predetermined. /
Desde el momento en que nació el universo, todo el destino nuestro ya está predeterminado.

< Line 11 > 너는 내 푸른 곰팡이. 나를 구원해 준 나의 천사, 나의 세상.

You are my green mould. My angel, and my world who kindly saved me. /
Eres mi moho verde. Mi angelita y mi mundo que amablemente me salvó.

< Line 12 > 난 네 삼색 고양이, 널 만나러 온. Love me now. Touch me now.
Just let me love you. Just let me love you.

I am your Calico kitty that came to see you. /
Soy tu gatito calicó que vino a verte.

< Line 13 > 우주가 처음 생겨났을 때부터, 모든 건 정해진 거였어.
Just let me love you.

Since the birth of the Universe all the destinies of ours already have been predetermined. /
Desde el momento en que nació el universo, todo el destino nuestro ya está predeterminado.

< Line 14 > 이젠 곁에 와 줘. 우리가 되어 줘. I don't want to let go. No.

이젠 = 이제는 = 이제 (now, ahora) + 는 [marker for emphasis] = (on the contrary) now / now
at last / eventually now / coming to now / (al contrario) ahora / ahora por fin / llegando a ahora
곁 = [pronunciation] 겯 = [noun] side / lado

곁에 = [pronunciation] 겨테 → 겨체 = 곁 + 에 (by, a) = by (my) side / al lado

오다 = [infinitive of verb] come / come to / approach / arrive / venir / venir a /
acercarse / llegar (a)

주다 = [infinitive of verb] kindly do / give as a favour / willing to do / please, /

amablemente hacer / dar con gusto / dispuesto a hacer / por favor,

와 주다 = kindly come / come as a favour / amablemente venir / venir con gusto

와 주어 = **와 줘** = familir ending for imperative mood of 와 주다 = Please, come near. / Please, come to me. / Por favor, acércate. / Por favor, vén

이젠 곁에 와 줘. 우리가 되어 줘. = Please come and stay by my side no later than now. / Por favor, vén y quédate a mi lado a más tardar ahora.

우리가 = 우리 (we, one team, couple, nosotros, un equipo, parejo) + 가 [marker for subject]

되다 = [infinitive of verb] become / turn into / volverse / convertirse / resultar / terminarse / hacerse / ser

주다 = [infinitive of verb] kindly do / give as a favour / willing to do / please, / amablemente hacer / dar con gusto / dispuesto a hacer / por favor,

되어 주다 = kindly become / willing to become / volverse con gusto / dispuesto a convertirse

되어 주어 = **되어 줘** = familiar ending for imperative mood of 되어 주다 = Please, become / Please let's be / Por favor, convirtamos / Por favor, hagamos

우리가 되어 줘. = Please let's turn into a 'one team'. / Please let's make a couple. Por favor, nos hagamos en 'un equipo'. / Por favor, nos convertimos en 'pareja'.

< Line 15 > 그냥 맡기면 되는 거야. 말 안 해도 느껴지잖아?

그냥 = [adverb] just / simply / as it is / simplemente / tal como está

맡기다 = [pronunciation] 맏끼다 = [infinitive of verb] trust / entrust / put in charge of / leave it to /confiar / encargar / encomendar / poner a cargo de / dejarlo a

맡기면 = [pronunciation] 맏끼면 = if trust / if entrust / if put in charge of / if leave to / si confiar / si encargar / si encomendar / si poner a cargo de / si dejarlo a

되다 = [infinitive of verb] be good [okay] / be well done / estar bien / estar bien hecho / ser bien

되는 = present adjective form of 되다 = being good / that is okay / estando bien hecho / que es bien

것이다 = 것 (the thing that ~, the fact that ~, el hecho que ~, lo que ~) + 이다 (be, ser)

것이야 = **거야** = familiar ending of 것이다

그냥 맡기면 되는 거야.

It will be okay if we just entrust ourselves (to the fate predetermined by the Universe). / Estará bien si simplemente nos encomiéndemos (al destino planeado por el universo).

말하다 = [infinitive of verb] say / tell / talk / speak / state / decir / hablar / referir

말 안 하다 = 말 아니 하다 = not say / not talk / no decir / no hablar

말 안 해도 = even if say nothing / even without talking / aunque no decir nada / incluso sin hablar

느끼다 = [infinitive of verb] feel / sense / perceive / sentir / percibir

느껴지다 = passive voice of 느끼다 = come to feel / get to sense / become to perceive / volverse sentir / llegar a percibir

느껴지지 = a noun-type cojugation of 느껴지다

아니 하다 = 안 하다 = 않다 = [pronunciation] 안타 = not do / no hacer

않아? = [pronunciation] 아나? = [tag questioning] You do, don't you? / it is right, isn't it? / haces, ¿no? / es correcto, ¿no?

느껴지지 않아? = 느껴지잖아? = [pronunciation] 느껴지자나? = [tag question] You see, you come to feel, don't you? / ¡Verás, te vuelves sentir, ¿no?

말 안 해도 느껴지잖아? = You see, you come to feel it even without saying a word, don't you? / Verás, te vuelves sentirlo aunque no decir nada, ¿no?

● This can be either a question or an emphasis. Therefore, ending tone is your choice.

< Line 16 > 별들은 떠 있고, 우린 날고 있어. 절대 꿈은 아냐.

별들은 = [pronunciation] 별드른 = 별 (star, estrella) + 들 [plural] + 은 [marker for subject] = stars / estrellas

뜨다 = [infinitive of verb] float / rise / emerge / come up / flotar / elevarse / émerger / subir

있다 = [pronunciation] 읻다 → 읻따 = [infinitive of verb] there is / be / exist / stay / remain / stand / hay / estar / existir / quedarse / permanecer / pararse

떠 있다 = [present progressive] stay [are] floating / have risen up / are being emerged up / permanecer flotando / estar flotando / se han levantado

떠 있고 = stay floating, and / be emerged up, and / permanecer flotando, y / se han levantado, y

우린 = 우리는 = 우리 (we, nosotros) + 는 [marker for subject]

날다 = [infinitive of verb] fly / soar / volarse / revolotear

있다 = [pronunciation] 읻다 → 읻따 = [infinitive of verb] there is / be / exist / stay / remain / stand / hay / estar / existir / quedarse / permanecer / pararse

날고 있다 = [present progressive] are flying / are soaring / estamos volando / estamos revoloteando

날고 있어 = formal ending of 날고 있다

별들은 떠 있고, 우린 날고 있어.

The stars stay floating in the air, and we are flying around. /
Las estrellas permanecen flotando en el aire, y nosotros estamos revoloteando.

절대 = [pronunciation] 절때 = [noun, also used as adverb] never / absolutely / completely / nunca / absolutamente / plenamente

● In Korean, the pronunciation of the first consonant just after ' ㄹ ' tends to become hard. However, this is not usually applicable within a word. Exceptions are mostly Sino-Korean words like «절대» which is pronounced as «절때».

꿈은 = [pronunciation] 꾸믄 = 꿈 (dream, illusion, sueño) + 은 [marker for subject]

아니다 = [infinitive of adjective] be not / be no / be different / no ser / ser diferente

아니야 = **아냐** = familiar ending of 아니다

절대 꿈은 아냐. = This is never a dream. / Esto nunca es un sueño.

< Line 17 > 떨지 말고, 내 손을 잡아. 이제 우리가 되는 거야. Let me love you. Just let me love you. Let me love, let me love you.

떨다 = [infinitive of verb] tremble / shake / shiver / quiver / temblar / estremecerse

떨지 = a noun-type conjugation of 떨다

말다 = [verb] quit doing / refrain from doing / not do any longer / dejar de hacer / no hacer

떨지 말다 = [verb phrase] Quit trembling / Refrain from shaking / Deja de temblar / Abstenerse de temblar

떨지 말고 = Quit trembling, and / Refrain from shaking, and / Deja de temblar, y /

Abstenerse de temblar, y

● In Korean, when two verbs combine, there is a tendency that the first verb does either a noun-type or an adverb-type conjugation. By doing so, the first verb serves like an object for the second verb [in case that the second verb is a transitive verb], or modifies the second verb like an adverb [in case that the second verb is an intransitive verb].

● By doing a noun-type conjugation the first verb can serve as an object of the second verb. [떨지 말다 = Quit trembling] Here, «떨지 (trembling)» is the object of «말다 (quit)».

내 = 나의 = 나 (I, yo) + 의 (marker for possession) = of me / my / of mine / mi

손을 = [pronunciation] 소늘 = 손 (hand, mano) + 을 (marker for object)

잡다 = [pronunciation] 잡따 = [infinitive of verb] hold / take hold of / grab / tomar / agarrar / coger

잡아 = [pronunciation] 자바 = [familiar ending for imperative mood] Do hold! / Do take hold of! / ¡Toma!

내 손을 잡아! = Hold my hand! / ¡Toma mi mano!

이제 우리가 되는 거야. = (우리는) 이제 우리가 되는 거야.

● Please note that the real subject, «우리는 (we, nosotros)», is omitted in this sentence.

Here, «우리가 (we, nosotros)» is just the subject of the verb «되다 (become, convertirse)».

(우리는) = 우리 (we, nosotros) + 는 [marker for subject]

이제 = [noun, also used as adverb] now / current moment / at this time / ahora / en este momento

우리가 = 우리 (we, one team, couple, nosotros, un equipo, pareja) + 가 [marker for subject]

되다 = [infinitive of verb] become / turn into / volverse / convertirse / resultar / terminarse / hacerse / ser

된다 = [pronunciation] 된다 = present form of 되다

● All the vowels and four consonants (ㄴ, ㄹ, ㅁ, ㅇ) are voiced sounds, which are soft. A consonant that is between any two of them becomes soft as well.
[되다 → 되다] [된다 → 된다] [떨다 → 떨다] [떨지 → 떨지] [말다 → 말다]

우리는 이제 우리가 된다 = 이제 우리는 우리가 된다 = Now we become us. / Ahora nos convertimos en nosotros. = Now you and I become one team. /

Ahora tú y yo nos convertimos en un solo equipo.

되는 = present adjective form of 되다

것이다 = 것 (thing, stuff, fact, case, cosa, hecho, caso, algo) + 이다 (be, ser)

것이야 = **거야** = familiar ending of 것이다

이제 우리가 되는 거야. = (The fact is that) now we turn into a 'one team'. /
From this moment we become a couple.

(El hecho es que) ahora nos hacemos en 'un equipo'. /
De este momento nos convertimos en 'pareja'.

< Line 13 > 우주가 처음 생겨났을 때부터, 모든 건 정해진 거였어.
Just let me love you.

Since the birth of the Universe all the destinies of ours have already been predetermined. /
Desde el momento en que nació el universo, todo el destino nuestro ya está predeterminado.

11. Mic Drop

Artist: BTS
Lyric Writers: Pdogg, Supreme Boi,
방시혁, J-Hope, RM

< Line 1 > Yeah. 누가 내 수저 더럽대?

Yeah. = 야 = [in Korean] Hey!

누가 = 누구 [pronoun] + 가 = 누구 (who, which person, quién) + 가 [marker for subject]

내 = 나의 = 나 (I, yo) + 의 [marker for possession] = of me / my / mi

수저 = [noun] spoon / spoon and chopsticks / cuchara / cuchara y palillos

더럽다 = [infinitive of adjective] = be dirty [filthy, grimy] / estar sucio [cochino, inmundo]

더럽대? = 더럽다고 해? = 더럽다 (dirty, sucio) + 이라고 해? [do say? / ¿dicc?]

이라고 하다 = 이라고 [a noun-type conjugation of 이다] + 하다 [do, hacer] = say / decir

이다 = [infinitive of marker that conjugates] be / ser

수저가 더럽다 = His spoon is dirty. / He is an underling. /
His spoon is made of neither gold or silver. / Su cuchara está sucia. /
Es un humilde. / Su cuchara no está hecha de oro ni plata.

누가 내 수저 더럽대? = Who says that my spoon is dirty? /
Who says that I am a lowling. / ¿Qien dice que mi cuchara esta sucia? /
¿Quien dice que soy humilde?

< Line 2 > I don't care. 마이크 잡음 금수저 여럿 패.

마이크 = [noun] mic / microphone / micrófono

잡다 = [infinitive of verb] hold / take hold of / grab / tomar / agarrar / mantener

잡음 = 잡으면 = if hold / if take hold of / if grap / si tomar / si agarrar / si mantener

금수저 = [noun] spoon of gold / golden spoon / cuchara de oro

여럿 = [pronunciation] 여런 = [noun] several guys / varios personas / varios tipos

패다 = [infintive of verb] thrash / hit / beat / surpass / prevail / golpear / batir /
superar / adelantar

패 = familiar ending of 패다

183

마이크 잡음 금수저 여럿 패.

If (I) take hold of a micrphone, (I) can supass several guys who have got gold spoons. /
Si tomo un micrófono, puedo superar a varios tipos que tienen chcharas de oro.

< Line 3 > 버럭해. 잘 못 익은 것들, 스테끼 여러 개.

버럭 = [adverb] abruptly / suddenly / of a sudden / abruptamente / repentinamente / de repente

화를 내다 = [verb phrase] get angry / lose one's temper / enojarse / enfadarse

버럭 화를 내다 = 버럭하다 = [pronunciation] 버럭카다 = abruptly get angry over /
suddenly lose one's temper / abruptamente enojarse / de repente enfadarse por algo

버럭해 = [pronunciation] 버러캐 = familiar ending of 버럭하다

잘 = [adverb] well / nicely / favourably / fully / properly / carefully / bien / bueno /
favorablemente / bastantemente / exactamente / con cuidado

못 = [pronunciation] 몯 = [adverb] not / unable / can't / incapable / won't /
no / no puede / incapaz

익다 = [infinitive of verb] cook / ripen / become mature / cocinar / cocerse / madurar

익은 = [pronunciation] 이근 = adjective form of 익다 = that is cooked / that is ripen /
que se cocina / que está maduro

것들 = [pronunciation] 걷들 → 걷뜰 = 것 (thing, stuff, cosa, hecho, caso) + 들 [plural]

스테끼 = [noun] steak / beefsteak / bistec / bisté / filete / bife

● **Please note the following double meanings:**

잘 못 익은 = not properly cooked / spiritually not mature / no bien cocinado /
espiritualmente no maduro

것 = [pronunciation] 걷 = thing / stuff / despisable person / cosa / persona despreciable

스테끼 = funny pronunciation of «steak» / similar to Korean foul word corresponding to
"bastard" / pronunciación divertida de bistec / similar a la sucia palabra coreana
correspondiente a «bastardo»

여러 = [adjective] several / varios

개 = [noun] couting units / unidades de conteo

버럭해. 잘 못 익은 것들, 스테끼 여러 개.

Abruptly I get angry over the several strips of steaks that are not properly cooked. /
Abruptly I get angry over those several guys of bastards who are spiritually immature.

Abruptamente me enojo por las varias tiras de filetes que no están bien cocinados. /
Abruptamente me enojo por esos varios tipos de bastardos que son espiritualmente inmaduros.

< Line 4 > 거듭해서 씹어줄께, 스타의 저녁에.

거듭하다 = [pronunciation] 거드파다 = [infinitive of verb] repeat /
do over and over again / repetir / hacer repetidamente / hacer una y otro vez
거듭해서 = [pronunciation] 거드패서 = adverb form of 거듭하다 = by doing repeatedly /
through doing over and over again / haciendo repetidamente / a través de hacer una y otra vez

● When 'ㅎ' combines with a consonant, the consonant becomes aspirated.
[ㄱ + ㅎ → ㅋ] [ㄷ + ㅎ → ㅌ] [ㅂ + ㅎ → ㅍ] [ㅈ + ㅎ → ㅊ]

씹다 = [pronunciation] 씹따 = [infinitive of verb] chew / masticate / masticar / mascar
● The word '씹다' is also used to imply 'speak ill / hablar mal' or 'criticize / criticar'.

주다 = [infinitive of verb] kindly do / give as a favour / willing to do / please, /
amablemente hacer / dar con gusto / dispuesto a hacer / por favor,
씹어 주다 = chew eagerly / willing to speak ill / dispuesto a masticar / dispuesto a hablar mal
씹어 줄께 = [pronunciation] 씨버 줄께 = I will chew eagerly / I am willing to speak ill /
voy a masticar con entusiasmo / estoy dispuesto a hablar mal

스타 = [noun] 별 = star / estrella = indicating the singer himself
스타의 = 스타 + 의 [marker for possession] = of the star / of myself / del estrella /
de mí mismo
저녁에 = 저녁 (evening, dinner, supper, noche, cena) + 에 (at, in, en)

거듭해서 씹어줄께, 스타의 저녁에.
I am willing to chew them over and over again at the dinner table of this star. /
I am willing to criticize them repeatedly at the dinner table of mine.

Estoy dispuesto a masticarlos una y otra vez en la mesa de esta estrella. /
Estoy dispuesto a criticarlos repetidamente en la mesa de la mía.

< Line 5 > World business 핵심. 섭외 일(1) 순위. 매진.

핵심 = [noun] core / key / essence / centre / núcleo / clave / esencia / médula
섭외 = [pronunciation] 서뵈 = [noun] negociation / invitation / casting /
negociación / invitación
순위 = [noun] ranking / order / standing / clasificación / orden / espera

매진 = [noun] sellout / being sold out / all gone / agotamiento / vendido por completo

World business 핵심. 섭외 일(1) 순위. 매진.
I am the core of the world business. I am at the top in the casting list.
Tickets are always sold out.

Soy el núcleo del negocio mundial. Estoy en lo más alto de la lista de casting.
Las entradas siempre agotadas.

< Line 6 > 많지 않지, 이 클래스. 가칠 만끽. 좋은 향기에 악췬 반칙. Mic, mic, bungee.

많다 = [pronunciation] 만타 = [infinitive of adjective] There are many [numerous] /
hay muchos
많지 = [pronunciation] 만치 = an adverb-type conjugation of 많다

아니하다 = 않다 = [pronunciation] 안타 = [infinitive of adjective] not be / no ser / no estar

● Here, «아니하다» or «않다» is not a verb, but an adjective, because it does not mean an action

많지 않다 = [pronunciation] 만치 안타 = There are not many / It is not common /
No hay muchos / No es común

● 많지 않다 = [만 + ㅎ + 지] + [안 + ㅎ + 다] = 만치 안타

많지 않지 = [pronunciation] 만치 안치 = familiar ending of 많지 않다
이 = [determiner] this / these / este / estos
클래스 = [noun] 급 = class / category / clase / categoría

많지 않지, 이 클래스 = Not many stars belong to this level of category. /
No muchas estrellas pertenecen a este nivel de categoría.

가칠 = 가치를 = 가치 (value, merit, valor, mérito) + 를 [marker for object]
만끽 = [noun] full amusement to one's content / diversión completa al contenido

가칠 만끽 = I am enjoying the merits fully to my content. /
Estoy disfrutando plenamente de esos méritos al contenido.

좋다 = [pronunciation] 조타 = [infinitive of adjective] be good [nice, satisfactory] /
ser bueno [agradable, satisfactorio]

● When 'ㅎ' combines with a consonant, the consonant becomes aspirated.

[ㄱ + ㅎ → ㅋ] [ㄷ + ㅎ → ㅌ] [ㅂ + ㅎ → ㅍ] [ㅈ + ㅎ → ㅊ]

좋은 = [pronunciation] 조은 = present tense of 좋다 = good [nice] / bueno [agradable]

향기에 = 향기 (fragrance, scent, aroma, fragncia) + 에 (towards, hacia)

악췬 = 악취는 = 악취 (odour, stink, stench, mal olor, hedor) + 는 [marker for subject]

반칙 = [noun] foul play / foul / cheating / juego sucio / falta / trampa

좋은 향기에 악췬 반칙

It is a foul play to bring stinking odour towards good fragrance. /
Es un juego sucio para traer mal olor hacia una buena fragancia.

**< Line 7 > Bright light, 전진! 망할 것 같았겠지만, I'm fine. Sorry.
미안해, Billboard. 미안해, Worldwide.**

전진 = [noun] advance / march / forward movement / avance / marcha / movimiento de avance

Bright light, 전진! = I march forward to the bright light. /
Marcho adelante hacia la luz brillante.

망하다 = [infinitive of verb] fail / go under / go to ruin / fallar / echar a perder

망할 = (future) adjective form of 망하다 = getting to fail / to go under / va a fallar /
echaré a perder

것 = [noun] the thing that ~ / the fact that ~ / la cosa que ~ / el hecho que ~ /
el caso que ~ / lo que ~

망할 것 = that we are going to fail / that I shall go under / lo que fallaría(n)

같다 = [pronunciation] 같따 = [infinitive of adjective] It looks like / It seems that /
Parecer que

같았다 = [pronunciation] 가탇따 = past tense of 같다 = It looked like /
It seemed like / Parecía que

같았겠다 = [pronunciation] 가타껟따 = Maybe it looked [seemed] like /
Tal vez parecía que

같았겠지만 = [pronunciation] 가타껟찌만 = Maybe it looked like, but /
Although it seemed like / Tal vez parecía que, pero

망할 것 같았겠지만, I'm fine. Sorry.

Maybe it looked like that I shall go under, but I'm fine. Sorry. /
Tal vez parecía que fallaría, pero estoy bien. Lo siento.

미안해, Billboard. 미안해, Worldwide.

[literal] I am sorry, Billoard. I am sorry Worldwide. / Lo siento, Billboard. Lo siento, Mundial.

● The above is a literal translation. The liberal and more correct translation shall be as follows:

[liberal] I am sorry, Bastards. I am a bright star at Billboard. You see, I am a worldwide star. /
I am sorry, Folks. I am a Billboard star. Sorry again, Folks, Now I am a worldwide star.

Lo siento, Bastardos. Soy una estrella brillante en Billoard. Verás, soy una estrella mundial. /
Lo siento, amigos. Soy una estrella de Billboard. Lo siento de nuevo, amigos. Ahora soy
una estrella mundial.

< Line 8 > 아들이 넘 잘 나가서 미안해, 엄마. 대신해 줘? 네가 못한 효도.

아들이 = 아들 (son, hijo) + 이 [marker for subject] = your son / tu hijo = I myself / yo mismo

넘 = 너무 = [adverb] too much [many] / excessively / demasiado / excessivamente / tanto bien

잘 = [adverb] well / nicely / favourably / fully / properly / carefully / bien / bueno /
favorablemente / bastantemente / exactamente / con cuidado
나가다 = [infintive of verb] advance / march / move forward / avanzar / marcha /
mover adelante
잘 나가다 = [verb phrase] make a speedy success / be so successful / hacer un éxito rápido /
ser tan exitoso
잘 나가서 = because make a speedy success / for being so successful /
porque hacer un éxito rápido / por siendo tan exitoso
미안하다 = [infinitive of verb] be sorry / feel apologetic / lo siento / sentir disculpado
미안해 = familiar ending of 미안하다

엄마 = [noun] Mom / Mamá = I would rather translate it into Korea or Motherland /
Corea o la madre patria.

아들이 넘 잘 나가서 미안해, 엄마.
Mom, I am sorry for this speedy success of your son. /
Korea, I am sorry that you have never expected this kind of worldwide sensation from us.

Mamá, lo siento por el rápido éxito de tu hijo. /
Corea, lo siento que nunca hayas esperado este tipo de sensación mundial de nosotros.

대신해 줘? 네가 못한 효도.

대신하다 = [infinitive of verb] take the place of / replace / tomar el lugar de / reemplazar

주다 = [infinitive of verb] kindly do / give as a favour / willing to do / please, / amablemente hacer / dar con gusto / dispuesto a hacer / por favor,

대신해 주어? = **대신해 줘?** = Do you want me kindly to take your place? ¿Quieres que tome tu lugar bondadosamente?

네가 = 너 (you, tú) + 이가 [marker for subject]

하다 = [infinitive of verb] do / act / make / hacer / realizar

못하다 = [infinitive of verb] cannot do / fail to do / not succeed doing / no poder hacer

못한 = past adjective form of 못하다 = that you couldn't do / that you failed to do / que no pudiste hacer /que fallaste en hacer

효도 = [noun] filial duty / filial piety / deber filial / piedad filial

● I would rather translate «효도 (filial piety)» into «patriotic activity», because the Singer has no reason to be filial to the Moms of the haters. And those haters were not able to represent their Mother Country, while the Singer was able to do so.

대신해 줘? 네가 못한 효도.
Do you want me kindly to take your place to perform the filial duties that you failed to do? / Do you want me kindly to take your place to perform the patriotic activities that you failed to do?

¿Quieres que tome tu lugar para cumplir con los deberes filiales que no pudist hacer? / ¿Quieres que tome tu lugar para cumplir con las actividades patrióticas que no pudist hacer?

< Line 9 > 우리 콘서트(에는) 절대 없어, 포도. I do it, I do it. 넌 맛없는 라따뚜이.

우리(의) = 우리 (we, nosotros) + 의 [marker for possession] = of us / our / de nosotros / nuestro

콘서트(에는) = 콘서트 (공연, concert, concierto) + 에는 (in, en)

절대 = [pronunciation] 절때 = [noun, also used as adverb] never / absolutely / completely / nunca / absolutamente / plenamente

● In Korean, the pronunciation of the first consonant just after ' ㄹ ' tends to become hard. However, this is not usually applicable within a word. Exceptions are mostly Sino-Korean words like «절대» which is pronounced as «절때».

없다 = [pronunciation] 업다 → 업따 = [infintive of adjective] there is no /
not exist / be absent / be without / no hay / no existir / estar ausente / estar sin

없어 = [pronunciation] 업써 = familiar ending of 없다

포도 = [noun] grape / uva = [slang] empty seats / asientos vacíos

우리(의) 콘서트(에는) 절대 없어, 포도
There are never empty seats in our concert. /
Nunca hay asientos vacíos en nuestro concierto.

넌 = 너는 = 너 (you, tú) + 는 [marker for subject]

맛없다 = [pronunciation] 맏 + 업따 → 마덥따 = [adjective] be tasteless / taste bad / be
insipid / ser desabrido / saborear malo / ser insípido.

● «맛없다» is the combination of two independent words 맛 and 없다. In that case, a sound-linking (or
liaison) is not allowed as «마섭따». The correct pronunciation is «마덥따».

맛없는 = [pronunciation] 맏 + 업는 → 맏 + 엄는 → 마덤는 = [present form] (that is)
tasteless / bad tasty / insipid / (que es) desabrido / no saboroso / insípido / de mal gusto.

라따뚜이 = [French noun] ratatouille

넌 맛없는 라따뚜이. = You are the tasteless ratatouille. / Your concert is insipid. /
Eres el ratatouille de mal gusto. / Tu concierto es insípido.

< Line 10 > 혹 배가 아프다면, 고소해. Sue it!

혹 = 혹시 = [adverb] by chance / possibly / on the chace that / tal vez / a lo major /
por casualidad

배가 = 배 (belly, stomach, abdomen, vientre, estómago, panza) + 가 [marker for subject]

아프다 = [infinitive of adjective] hurt / be ill [sick, painful, sore, hurting] / be tormented /
doler / ser doloroso / estar enfermo [dolorido, herido] / atormentarse

아프다면 = if hurt / if be ill / si doler / si ser doloroso / is estar enfermo

배가 아프다면
if your belly hurts / if your belly torments you / if you feel pain out of jealousy [envy] /
si te duele el vientre / si te atormenta el vientre / si te sientes dolor por celos [envidia]

고소하다 = [infinitive of verb] sue / file a lawsuit / demandar / archivar una demanda judicial

고소해 = familiar ending for imperative mood of 고소하다

혹(시) 배가 아프다면, 고소해.

If you happen to feel jealous and got stomach sick, sue me. /
Si te sientes celoso y te duele el estómago, demándame.

< Line 11 > [Did you see my bag? X 2] It's hella trophies, it's hella thick.
[What do you think 'bout that? X 2] I bet, it got my haters hella sick.

Come and follow me. Follow me, with your signs up.

I'm so firing, firing. Boy, your time's up.
Keep on running and running until I catch up. [How you dare? X 3]
Another trophy. My hands carry 'em. Too many that I can't even count 'em.
Mic drop, 발발 조심. 너네 말 말 조심.

Mic drop, 발발 조심. 너네 말 말 조심.

Mic drop. Foot, foot, watch out. Guys, tongue, tongue, watch out.
Mic drop. Pie, pie, cuidado. Chicos, lengua, lengua, cuidado.

발 = [noun] foot / pie

조심 = [noun] caution / watch out / beware / caución / precaución / cuidado

너네 = 너 (you, tú) + 네 [plural] = you guys / chicos

말 = [noun] words / saying / palabras = tongue / mouth / lengua / boca

< Line 12 > Somebody stop me. I'm 'bouta pop off. Too busy.
You know, my body ain't enough. Mic drop, 발발 조심. 너네 말 말 조심.

Too busy. You know, I need far more than one body. /
Estoy muy ocupado. Sabes, necesito mucho más de un cuerpo.

Mic drop. Foot, foot, watch out. Guys, tongue, tongue, watch out. /
Mic drop. Pie, pie, cuidado. Chicos, lengua, lengua, cuidado.

< Line 13 > Baby, watch your mouth. It comes back around.
Once upon a time, we learnt how to fly.

Go look at your mirror. Same day clothes. You know how I feel. 개행복!

How many hours do we fly? I keep on dreaming on the cloud.

Yeah, I'm on the mountain. Yeah, I'm on the bay.
Every day we vibing. Mic drop. Bam!

개행복! = 개 (dog, perro) + 행복 (happiness, felicidad) = [slang] Couldn't be better! /
¡No podría estar mejor! / ¡No podría ser mejor!

개 = [noun] dog / perro = [slang] extravagant / excessive / extraordinary / damn /
excesivamente / excesivo / extraordinario / muchísimo

< Line 11> [Did you see my bag? X 2] It's hella trophies, it's hella thick.
[What do you think 'bout that? X 2] I bet, it got my haters hella sick.

Come and follow me. Follow me, with your signs up.
I'm so firing, firing, boy. Your time's up.

Keep on running and running until I catch up. [How you dare? X 3]
Another trophy. My hands carry 'em. Too many that I can't even count 'em.
Mic drop, 발발 조심. 너네 말 말 조심.

Mic drop. Foot, foot, watch out. Guys, tongue, tongue, watch out.
Mic drop. Pie, pie, cuidado. Chicos, lengua, lengua, cuidado.

< Line 12 > Somebody stop me. I'm 'bouta pop off. Too busy.
You know, my body ain't enough. Mic drop, 발발 조심. 너네 말 말 조심.

Mic drop. Foot, foot, watch out. Guys, tongue, tongue, watch out.
Mic drop. Pie, pie, cuidado. Chicos, lengua, lengua, cuidado.

< Line 14 > Haters gon' hate. Players gon' play. Live a life, man. Good luck.
[더 볼 일 없어. 마지막 인사야. 할 말도 없어. 사과도 하지 마! X 2]

더 = [adverb] more / further / aditionally / más / de nuevo

보다 = [infinitive of verb] see / watch / look at / observe / ver / mirar / observar

볼 = adjective form of 보다

일 = [noun] work / affair / incident / event / case / thing / trabajo / asunto / incidente /
suceso / caso / cosa / aventura

없다 = [pronunciation] 업다 → 업따 = [infintive of adjective] there is no / not exist /
be absent / be without / no hay / no existir / estar ausente / estar sin

없어 = [pronunciation] 업써 = familiar ending of 없다

더 볼 일 없어. = (I) have no affair [reason] to see you again. /
No tengo ninguna cosa [razón] por verte de nuevo.

마지막 = [noun, also used as adjective] the end / closing / last / final / último

인사 = [noun] greeting / salute / hi / saludo / hola

이다 = [infinitive of marker that conjugates] be / ser

이야 = **야** = familiar ending of 이다

마지막 인사야. = This is my last 'hi' to you. / Este es mi último 'hola' para ti.

하다 = [infinitive of verb] do / act / make / hacer / realizar

할 = adjective form of 하다

말도 = 말 (words, saying, palabras) + 도 [marker] (neither, not even, ni, ni siquiera)

● In principle, «도» itself is not negative, but here, one can expect that a negative expression would come along.

없다 = [pronunciation] 업다 → 업따 = [infintive of adjective] there is no / not exist /
be absent / be without / no hay / no existir / estar ausente / estar sin

없어 = [pronunciation] 업써 = familiar ending of 없다

할 말도 없어. = I have not even a thing to say. / Ni siquiera tengo nada que decir.

사과도 = 사과 (apology, excuse, disculpa, excusa) + 도 [marker] (neither, not at all, ni, ni siquiera)

하다 = [infinitive of verb] do / act / make / hacer / realizar

사과하다 = [infinitive of verb] apologize / make an apology / disculparse /
pedir perdón

말다 = [verb] quit doing / refrain from doing / not do any longer / dejar de hacer /
no hacer

마 = familiar ending of 말다

하지 마! = [imperative mood] Don't do it! / Refrain from doing! / ¡No lo hagas! /
¡Absente de hacerlo!

사과도 하지 마! = Don't even apologize! / ¡Ni siquiera te disculpes!

< Line 15 > 잘 봐! 넌 그 꼴 나지. 우린 탁 쏴. 마치 콜라지. 너의 각막 깜짝 놀라지. 꽤 꽤 폼나지. 폼나지. Yeh.

잘 = [adverb] well / nicely / favourably / fully / properly / carefully / bien / bueno / favorablemente / bastantemente / exactamente / con cuidado
보다 = [infinitive of verb] see / watch / look at / observe / ver / mirar / observar
보아! = **봐!** = [imperative mood] see! / look! / take a look! / ¡ve! / ¡mira! / ¡echa un vistazo!

잘 봐! = Look carefully! / ¡Mira con cuidado!

넌 = 너는 = 너 (you, tú) + 는 [marker for subject]
그 = [determiner] the / that / those / ese / tal
● A determiner is an unconjugating adjective.

꼴 = [noun] terrible shape / undesirable state / forma terrible / estado indeseable
나다 = [infinitive of verb] end up / becoming / terminar convirtiéndose / terminar siendo
나지 = familiar ending of 나다

넌 그 꼴 나지. = You ended up looking terrible like that. /
Terminaste pareciéndote terrible así.

우린 = 우리는 = 우리 (we, nosotros) + 는 [marker for subejct]
탁 = [adverb] with a pop / with a popping flavour / con un pop / con un sabor a popping
쏘다 = [infinitive of verb] sting / sting the tongue / stimulate / picar / picar la lengua / estimular
쏴 = familiar ending of 쏘다

우린 탁 쏴. = We stimulate your tongue with a pop. /
Estimulamos la lengua con un sabor a popping.

마치 = [adverb] like / as if / as / a kind of / como / una especie de

콜라 = [noun] cola / soda

이다 = [infinitive of marker that conjugates] be / ser

이지 = **지** = familiar ending of 이다 [assertive tone]

마치 콜라지. = We are kind of a cola. / Somos una especie de soda.

너의 = 너 (you, tú) + 의 [marker for possession] = of you / your / tu / tus

각막 = [noun] cornea / córnea

깜짝 = [mimetic adverb] with surprise / startlingly / con sorpresa / asombrosamente

놀라다 = [infinitive of verb] be surprised / be amazed / estar sorprendido / estar asustado

놀라지 = familiar ending of 놀라다 [assertive tone]

너의 각막 깜짝 놀라지. = Your corneas get to experience a startling amazement. /
Tus córneas pueden experimentar un asombro sorprendente.

꽤 = [adverb] quite / pretty / rather / bastante / considerablemente / mucho

폼나다 = [infinitive of verb] be stylish / look cool / look dandy / ser elegante /
verse genial / ser excelente

폼나니? = familiar ending for questioning of 폼나다 = Do we look dandyish? /
¿Nos vemos geniales?

폼나지? = familiar ending for tag questioning of 폼나다 = We look danyish, don't we? /
Nos vemos geniales, ¿no?

꽤 꽤 폼나지? = We look quite quite dandyish, don't we? /
Mucho, mucho nos vemos geniales, ¿no?

12. Blood Sweat and Tears (피 땀 눈물)

Artist: BTS
Lyric Writers: Pdogg, RM, Suga, J-Hope, 방시혁, 김도훈 (RBW)

< Line 1 > 내 피 땀 눈물, 내 마지막 춤을 다 가져가.
내 피 땀 눈물, 내 차가운 숨을 다 가져가. 내 피 땀 눈물.

내 = 나의 = 나 (I, yo) + 의 [marker for object] = my / of me / mi

피 = [noun] = blood / sangre

땀 = [noun] sweat / perspiration / sudor / traspiración

눈물 = [noun] tears / lágrimas

마지막 = [noun, also used as adjective] the end / closing / last / final / último

춤을 = 춤 (dance, baile, danza) + 을 [marker for object]

다 = [adverb] all / everything / everyone / totally / completely / todo(s) / totalmente / completamente

가져가다 = [infinitive of verb] take along with / take away / carry away / bring / llevar

가져가 = familiar ending for imperative mood of 가져가다

차갑다 = [pronunciation] 차갑따 = [infinitive of adjective] be cold [freezing, icy, chilly] / ser frío

차가운 = present tense of 차갑다 = cold / freezing / icy / chilly / frío

숨을 = [pronunciation] 수믈 = 숨 (breaths, alientos, resperaciones) + 을 [mareker for object]

내 피 땀 눈물, 내 마지막 춤을 다 가져가.

My blood, sweat and tears. My last dance as well, take all of them along with you. /
Mi sangre, sudor y lágrimas. Mi último baile también, llévatelos a todos contigo.

내 피 땀 눈물, 내 차가운 숨을 다 가져가.

My blood, sweat and tears. My cold breaths as well, take all of them along with you. /
Mi sangre, sudor y lágrimas. Mis alientos fríos también, llévalos a todos contigo.

내 피 땀 눈물 = My blood, sweat and tears. / Mi sangre, sudor y lágrimas.

< Line 2 > 내 피 땀 눈물도, 내 몸 마음 영혼도 너의 것인 걸 잘 알고 있어.
이건 나를 벌받게 할 주문.

내 = 나의 = 나 (I, yo) + 의 [marker for object] = my / of me / mi

몸 = [noun] body / cuerpo

마음 = [noun] mind / heart / feelings / caring heart / mente / corazón

영혼도 = 영혼 (soul, spirit, espíritu, alma) + 도 [marker] (as well, also, too, también, tampoco, y además)

너의 = 너 (you, tú) + 의 [marker for possession] = of you / your / tu

것 = [pronunciation] 걷 = [noun] thing / stuff / fact / case / cosa / hecho / caso / algo

너의 것 = [pronunciation] 너에 걷 = [noun phrase] yours / el tuyo

이다 = [infinitive of marker that conjugates] be / ser

인 = adjective form of 이다

걸 = 것을 = 것 [the thing that ~ / the fact that ~ / el hecho que ~/ lo que ~] + 을 [marker for object]

너의 것인 걸 = the fact that it is yours / el echo de que es [sea] tuyo

잘 = [adverb] well / nicely / favourably / fully / properly / carefully / bien / bueno / favorablemente / bastantemente / exactamente / con cuidado

알다 = [infinitive of verb] know / be aware of / recognize / notice / saber / conocer / notar

알고 = an adverb-type conjugation of 알다

있다 = [pronunciation] 읻다 → 읻따 = [infinitive of verb] there is / be / exist / stay / remain / stand / hay / estar / existir / quedarse / permanecer / pararse

있어 = [pronunciation] 이써 = familiar ending of 있다

잘 알고 있다 = [simultaneous action] be in the state of knowing it well / know it well / estar en el estado de saberlo bien / saberlo bien

● The simultaneous action with the verb «있다» can be also the present progressive tense.

잘 알고 있어 = familiar ending of 잘 알고 있다 = I am in the state of knowing it well. / I know it well. / Estoy en el estado de saberlo bien. / Lo sé bien.

내 피 땀 눈물도, 내 몸 마음 영혼도 너의 것인 걸 잘 알고 있어.

I know it well that all is yours including my body, mind and soul as well as my blood, sweat and tears. /
Sé bien que todo es tuyo, incluyendo mi cuerpo, mente y alma, así como mi sangre, sudor y lágrimas.

이건 = 이것은 = 이것 (this, this thing, esto) + 은 [marker for subject]

나를 = 나 (I, yo) + 를 [marker for object] = me

벌 = [noun] punishment / penalty / castigo / pena

벌받다 = [pronunciation] 벌받따 = [infinitive of verb] suffer punishment / be punished / take the penalty / sufrir castigo / ser catigado / recibir la pena

● All the vowels and four consonants (ㄴ, ㄹ, ㅁ, ㅇ) are voiced sounds, which are soft. A consonant that is not between any two of them becomes hard (or fortis), if applicable like [ㄱ → ㄲ] [ㄷ → ㄸ] [ㅂ → ㅃ] [ㅅ → ㅆ] [ㅈ → ㅉ].
[벌받다 → 벌받따] [벌받게 → 벌받께]

벌받게 하다 = [pronunciation] 벌받께 하다 = [causative verb] let suffer punishment / make be punished / let take the penalty / dejar sufrir castigo / hacer ser castigado / dejar que tome la pena

벌받게 할 = (future) adjective form of 벌받게 하다

주문 = [noun] spell / incantation / hechizo / palabra mágica

이건 날 벌 받게 할 주문 = This is a spell that will make me be punished /
Este es un hechizo que me hará ser castigado.

< Line 3 > Peaches and cream, sweeter than sweet.
Chocolate cheeks and chocolate wings.
But 너의 날개는 악마의 것. 너의 그 Sweet 앞엔 Bitter, Bitter.

너의 = 너 (you, tú) + 의 [marker for possession] = of you / your / tu

날개는 = 날개 (wings, alas) + 는 [marker for subject]

악마의 = 악마 (devil, demon, diablo, demonio) + 의 [marker for possession] = of the deveil / del diablo

것 = [pronunciation] 걷 = [noun] thing / stuff / fact / case / cosa / hecho / caso / algo

너의 날개는 악마의 것 = Your wings are those of the devil. /
Your wings belong to the devil. / Tus alas son las del diablo. / Tus alas pertenecen al diablo.

너의 = 너 (you, tú) + 의 [marker for possession] = of you / your / tu

그 = [determiner] the / that / those / ese / tal

앞 = [pronunciation] 압 = [noun] the front / el frente

앞엔 = [pronunciation] 아펜 = 앞에는 = 앞 + 에는 (in, at, en) = in front of / en frente de

너의 그 Sweet 앞엔 Bitter, Bitter.
Everything is bitter, bitter in front of your sweetness. /
Todo es amargo, amargo frente a tu dulzura.

< Line 4 > Kiss me. 아파도 돼. 어서 날 조여 줘. 더 이상 아플 수도 없게.

아프다 = [infinitive of adjective] hurt / be ill [sick, painful, sore, hurting] / be tormented /
doler / ser doloroso / estar enfermo [dolorido, herido] / atormentarse

아파도 = even if it hurts / even if it is painful / aunque duela / incluso si es doloroso

되다 = [infinitive of verb] become fine / goes well / be good / se convierten en todo bien /
va bien / llegar a estar bien / estar bien hecho

되어 = **돼** = familiar ending of 되다

아파도 돼.

It is okay to be painful. / You can torment me. / I don't mind being tormented by you. /
Está bien ser doloroso. / Puedes atormentarme. / No me importa ser atormentado por ti.

어서 = [adverb] quick / fast / promptly / without delay / rápido / deprisa / pronto / sin retraso

날 = 나를 = 나 (I, yo) + 를 [marker for object] = me

조이다 = [infinitive of verb] strangle / tighten / squeeze / choke / estrangular / estrechar /
ceñir / atragantar / apretar

주다 = [infinitive of verb] kindly do / give as a favour / willing to do / please, /
amablemente hacer / dar con gusto / dispuesto a hacer / por favor,

조여 주다 = kindly squeeze / willing to strangle / amablemente apretar / estrangular con gusto

조여 주어 = **조여 줘** = familiar ending for imperative mood of 주다 = Please, strangle me! /
¡Por favor, estrangulame!

어서 날 조여 줘.

Do me a favour quickly by squeezing me tight. / Please squeeze me tight and quick. / Hazme un favor rápidamente apretándome fuerte. / Por favor, apriétame fuerte y rápido.

더 이상 = [adverb phrase] no more / not anymore / no further / no aditionally / no más / no adicionalmente

● The words «더 이상» itself is not negative. But one can expect that a negative expression will come along eventually.

아프다 = [infinitive of adjective] hurt / be ill [sick, painful, sore, hurting] / be tormented / doler / ser doloroso / estar enfermo [dolorido, herido] / atormentarse

아플 = (future) adjective form of 아프다

수 = [noun] means / resource / possibility / likelihood / medio / recurso / posibilidad / probabilidad

도 = [marker] neither, not even, ni, ni siquiera

없다 = [pronunciation] 업다 → 업따 = [infintive of adjective] there is no / not exist / be absent / be without / no hay / no existir / estar ausente / estar sin

없게. = [pronunciation] 업께 = adverb ending of 없다 = to make it not be / para que no sea

할 수 없게 = to make it impossible to do / para que sea imposible de hacer

할 수도 없게 = to make it even impossible to do / para que sea incluso imposible de hacer

더 이상 아플 수도 없게. = [pronunciation] 더 이상 아플 쑤도 업께

To make it even impossible to torment me more painfully /
Para que sea incluso imposible atormentarme más dolorosamente /
Para hacer incluso imposible atormentarme más dolorosamente

< Line 5 > Baby. 취해도 돼. 이제 널 들이켜, 목 깊숙이. 너란 위스키.

취하다 = [infinitive of verb] get drunk / get intoxicated / be overcome with liquor / emborracharse / embriagarse / estar abrumado por el licor

취해도 = even if I get intoxicated / incluso si me emborracho

되다 = [infinitive of verb] become fine / goes well / be good / se convierten en todo bien / va bien / llegar a estar bien / estar bien hecho

되어 = **돼** = familiar ending of 되다

취해도 돼 = I don't mind getting intoxicated. / No me importa emborracharme.

이제 = [noun, also used as adverb] now / current moment / at this time / ahora / en este momento

널 = 너를 = 너 (you, tú) + 를 [marker for object] = you / te

들이키다 = [infinitive of verb] drink up / beber (todo) / chiflar

들이키어 = **들이켜** = familiar ending of 들이키다

목(구멍) = [noun] throat / gullet / garganta

깊숙이 = [pronunciation] 깁쑤기 = [adverb] deep / deep down / profundamente / hondamente

너란 = 너라는 = 너 (you, tú) + (이)라는 = that is called the 'You' / que se llama la 'Tú'

이다 = [infinitive of marker that conjugates] be / ser

(이)라는 = that is called (as) / so-called / that is named as / being known as / que se llama (como) / así se llama / que se conoce como

위스키 = [noun] whisky / whiskey / güisqui / whiski

이제 널 들이켜, 목 깊숙이. 너란 위스키.

Now I drink up deep into the throat the whiskey that is called the 'You'.
Ahora bebo profundamente en la garganta el whisky que se llama la "Tú".

< Line 1 > 내 피 땀 눈물, 내 마지막 춤을 다 가져가.

내 피 땀 눈물, 내 차가운 숨을 다 가져가.

My blood, sweat and tears. My last dance as well, take all of them along with you. / Mi sangre, sudor y lágrimas. Mi último baile también, llévatelos a todos contigo.

My blood, sweat and tears. My cold breaths as well, take all of them along with you. / Mi sangre, sudor y lágrimas. Mis alientos fríos también, llévalos a todos contigo.

< Line 6 > 원해 [많이 X 4] , 원해 [많이 X 6], 원해 [많이 X 4], 원해 [많이 X 6]

원하다 = [infinitive of verb] = want / wish / desire / querer / desear

원해 = familiar ending of 원하다

많이 = [pronunciation] 마니 = [adverb] a lot / much / many / aplenty / abundantly / quite / in profusion / mucho(s) / abundantemente / en profusion / tanto

원해, 많이, 많이 = I want you, a lot, a lot. / Te deseo, mucho, mucho.

< Line 7 > 아파도 돼. 날 묶어줘. 내가 도망칠 수 없게.

아파도 돼

It is okay to be painful. / You can torment me. / I don't mind being tormented by you. / Está bien ser doloroso. / Puedes atormentarme. / No me importa ser atormentado por ti.

날 = 나를 = 나 (I, yo) + 를 [marker for object] = me

묶다 = [pronunciation] 묵따 = [infinitive of verb] tie up / bind / atar / ligar / amarrar

주다 = [infinitive of verb] kindly do / give as a favour / willing to do / please, / amablemente hacer / dar con gusto / dispuesto a hacer / por favor,

묶어 주다 = [pronunciation] 무꺼 주다 = kindly bind / ambablemente amarrar

묶어 주어 = **묶어 줘** = [pronunciation] 무꺼 줘 = familiar ending for imperative mood of

묶어 주다 = Please, tie me! / ¡Por favor, átame!

날 묶어줘. = Do me a favour by tying me up. / Please tie me up. / Hazme un favor atándome. / Por favor, átame.

내가 = 나 + 이가 = 나 (I, yo) + 이가 [marker for subject]

도망치다 = [infinitive of verb] run away / get away / escape / flee / huir / escaparse / desertar

도망칠 = adjective form of 도망치다

수 = [noun] means / resource / possibility / likelihood / medio / recurso / posibilidad / probabilidad

없다 = [pronunciation] 업다 → 업따 = [infintive of adjective] there is no / not exist / be absent / be without / no hay / no existir / estar ausente / estar sin

없게 = [pronunciation] 업께 = adverb ending of 없다 = to make it not be / para que no sea

내가 도망칠 수 없게. = [pronunciation] 내가 도망칠 쑤 업께

In order to make it impossible for me to run away. / To make me not to escape. / Con el fin de hacer imposible para mí huir. / Para hacerme no escapar.

< Line 8 > 꽉 쥐고 날 흔들어 줘. 내가 정신 못 차리게.

꽉 = [adverb] quite tight / quite firmly / bastante fuerte / bastante firme

쥐다 = [infinitive of verb] hold / grasp / grip / seize / clench / tomar / sostener / agarrar / sujetar

쥐고 = hold [grasp, grip, seize, clench], and / tomar [sostener, agarrar, apretar], y

날 = 나를 = 나 (I, yo) + 를 [marker for object] = me

흔들다 = [infinitive of verb] = shake / rock / sway / sacudir / agitar / mecer

주다 = [infinitive of verb] kindly do / give as a favour / willing to do / please, / amablemente hacer / dar con gusto / dispuesto a hacer / por favor,

흔들어 주다 = [verb phrase] rock as a favour / sacudir con gusto

흔들어 주어 = **흔들어 줘** = familiar ending for imperative mood of 흔들어 주다

= Plese, rock me! / ¡Por favor, agítame!

꽉 쥐고 날 흔들어 줘. = Hold me quite tight and shake me, please. / Agarrame fuerte, y sacúdeme, por favor.

내가 = 나 + 이가 = 나 (I, yo) + 이가 [marker for subject]

정신 = spirit / mind / mental sanity / espíritu / mente / cordura mental

정신차리다 = [infinitive of verb] collect [maintain] one's mind / come to one's senses / recoger la mente / llegar a los sentidos

정신 못 차리다 = [verb phrase] lose one's mind / knock galley-west / feel dizzy / perder la cabeza / perder a los sentidos / sentirse mareado

정신 못 차리게 = poetic or familiar ending of 정신 못 차리다

내가 정신 못 차리게. = [pronunciation] 내가 정신 몯 차리게

In order to make it impossible for me to maintain my mind / Para hacer me impossible mantener la mente

< Line 9 > Kiss me on the lips, lips. 둘 만의 비밀. 너란 감옥에 중독돼, 깊이.

둘 = [noun] two persons / us two / dos personas / nosotros dos / los dos

만의 = 만 (only, just, solo, solamente) + 의 [marker for possession]

둘 만의 = [adjective phrase] just between us / just between you and me / of only us two / of the two / sólo entre nosotros / sólo entre tú y yo / de sólo nosotros dos / de los dos

비밀 = [noun] secret / confidentiality / confidence / secreto / confidencialidad / confianza

둘 만의 비밀. = This is a secret just between you and me. / Este es un secreto sólo entre tú y yo.

너란 = 너라는 = 너 (you, tú) + (이)라는

이다 = [infinitive of marker that conjugates] be / ser

(이)라는 = that is called (as) / so-called / that is named as / being known as / que se llama (como) / así se llama / que se conoce como

감옥에 = [pronunciation] 가모게 = 감옥 (prison, jail, prisión, cárcel) + 에 (by, to, por, a)

너란 감옥에 = by the prison that is named as 'You'. / por la prisión que se llama 'Tú'.

중독 = [noun] addiction / intoxication / adicción / intoxicación

중독되다 = [pronunciation] 중독뙤다 = [infinitive of verb] be addicted / get intoxicated / ser adicto / intoxicarse

● All the vowels and four consonants (ㄴ, ㄹ, ㅁ, ㅇ) are voiced sounds, which are soft. A consonant that is not between any two of them becomes hard (or fortis), if applicable like [ㄱ → ㄲ] [ㄷ → ㄸ] [ㅂ → ㅃ] [ㅅ → ㅆ] [ㅈ → ㅉ]. [중독되다 → 중독뙤다]

중독되어 = [pronunciation] 중독뙤어 = **중독돼** [중독뙈] = familiar ending of 중독되다

깊이 = [pronunciation] 기피 = [adverb] deeply / profoundly / profundamente / hondamente

너란 감옥에 중독돼, 깊이. = I am addicted to the the prison that is named as 'You'. / Soy adicto a la prisión que se llama "Tú".

< Line 10 > 네가 아닌 다른 사람 섬기지 못해. 알면서도 삼켜버린 독이 든 성배.

네가 아닌 다른 사람 섬기지 못해.

The real subject '나는 (I, yo)' is missed in the above sentence.

(나는) = 나 (I, yo) + 는 [marker for subject]

네가 = 너 (you, tú) + 이가 [marker for subject]

● Many Korean speakers including BTS pronounce «네가» as «니가». That's because «네가» sounds similar to «내가», in order to avoid misunderstading, they tend to pronounce «네가» as «니가». Nevertheless, it is not correct.

아니다 = [infinitive of adjective] be not / be no / be not correct / no ser / no ser correcto

아닌 = present tense of 아니다

다르다 = [infinitive of adjective] be different / ser diferente

다른 = present tense of 다르다 = different / another / diferente / otro

사람 = [noun] person / human / persona / ser humano

네가 아닌 다른 사람 = any other person that is not you / any person other than you / cualquier otra persona que no sea tú / cualquier persona excepto tú

다른 사람(을) = 다른 사람 (another person, otra persona) + 을 [marker for object]

섬기다 = [infinitive of verb] serve / service / worship / servir / adorar

섬기지 = a noun-type conjugation of 섬기다

● «noun form» can be regarded as a noun, «adverb-form» can be regarded as an adverb, while «a noun-type conjuation» or «an adverb-type conjugation» is regarded as a verb.

● In Korean, when two verbs combine, there is a tendency that the first verb does either a noun-type or an adverb-type conjugation. By doing so, the first verb serves like an object for the second verb [in case that the second verb is a transitive verb], or modifies the second verb like an adverb [in case that the second verb is an intransitive verb].

하다 = [infinitive of verb] do / act / make / hacer / realizar

못하다 = [infinitive of verb] cannot do / fail to do / not succeed doing / no poder hacer

섬기지 못하다 = [pronunciation] 섬기지 모타다 = [verb phrase] cannot do worshiping / no poder adorar

못해 = [pronunciation] 몯해 → 모태 = familiar or poetic ending of 못하다

● By doing a noun-type conjugation the first verb can serve as an object of the second verb. [섬기지 못하다 = cannot do worshiping] Here, «섬기지 (worshiping)» serves as the object of the verb «못하다 (cannot do)».

네가 아닌 다른 사람 섬기지 못해. = I cannot worship any person other than you. /
No puedo adorar a ninguna persona que no seas tú.

알면서도 삼켜버린 독이 든 성배

알다 = [infinitive of verb] know / be aware of / recognize / notice / saber / conocer / notar

알면서도 = even though I know that ~ / in spite of knowing that ~ /
aunque saber que ~ / a pensar de saber que ~

삼키다 = [infinitive of verb] swallow / engulf / take in / drink in / tragar / ingerir /
sorber / beber

삼켜버리다 = stronger expression than 삼키다

삼켜버린 = past adjective form of 삼켜버리다 = that swallowed / que sorbí

독이 = [pronunciation] 도기 = 독 (poison, toxin, venom, tóxico, venono) + 이 [marker for subject]

들다 = [infinitive of verb] hold / be contained with / contener / estar contenido con

든 = adjective form of 들다 = that holds / that is contained with / que contiene /
que está contenido con

성배 = [noun] holy grail / sangrail / chalice / calix / santo grial / vaso sagrado / calce / cáliz

독이 든 성배 = the holy grail that is contained with poison / the holy grail that holds poison /
el santo grial que está contenido con veneno / el santo grial que tiene veneno

알면서도 삼켜버린 독이 든 성배.
In spite of knowing it, I couldn't help but take in from the the holy grail that holds poison. /
A pesar de saberlo, no pude evitar sorber del santo grial que contiene veneno.

< Line 1 > 내 피 땀 눈물, 내 마지막 춤을 다 가져가.
내 피 땀 눈물, 내 차가운 숨을 다 가져가.

My blood, sweat and tears. My last dance as well, take all of them along with you. /
Mi sangre, sudor y lágrimas. Mi último baile también, llévatelos a todos contigo.

My blood, sweat and tears. My cold breaths as well, take all of them along with you. /
Mi sangre, sudor y lágrimas. Mis alientos fríos también, llévalos a todos contigo.

< Line 6 > 원해 [많이 x 4] , 원해 [많이 x 6], 원해 [많이 x 4], 원해 [많이 x 6]

원해, 많이, 많이 = I want you, a lot, a lot. / Te deseo, mucho, mucho.

< Line 11 > 나를 부드럽게 죽여 줘. 너의 손길로 눈 감겨 줘.

나를 = 나 (I, yo) + 를 [marker for object] = me

부드럽다 = [pronunciation] 부드럽따 = [infinitive of adjective] = be soft [smooth, gentle, tender] / ser suave / ser tierno

부드럽게 = [pronunciation] 부드럽께 = adverb form of 부드럽다 = softly / smoothly / tenderly / suavemente / tiernamente

죽이다 = [pronunciation] 주기다 = [infinitive of verb] kill / murder / slay / matar / eliminar / tumbar

주다 = [infinitive of verb] kindly do / give as a favour / willing to do / please, / amablemente hacer / dar con gusto / dispuesto a hacer / por favor,

죽이어 주다 = 죽여 주다 = kindly kill / amablemente matar

죽여 주어 = **죽여 줘** = familiar ending for imperative mood of 주다 = please, kill / por favor, mátame

나를 부드럽게 죽여 줘.

Do me a favour by killing me softly. / Please kill me tenderly. /
Hazme un favor matándome suavemente. / Por favor, mátame tiernamente.

너의 = 너 (you, tú) + 의 [marker for possession] = of you / your / tu / tus

손길로 = 손길 (hand touch, toque de la mano) + 로 (with, con)

너의 손길로 = with the hand-touch of yours / con el toque de tu mano

눈(을) = 눈 (the eyes, los ojos) + 을 [marker for object]

감다 = [infinitive of verb] = close / shut / cerrar

감기다 = [infinitive of verb] = let close / dejar cerrar / hacer cerrar

주다 = [infinitive of verb] kindly do / give as a favour / willing to do / please, / amablemente hacer / dar con gusto / dispuesto a hacer / por favor,

감기어 주다 = **감겨** 주다 = kindly close / amablementer cerrar

감겨 주어 = **감겨 줘** = familiar ending for imperative mood of 주다 = please, close / Por favor, cerra

너의 손길로 눈 감겨 줘 = Please, let your own hand-touch close my eyes. / Por favor, deja que el toque de tu mano pueda cerrar mis ojos.

< Line 12 > 어차피 거부할 수조차 없어. 더는 도망갈 수조차 없어. 네가 너무 달콤해, 네가 너무 달콤해, 너무 달콤해서.

어차피 = [adverb] anyhow / anyway / one way or the other / in any case / after all / de todas maneras [formas] / de todos modos / en cualquier caso / después de todo

거부하다 = [infinitive of verb] refuse / deny / veto / resist / rechazar / negar / vetar / resistir

하다 = [infinitive of verb] do / act / make / hacer / realizar

할 = (future) adjective form of 하다

● In case of Korean (future) adjective forms, sometimes it is more natural to translate them into the present tense or the infinitive form in European languages.

수 = [noun] means / resource / possibility / likelihood / medio / recurso / posibilidad / probabilidad

● In Korean, the pronunciation of the first consonant just after ' ㄹ ' tends to become hard. [할 수 → 할 쑤]

조차 = [marker for emphasis] even / as well / but also / incluso / también / (ni) siquiera

없다 = [pronunciation] 업다 → 업따 = [infintive of adjective] there is no / not exist / be absent / be without / no hay / no existir / estar ausente / estar sin

없어 = [pronunciation] 업써 = familiar ending of 없다

어차피 거부할 수조차 없어 = [pronunciation] 어차피 거부할 쑤조차 업써
In any case, I cannot even resist it. / En cualquier caso, ni siquiera puedo resistirme.

더 = [adverb] more / further / aditionally / más / de nuevo

더는 = [adverb phrase] 더 + 는 [marker for emphasis] = 더 + 는 (not any longer / ya no más)

도망가다 = [infinitive of verb] run away / get away / escape / flee / huir / escaparse / desertar

도망갈 = (future) adjective form of 도망가다

수 = [noun] means / resource / possibility / likelihood / medio / recurso / posibilidad / probabilidad

조차 = [marker for emphasis] even / as well / but also / incluso / también / (ni) siquiera

없다 = [pronunciation] 업다 → 업따 = [infintive of adjective] there is no / not exist / be absent / be without / no hay / no existir / estar ausente / estar sin

없어 = [pronunciation] 업써 = familiar ending of 없다

더는 도망갈 수조차 없어. = [pronunciation] 더는 도망갈 쑤조차 업써

I cannot even escape any further. / Ni siquiera puedo escapar más.

네가 = 너 (you, tú) + 이가 [marker for subject]

너무 = [adverb] too much [many] / excessively / quite / demasiado / excessivamente / tanto bien

달콤하다 = [infinitive of adjective] be sweet / be sugary / ser dulce / ser azucarado

달콤해 = familiar ending of 달콤하다

달콤해서 = because be sweet / porque ser dulce

네가 너무 달콤해(서) = because you are too sweet / porque eres demasiado dulce

< Line 1-1 > 내 피 땀 눈물. 내 피 땀 눈물.

My blood, sweat and tears. /
Mi sangre, sudor y lágrimas.

13. Lovesick Girl

Artist: Blackpink
Lyric Writers: Teddy Park, Løren,
지수, 제니, Danny Chung

< Line 1 > 영원한 밤. 창문없는 방에 우릴 가둔 Love. (Love)

영원하다 = [infinitive of adjective] be eternal / be permanent / ser eterno / ser perpetuo
영원한 = present tense of 영원하다 = eternal / permanent / eterno / perpetuo
밤 = [noun] night / night-time / noche

영원한 밤 = the eternal night / la noche eterna

창문 = [noun] window / ventana
없다 = [pronunciation] 업다 → 업따 = [infintive of adjective] there is no / not exist / be absent / be without / no hay / no existir / estar ausente / estar sin
없는 = [pronunciation] 업는 → 엄는 = present tense of 없다
방에 = 방 (room, chamber, habitación, cámara) + 에 (in, en) = in the room / en la habitación

우릴 = 우리를 = 우리 (we, nosotros) + 를 [marker for object]
가두다 = [infinitive of verb] lock up / put in / confine / encerrar / poner en / confinar
가둔 = past adjective form of 가두다

창문없는 방에 우릴 가둔 **Love** = The love that locked us up in a room without window / El amor que nos encerró en una habitación sin ventana

< Line 2 > **What can we say?** 매번 아파도 외치는 **Love.**

매번 = [adverb] every time / each occasion / constantly / cada vez / cada ocasión / constantemente
아프다 = [infinitive of adjective] hurt / be ill [sick, painful, sore, hurting] / be tormented / doler / ser doloroso / estar enfermo [dolorido, herido] / atormentarse
아파도 = in spite of feeling painful / even if it hurts me / although I feel sick / a pesar de sentirme doloroso / incluso si me duele / aunque me sienta mal

210

외치다 = [infinitive of verb] shout / cry out / cry for / yell / gritar / clamar / clamorear

외치는 = present adjective form of 외치다

매번 아파도 외치는 **Love.**
Love that I cry for in spite of the pain that comes to me again and again /
Amor por el que clamo a pesar del dolor que me llega una y otra vez

< Line 3 > 다치고 망가져도, 나, 뭘 믿고 버티는 거야?

다치다 = [infinitive of verb] get hurt / get injured / be wounded / ser herido / lastimarse

다치고 = get hurt, and / be injured, and / be wounded, and / ser herido, y / lastimarse, y

망가지다 = [infinitive of verb] break down / be damaged [wrecked, be ruined] /
go wrong / romperse / dañarse / arruinarse / fracasarse / salir mal

다치고 **망가져도** = in spite of getting hurt and damaged / even though getting injured
and wrecked / although getting wounded and ruined / a pesar de resultar herido y dañado /
incluso si me lastime y sea destrozado / aunque sea herido y arruinado

나(는) = 나 (I, yo) + 는 [marker for subject]

뭘 = 무얼 = 무엇을 = 무엇 (what, something, qué, algo) + 을 [marker for object]

믿다 = [pronunciation] 믿따 = [verb] believe (in) / trust / confide / rely on / confiar / creer

믿고 = [pronunciation] 믿꼬 = an adverb-type conjugation of 믿다 = by believing /
by trusting / through confiding / por creer / por confiar

버티다 = [infinitive of verb] withstand / endure / maintain / sustain / mantener /
sostener / soportar

믿고 버티다 = [simultaneous action] withstand while trusting / sustain through believing /
mantener mientras confiando / sostenerse creyendo

버틴 = past adjective form of 버티다 = withstood / endured / that maintained /
that sustained / que mantuvo / que sostuvo / que ha soportado

버틸 = (future) adjective form of 버티다 = that will sustain / que sostendré

버티는 = [present adjective form] withstanding / that sustain / manteniendo / que sostiene

것이다 = 것 (the scene that ~, the fact that ~, el hecho que ~, lo que ~) + 이다 (be, ser)

것이야? = **거야?** = soliloquy questioning of 것이다

나(는) 뭘 믿고 버티는 거야?

By trusting what, is it possible that I sustain myself? / What do I rely on to sustain myself? / Confiando en qué, ¿es possible que me sostenga? / ¿En qué confío para mantenerme?

< Line 4 > 어차피 떠나면, 상처투성(이)인 채로 미워하게 될 걸!

어차피 = [adverb] anyhow / anyway / one way or the other / in any case / after all / de todas maneras [formas] / de todos modos / en cualquier caso / después de todo

떠나다 = [infinitive of verb] leave / depart / go away / be going / irse / partir / eliminarse

떠나면 = if you leave / if you go away / si te vas / si te elimines

상처 = [noun] wound / scar / bruise / herida / cicatriz / herida / moretón

투성이 [noun suffix] = status being covered with / status being full of / condition being smeared with / estado cubierto con / estado lleno de / condición manchada con

이다 = [infinitive of marker that conjugates] be / ser

상처투성(이) 이다 = be covered with bruises / be full of wounds / be smeared with scars / estar cubierto de moretones / estar lleno de heridas / ser manchado con cicatrices

인 = present adjective form of 이다 (be, ser)

채 = [noun, also used as adverb] state / condition / status / situation / in the state of / just as it is / el estado / condición / situación / en el estado de / tal como es

로 = [marker for condition] as / being / while / como en / estando / mientras

상처투성(이)인 채로 = as in the state of being covered with bruises / being full of wounds / while being smeared with scars / como en el estado de estar cubierto de moretones / estando lleno de heridas / mientras soy manchada con cicatrices

미워하다 = [infinitive of verb] hate / detest / odiar / detestar

(하게) 되다 = [infinitive of verb with another verb] come to / get to / ir a / llegar a

미워하게 되다 = [verb phrase] get to hate / come to detest / ir a odiar / llegar a detestar

될 = adjective form of 되다

것이다 = 것 (the scene that ~, the fact that ~, el hecho que ~, lo que ~) + 이다 (be, ser)

것을! = **걸!** = poetic ending of 것이다

미워하게 될 걸! = [pronunciation] 미워하게 될 껄!
will get to hate you! / will come to hate you! / ¡llegará a odiarte! / se convertiré en odiarte!

어차피 떠나면, 상처투성(이)인 채로 미워하게 될 걸!

In any case, if you leave me, I will get to hate you in the state of being covered with bruises.
/ En cualquier caso, si me dejas, llegaré a odiarte en el estado de estar cubierto de moretones.

< Line 5 > 끝장을 보기 전(에) 끝낼 순 없어. 이 아픔을 기다린 것처럼.

끝장을 = [pronunciation] 끋짱을 = 끝장 (the final ending, the final result, el fin final, el resultado final) + 을 [marker for object]

보다 = [infinitive of verb] see / watch / look at / observe / ver / mirar / observar

보기 = noun form of 보다

끝장을 보다 = look at the final ending / experience the final result / it is over completely / mirar el fin final / experimentar el resultado final / se acaba por completo

전(에) = before / prior to / antes / previo

끝장을 보기 전(에) = Before it is over completely / Antes de que termine por completo

끝나다 = [pronunciation] 끋나다 → 끈나다 = [infinitive of verb] it ends / come to an end / it closes / be finished / terminarse / llegar al fin / cerrarse / acabarse

끝내다 = [pronunciation] 끋내다 → 끈내다 = [infinitive of verb] end it / finish off / fainalize / terminate it / make an end of / bring to a close / terminarlo / cerrar / finalizar / hacer un final de / llevar a un final

끝낼 = [pronunciation] 끋낼 → 끈낼 = adjective form of 끝내다

수 = [noun] means / resource / possibility / likelihood / medio / recurso / posibilidad / probabilidad

순 = 수는 = 수 + 는 [marker for emphasis]

없다 = [pronunciation] 업다 → 업따 = [infintive of adjective] there is no / not exist / be absent / be without / no hay / no existir / estar ausente / estar sin

없어 = [pronunciation] 업써 = familiar ending of 없다

끝장을 보기 전 끝낼 순 없어 = [pronunciation] 끋짱을 보기 전 끈낼 쑨 업써
We shouldn't end it before it is over completely. /
No deberíamos terminarlo antes de que se acabe por completo.

이 아픔을 기다린 것처럼.

이 = [determiner] this / these / este / estos

아픔을 = 아픔 (pain, agony, torment, dolor, pena, agonía) + 을 [marker for object]

기다리다 = [infinitive of verb] expect / wait (for) / await / esperar / aguardar / atender

기다린 = past adjective form of 기다리다

것처럼 = 것 (the thing ~, the fact ~, el echo que ~) + 처럼 (like, as if, como, como si)

(느껴져) = I feel that ~ / It seems to me that ~ / Siento que ~ / Me parece que ~

이 아픔을 기다린 것처럼 = I feel as if I have expected this kind of pain. / You see, I am ready for this type of agony.

Siento como si hubiera esperado este tipo de dolor. / Verás, estoy listo para este tipo de agonía.

< Line 6 > 아마 다 잠깐일지도 몰라. 우린 무얼 찾아서 헤매는 걸까?

아마 = [adverb] maybe / perhaps / probably / possibly / quizá / tal vez / probablemente / posiblemente

다 = [adverb] all / everything / everyone / totally / completely / todo(s) / totalmente / completamente

잠깐 = [noun, also used as adverb] moment / instant / for a short while / temporarily / momento / instante/ por un rato / momentáneamente

이다 = [infinitive of marker that conjugates] be / ser

일지 = [pronunciation] 일찌 = a noun-type conjugation of 이다 = if it could be / (whether) it might be / si pudiera ser / (si) podría ser

일지도 = [pronunication] 일찌도 = stronger expression than 일지

● '지' was originally an independent word, whose meaning is «uncertainty», «probability» or «whether». Now it is combined with a verb for making a noun form.

● In Korean, the pronunciation of the first consonant after '르' tends to become hard.
[일지도 = 일 + 지도 → 일찌도]

모르다 = [infinitive of verb] not know [aware, realize, notice, understand, learned] / no saber [aprendí] / desconocer / no darse cuenta

몰라 = familiar ending of 모르다

일지도 몰라 = Maybe it could be / You never know whether it might be / I wonder if it is / Tal vez podría ser / Nunca se sabe si podría ser / Me pregunto si es

아마 다 잠깐인지도 몰라. = Maybe everything might last only for a short while. / Quizás todo pueda durar poco tiempo. / Tal vez todo dure sólo por un rato.

우린 = 우리는 = 우리 (we, people, nosotros, la gente) + 는 [marker for subejct]

무얼 = 무엇을 = 무엇 (what, something, qué, algo) + 을 [marker for object]

찾다 = [pronunciation] 찰따 = [infinitive of verb] look for / find / search / seek / buscar / averiguar

찾아서 = [pronunciation] 차자서 = an adverb-type conjugation of 찾다 = searching for / buscando

● an adverb-type conjugation is to imply a simultaneous action or the object of an action.

헤매다 = [infinitive of verb] wander / roam / hover / deambular / vagar / brujulear / dar vueltas

찾아서 헤매다 = be roaming for finding (something) / estar vagando por descubrir (alguno)

찾아서 헤매는 = present adejctive form of 찾아서 헤매다 [차자서 헤매다]

것이다 = 것 (the scene that ~, the fact that ~, el hecho que ~, lo que ~) + 이다 (be, ser)

것일까? = **걸까?** = soliloquy questioning of 것이다

우린 무얼 찾아서 헤매는 걸까? = In searching of what are we roaming? / In searching of what are people roaming?

¿En la búsqueda de lo qué estamos vagando? / ¿En la búsqueda de lo qué está la gente vagando?

< Line 7 > But I don't care. I'll do it over and over. 내 세상 속엔 너만 있으면 돼.

내 = 나의 = 나 (I, yo) + 의 [marker for possession] = of me / my / mi

세상 = [noun] the world / the earth / our era / el mundo / la tierra / nuestra era

속엔 = 속에는 = 속 (the inside, the bottom, mind, el interior, mente) + 에는 (in, at, en)

너만 = 너 (you, tú) + 만 (only, just, sólo, solamente) = nobody else but you / nadie más que tú

있다 = [pronunciation] 읻다 → 읻따 = [infinitive of verb] there is / be / exist / stay / remain / stand / hay / estar / existir / quedarse / permanecer / pararse

있으면 = if there is / if exist / if stay / if be doing / si hay / si estar / si existir / si quedar

되다 = [infinitive of verb] become fine / goes well / be good / se convierten en todo bien / va bien / llegar a estar bien / estar bien hecho

돼 = familiar ending of 되다

내 세상 속엔 너만 있으면 돼. = It is all right for me only if you stay in my world. / Está bien para mí sólo si te quedas en mi mundo.

< Line 8 > We are the lovesick girls. 네 멋대로 내 사랑을 끝낼 순 없어.

네 = 너의 = 너 (you, tú) + 의 [marker for possession] = of you / your / tu

멋 = [pronunciation] 먿 = dandyism / relish / taste / zest / mood / whim / dandismo / gusto / estado de ánimo / capricho / antojo

대로 = [adverb] accroding to / following / as one pleases / by / según / siguiendo / como se agrada / por

네 멋대로 = [pronunciation] 네 먿대로 → 네 먿때로 =
following [according to] your whim / at your whim / by your own mood / as you pleases / según su capricho / por tu propio estado de ánimo / como te agrada [plazca] / a tu antojo

내 = 나의 = 나 (I, yo) + 의 [marker for possession] = of me / my / mi

사랑을 = 사랑 (love, amor) + 을 [marker for object]

끝내다 = [pronunciation] 끝내다 → 끈내다 = [infinitive of verb] end it / we close / finish off / fainalize / terminate it / make an end of / bring to a close / cerrar / acabar / finalizar / terminarlo / hacer un final de / llevar a un final

끝낼 = adjective form of 끝내다

수 = [noun] means / resource / possibility / likelihood / medio / recurso / posibilidad / probabilidad

순 = 수는 = 수 + 는 [marker for emphasis]

없다 = [pronunciation] 업다 → 업따 = [infintive of adjective] there is no / not exist / be absent / be without / no hay / no existir / estar ausente / estar sin

없어 = [pronunciation] 업써 = familiar ending of 없다

네 멋대로 내 사랑을 끝낼 순 없어 = [pronunciation] 네 먿때로 내 사랑을 끈낼 쑨 업써
You shouldn't finish off my love following your own whim. [at your whim] /
No deberías acabar con mi amor siguiendo tu propio capricho. [a tu antojo]

< Line 9 > We are the lovesick girls. 이 아픔 없인 난 아무 의미가 없어.

이 = [determiner] this / these / este / estos

아픔 = [noun] pain / agony / torment / dolor / pena / agonía

없다 = [pronunciation] 업다 → 업따 = [infintive of adjective] there is no / not exist / be absent / be without / no hay / no existir / estar ausente / estar sin

없인 = 없이는 = if there is no / if not exist / if be without / si no hay / si no existir / si estar sin

난 = 나는 = 나 (I, yo) + 는 [marker for subject]

아무 = [determiner] (not) any / alguno / ningún

● In principle, «아무» itself is not negative, but here, one can expect that a negative expression would come along.

의미가 = 의미 (meaning, sense, signification, point, sentido) + 가 [marker for subject]

없다 = [pronunciation] 업다 → 업따 = [infintive of adjective] there is no / not exist / be absent / be without / no hay / no existir / estar ausente / estar sin

없어 = [pronunciation] 업써 = familiar ending of 없다

이 아픔 없인 난 아무 의미가 없어.
If there is no such a pain, my life will have no senses. /
I am quite meaningless without this kind of pain. /

Si no hay tal dolor, mi vida no tendrá sentido. /
No tendré ningún sentido sin este tipo de dolor.

< Line 10 > But we are born to be alone. Yeah, we are born to be alone. Yeah, we are born to be alone. But why we still looking for love?

< Line 11 > No love letters. No X, no O's. No love never, my exes know. No diamond rings that set in stone. To the left, better left alone. Didn't wanna be a princess. I'm priceless. A prince not even on my list. Love is a drug that I quit. No doctor could help when I'm lovesick.

< Line 6 > 아마 다 잠깐인지도 몰라. 우린 무얼 찾아서 헤매는 걸까?

Maybe everything might last only for a short while. / Tal vez todo dure sólo por un rato.

In searching of what are we roaming? / ¿En la búsqueda de lo qué estamos vagando?

< Line 12 > 불안한 내 눈빛 속에 널 담아. 아프더라도 너만 있으면 돼.

불안하다 = [infinitive of adjective] = be uneasy [insecure, restless, anxious] / estar inquieto [inseguro, intranquilo, preocupado, ansioso]

불안한 = present tense of 불안하다

내 = 나의 = 나 (I, yo) + 의 [marker for possession] = of me / my / mi

눈빛 = [pronunciation] 눈삗 = [noun] 눈 (eyes, ojos) + 빛 (light, luz) = gaze / look / sight / straring / glittering look / mirada / vista / mirada brillante

● When two independent words combine, the first consonant of the second word becomes strong. [눈빛 → 눈빋 →눈삗]

속에 = [pronunciation] 소게 = 속 (the inside, the bottom, mind, el interior, mente) + 에 (in, at, en)

널 = 너를 = 너 (you, tú) + 를 [marker for object] = you / te

담다 = [pronunciation] 담따 = [infinitive of verb] put in / include / hold / contain / poner en / incluir / encestar / contener

담아 = [pronunciation] 다마 = familiar ending of 담다

불안한 내 눈빛 속에 널 담아. = [pronunciation] 부란한 내 눈삗 쏘게 널 다마
I put you in my uneasy sight. / Te pongo en mi vista inquieta.

아프다 = [infinitive of adjective] hurt / be ill [sick, painful, sore, hurting] / be tormented / doler / ser doloroso / estar enfermo [dolorido, herido] / atormentarse

아프더라도 = even if I am hurt / although I feel painful / incluso si estoy herido / aunque me siento doloroso

너만 = 너 (you, tú) + 만 (only, just, sólo, solamente) = nobody else but you / nadie más que tú

있다 = [pronunciation] 읻다 → 읻따 = [infinitive of verb] there is / be / exist / stay / remain / stand / hay / estar / existir / quedarse / permanecer / pararse

있으면 = [pronunciation] 이쓰면 = if there is / if exist / if stay / if be doing / si hay / si estar / si existir / si quedar

되다 = [infinitive of verb] become fine / goes well / be good / se convierten en todo bien / va bien / llegar a estar bien / estar bien hecho

되어 = 돼 = familiar ending of 되다

아프더라도 너만 있으면 돼. = [pronunciation] 아프더라도 너만 이쓰면 돼.
Although I feel painful, it is all right for me only if you stay by me. /
Aunque me siento doloroso, está bien para mí sólo si te quedas a mi lado.

< Line 8 > We are the lovesick girls. 네 멋대로 내 사랑을 끝낼 순 없어.

You shouldn't finish off my love following your own whim. [at your whim]

No deberías acabar con mi amor siguiendo tu propio capricho. [a tu antojo]

< Line 9 > We are the lovesick girls. 이 아픔없인 난 아무 의미가 없어.

If there is no such a pain, my life will have no senses. /
I am quite meaningless without this kind of pain.

Si no hay tal dolor, mi vida no tendrá sentido. /
No tendré ningún sentido sin este tipo de dolor.

**< Line 11 > But we are born to be alone. Yeah, we are born to be alone.
Yeah, we are born to be alone. But why we still looking for love?**

**< Line 13 > 사랑은 slippin' and fallin'. 사랑은 killin' and darlin'.
아프다(가) 아물면 또 찾아오는 이 겁 없는 떨림.**

사랑은 = Love is / Amore es

아프다 = [infinitive of adjective] hurt / be ill [sick, painful, sore, hurting] / be tormented /
doler / ser doloroso / estar enfermo [dolorido, herido] / atormentarse
아물다 = [infinitive of verb] heal [up] / be healed / currarse / cerrarse / cicatrizarse

아프다(가) 아물면 = Whenever it heals up after suffering from pain /
Cada vez que se cura después de sufrir de dolor

또 = [adverb] again / still / even now / moreover / otra vez / todavía / incluso ahora / de nuevo
찾아오다 = [pronunciation] 차자오다 = [infinitive of verb] come back / come around /
come by / visit / volver / venir / visitar
찾아오는 = [pronunciation] 차자오는 = present adjective form of 찾아오다

이 = [determiner] this / these / este / estos
겁 = [noun] fear / fright / terror / scare / miedo / pánico / temor / horror
없다 = [pronunciation] 업다 → 업따 = [infintive of adjective] there is no / not exist /
be absent / be without / no hay / no existir / estar ausente / estar sin
없는 = [pronunciation] 업는 → 엄는 = present adjective form of 없다

겁 없는 = [pronunciation] 겁 업는 → 겁 엄는 → 거 범는 = [adjective form] fearless /
bold / daring / sin miedo / atrevido / osado / audaz

떨다 = [infinitive of verb] throb / palpitate / pulsate / quiver / latir / palpitar / estremecer

떨림 = noun form of 떨다 = heartthrob / palpitation / pulsation / el latido / palpitación /
pulsación

아프다 아물면 또 찾아오는 이 겁 없는 떨림.

This bold heartthrob that surely comes back whenever the scar heals up after suffering from pain. /

Este osado latido de corazón que seguramente vuelve cada vez que la cicatriz se cura después de sufrir de dolor.

< Line 14 > 들리지 않아 **what you say.** 이 아픔이 난 행복해.

나를 불쌍해 하는 네가 내 눈엔 더 불쌍해.

들리다 = [infinitive of verb] hear / be heard / oírse / escuchar / ser escuchado

들리지 = [pronunciation] 들리지 = a noun-type conjugation of 들리다

아니 하다 = 안 하다 = 않다 = [pronunciation] 안타 = not do / no hacer

않아 = [pronunciation] 안아 → 아나 = familiar ending of 않다

들리지 않아 = [verb phrase] I cannot hear / It cannot be heard / No puedo oír /
No se puede oír [escuchar]

들리지 않아 **what you say.** = I cannot hear what you say. / No puedo oír lo que dices.

이 = [determiner] this / these / este / estos

아픔이 = [pronunciation] 아프미 = 아픔 (pain, agony, torment, dolor, pena, agonía)
+ 이 [marker for subject]

난 = 나는 = 나 (I, yo) + 는 [marker for subject]

행복하다 = [pronunciation] 행보카다 = [infinitive of adejctive] be happy /
enjoy well-being / be fortunate / ser feliz [afortunado]

행복해 = [pronunciation] 행보캐 = familiar ending of 행복하다

이 아픔이 난 행복해. = Owing to this pain I feel happy. / This agony makes me happy. /
Por este dolor me siento feliz. / Esta agonía me hace feliz.

나를 불쌍해 하는 네가 내 눈엔 더 불쌍해.

나를 = 나 (I, yo) + 를 [marker for object] = me

불쌍하다 = [infinitive of adjective] = be pitiful [pathetic, piteous] /
ser lastimoso [patético, infortunado]

불쌍해 하다 = sympasize / feel sympathy for / regard one as piteous / simpatizar /
sentir simpatía por

불쌍해 하는 = present adjective form of 불쌍해 하다

네가 = 너 (you, tú) + 이가 [marker for subject]

내 = 나의 = 나 (I, yo) + 의 [marker for possession] = of me / my / mi

눈엔 = [pronunciation] 누넨 = 눈에는 = 눈 (eyes, ojos) + 에는 (in, to, en, a) = to the eyes / a los ojos

더 = [adverb] more / further / aditionally / más / de nuevo

불쌍해 = familiar ending of 불쌍하다

나를 불쌍해 하는 네가 내 눈엔 더 불쌍해.
To my eyes, the more piteous one is you who are treating me as a piteous one. /
A mis ojos, el más lastimoso eres tú que me tratas como un lastimoso.

< Line 8 > We are the lovesick girls. 네 멋대로 내 사랑을 끝낼 순 없어.

You shouldn't finish off my love following your own whim. [at your whim] /
No deberías acabar con mi amor siguiendo tu propio capricho. [a tu antojo]

< Line 9 > We are the lovesick girls. 이 아픔없인 난 아무 의미가 없어.

If there is no such a pain, my life will have no meaning. /
I am quite meaningless without this kind of pain.

Si no hay tal dolor, mi vida no tendrá sentido. /
No tendré ningún sentido sin este tipo de dolor.

< Line 15 > One, Two, Lovesick girls. 모두 결국 떠나가고. Lovesick girls.
내 눈물이 무뎌져도. Lovesick girls. 아프고, 또 아파도. Lovesick girl.
But we are still looking for love.

모두 = [adverb] all / the whole / all of us / all of them / every / todo(s) / cada

결국 = [pronunciation] 결국 = [noun, also used as adverb] eventually / finally / at last / in the end / al final / por fin

● In Korean, the pronunciation of the first consonant just after ' ㄹ ' tends to become hard. However, this is not usually applicable within a word.

떠나가다 = [infinitive of verb] leave / go away / get away / depart / eliminarse / despejar

떠나가고 = leave, and / go away, and / get away, and / derpart, and / se elimina, y / despeja, y

내 = 나의 = 나 (I, yo) + 의 [marker for possession] = of me / my / mi

눈물이 = 눈물 (tears, lágrimas) + 이 [marker for subject]

무디다 = [infinitive of adjective] be blunt [dull, numb, pointless, obtuse] / ser embotado [romo, entumecido]

무디어지다 = 무뎌지다 = become blunt / get to be numb [pointless] / convertir embotado [entumecido]

무디어져도 = **무뎌져도** = in spite of becoming blunt [dull] / although it becomes numb [pointless] / a pesar de volverse embotado [romo] / incluso si se vuelve entumecido [obtuso]

아프다 = [infinitive of adjective] hurt / be ill [sick, painful, sore, hurting] / be tormented / doler / ser doloroso / estar enfermo [dolorido, herido] / atormentarse

또 = [adverb] again / still / even now / moreover / otra vez / todavía / incluso ahora / de nuevo

아프고, 또 아파도 = although it hurts me again and again / even if it is painful and painful again / aunque me duela una y otra vez / incluso si es doloroso y dolorso de nuevo

모두 결국 떠나가고, 내 눈물이 무뎌져도. 아프고, 또 아파도.
But we are still looking for love.

Everyone leaves me eventually, thus I shed tears until I get numb. Even if it is painful and painful again, but we are still looking for love.

Todos me dejan eventualmente, así que derramé lágrimas hasta que me entumezco. Incluso si es doloroso y doloroso de nuevo, pero todavía estamos buscando el amor.

14. Yes or Yes

Artist: *Twice*

Lyric Writer: 심은지

< Line 1 > Hey, boy! Look! I'm gonna make this simple for you.
You got two choices … Yes or Yes. 둘 중에 하나만 골라! Yes or Yes.

둘 = [noun] two things / two options / dos cosas

중에 = 중 (between, among, entre) + 에 (out of, from, de)

하나만 = 하나 (one thing, una cosa) + 만 (just, only, simply, sólo, solamente)

고르다 = [infinitive of verb] choose / pick out / select / elegir / escoger / seleccionar

골라! = imperative mood of 고르다 = do pick out! / select! / ¡escoge! / ¡seleccione!

둘 중에 하나만 골라! Yes or Yes. = [pronunciation] 둘 쭝에 하나만 골라!
Pick out only one from these two! / ¡Escoge sólo uno de estos dos!

< Line 2 > 하나만 선택해, 어서! Yes or Yes.

하나만 = 하나 (one thing, una cosa) + 만 (just, only, simply, sólo, solamente)

선택하다 = [pronunciation] 선태카다 = [infinitive of verb] choose / pick out / select /
elegir / escoger / seleccionar

선택해! = [pronunciation] 선태캐! = imperative mood of 고르다 = do choose [select]! /
¡elige! / ¡selecciona!

어서 = [adverb] quick / fast / promptly / rápido / deprisa / pronto

하나만 선택해, 어서! Yes or Yes. = Choose only one, quick! / ¡Elige sólo uno, rápido!

< Line 3 > 내가 이렇게도 이기적이었던가?

내가 = 나 + 이가 = 나 (I, yo) + 이가 [marker for subject]

이러하다 = [infinitive of adjective] be this way / be like this / be as follows / ser así /
ser la siguiente / ser como sigue / ser como éste

이러하게 = adverb form of 이러하다 = 이렇게 = [pronunciation] 이러케 = so / like this /
like such / como esto / como tal

이렇게도 = [pronunciation] 이러케도 = 이렇게 + 도 [marker for emphasis] = as much [many] as this / tanto[s] como esto

이기적 = [determiner] selfish / egoistic / egocentric / egoísta / egocéntrico

이다 = [infinitive of marker that conjugates] be / ser

이었다 = [pronunciation] 이얻따 = past tense of 이다 = was / has been / fue / ha sido

이었던가? = [pronunciation] 이얻떤가? = soliloquy questiong of 이었다

내가 이렇게도 이기적이었던가? = Have I been [Am I] egocentric as much as this? / ¿He sido [Soy] egocéntrica tanto como esto?

< Line 4 > 뭔가 이렇게 갖고 싶던 적이 있었나, 있었나?
다 놀라. 다 놀라. 내 뻔뻔함에. (Come on, and tell me yes.)

(내가) = 나 (I, yo) + 이가 [marker for subject]
● The above subject is omitted. Este sujeto se omite.

무엇인가 = 무언가 = **뭔가** = 무엇 (what, something, qué, algo) + 인가 [marker for uncertain object]
● «이다 (be, ser)» is the only marker that conjugates. «인가» is a noun form of «이다» for uncertainty. «무엇인가» indicates someone who is uncertain or undesignated. «를» is a marker for object which is omitted in this line.

뭔가(를) = something that is undesignated / algo que no está designado

이러하다 = [infinitive of adjective] be like this [this way, as follows] / ser así [éste, la siguiente]
이러하게 = adverb form of 이러하다 = **이렇게** = [pronunciation] 이러케 = so / like this / like such / como éste / como tal

갖다 = [pronunciation] 갇따 = [infinitive of verb] own / take / keep / poseer / tomar / mantener

싶다 = [pronunciation] 십다 → 십따 = [infinitive of verb] feel like / would like / want / wish / desire / querer / gustar

갖고 싶다 = [pronunciation] 갇꼬 십따 = [verb phrase] feel like keeping / want to own / wish to take / quiero poseer / deseo tomar / tengo ganas de mantener

갖고 싶던 = [pronunciation] 갇꼬 십떤 = past adjective form of 갖고 싶다 =
that I wanted to own [keep] / lo que lo que quería poseer [tener, mantenar]

적이 = [pronunciation] 저기 = 적 (time, occasion, case, when, vez, ocasión, caso, cuando)
+ 이 [marker for subject]
있다 = [pronunciation] 읻다 → 읻따 = [infinitive of verb] there is / be / exist / stay / remain / stand /
hay / estar / existir / quedarse / permanecer / pararse
있었다 = [pronunciation] 이썯따 = past tense of 있다

있었나? = [pronunciation] 이썯나? → 이썬나? = questioning form of 있었다

뭔가 이렇게 갖고 싶던 적이 있었나? =
[pronunciation] 뭔가 이러케 갇꼬 십떤 저기 이썬나?
Have I ever wanted something as much as like this? / ¿Alguna vez he querido algo como esto?

다 = [adverb] all / everything / everyone / totally / completely / todo(s) / totalmente /
completamente
놀라다 = [infinitive of verb] be surprised / be amazed / estar sorprendido / estar asustado
놀라 = familiar ending of 놀라다
다 놀라 = Everyone got surprised. / It is completely surprising. /
Todos se sorprendieron. / Es completamente sorprendente.

내 = 나의 = 나 (I, yo) + 의 [marker for possession] = of me / my / mi
뻔뻔하다 = [infinitive of adjective] be impudent [cheeky, audacious, shameless,
brazen-faced] / tener cara dura / ser descarado [desvergonzado, sinvergüenza]
뻔뻔함 = noun form of 뻔뻔하다 = impudence / descaro
뻔뻔함에 = [pronunciation] 뻔뻔하메 = 뻔뻔함 + 에 (at, by, with, to, de, por, con, a)

다 놀라. 내 뻔뻔함에. = Everyone got surprised at my impudence. /
Todos se sorprendieron de mi descaro.

< Line 5 > 생각보다 과감해진 나의 시나리오. 이 정도 플랜이면 완벽해.
만족해, 만족해. I don't care, I don't care 누가 뭐래도. (You better tell me yes.)

생각 = [noun] thought / consideration / initial intention / pensamiento / consideración /
intención inicial

보다 = [marker] than / more than / más que

과감하다 = [infinitive of adjective] be bold [daring, drastic, defiant] /
ser audaz [atrevido, drástico, valiente]

과감해지다 = become bold [daring] / get to be drastic [defiant] / se vuelve audaz [atrevido] /
llegar a ser drástico [valiente]

과감해진 = past adjective form of 과감해지다

나의 = 나 (I, yo) + 의 [marker for possession] = of me / my / mi

시나리오 = [in Korean] 각본 / 대본 = [noun] scenario / escenario / guión

생각보다 과감해진 나의 시나리오.
The scenario that has become bolder than my initial intention /
El guión que se ha vuelto más audaz que mi intención inicial

이 = [determiner] this / these / este / estos

정도 = [noun] level / degree / extent / boundary / nivel / grado / extensión / límite

플랜 = [in Korean] 계획 / 기획 = [noun] projection / plan / proyecto

이다 = [infinitive of marker that conjugates] be / ser

이면 = 이다 (be, ser) + 면 = if it is / si es

완벽하다 = [pronunciation] 완벼카다 = [infinitive of adejctive] be perfect [flawless,
immaculate, complete] / ser perfecto [impecable, inmaculado, completo]

완벽해 = [pronunciation] 완벼캐 = infirmal eding of 완벽하다 [완벼카다]

이 정도 플랜이면 완벽해. = This level of plan can be said perfect. /
If a plan is this much sophisticated, I can say that it is perfect.

Este nivel de plan se puede decir perfecto. /
Si un plan es tan sofisticado, puedo decir que es perfecto.

만족하다 = [pronunciation] 만조카다 = [infinitive of adjective] be satisfactory [content] /
estar satisfecho [contento]

(나는) **만족해** = [pronunciation] 만조캐 = familiar ending of 만족하다 = I am contented. /
Esoty contenta.

누가 = 누구가 = 누구 (who, whoever, quién, la gente) + 가 [marker for subject]

뭐라(고) 하다 = 무엇 (what, whatever, qué) + (이)라고 하다 (say, tell, decir, hablar)

뭐라(고) 하여도 = **뭐래도** = regardless of whatever they say / aunque qué diga la gente

I don't care 누가 뭐래도. = I don't care, even if whoever says whatever. /
I don't care, regardless of what people say. / No me importa, aunque qué diga la gente. /
No me importa, independientemente de lo que diga la gente

< Line 6 > 내 맘은 정했어, Yes. 그럼 이제 네 답을 들을 차례.

내 = 나의 = 나 (I, yo) + 의 [marker for object] = my / of me / mi

맘은 = 마음 (mind, feelings, thought, mente, corazón, pensamiento) + 은 [marker for subject]

정하다 = [infinitive of verb] decide / determine / choose / decidir / determinar / elegir

정하였다 = [pronunciation] 정하엳따 = 정했다 [정핻따] = past tense of 정하다

정했어 = [pronunciation] 정해써 = familiar ending of 정했다

● In priciple, «을 [marker for object] » should be used. However, for the purpose of
comparison, Korean speakers use '은' instead of '을'.
  - 시작은 좋았다. 그러나, 끝은 나빴다. The beginning was good. But the ending was bad.
  - 내 맘은 정했어. 그런데, 네 맘은? My mind has been determined. And how about yours?

내 맘은 정했어. = [pronunciation] 내 마믄 정해써.
My mind has been determined. / My thought was decided. /
Mi mente ha sido determinada. / Mi pensamiento estaba decidido.

그러하다 = [infinitive of adjective] be (like) such / be like that / ser así / ser como tal
그러하면 = 그러면 = **그럼** = adverb form of 그러하다 = if it is such / if it is like that /
then / si ser / ser así / entonces

네 = 너의 = 너 (you, tú) + 의 [marker for possession] = of you / your / tu

답을 = 답 (reply, answer, solution, decision, respuesta, solución, decisión) + 을 [marker for
object]

듣다 = [pronunciation] 듣따 = [infinitive of verb] hear / listen to / oír / escuchar

들을 = [pronunciation] 드를 = (future) ajective form of 듣다

차례 = [noun] order / turn / sequence / time / ordern / turno / secuencia / tiempo

그럼 이제 네 답을 들을 차례. = Then, it is the turn [time] to hear your decision. /
Entonces, es el turno [tiempo] de escuchar su decisión.

< Line 7 > 힘들면 보기를 줄께. 넌 고르기만 해! 고민할 필요도 없게 해줄께.

힘들다 = [infinitive of verb] be hard / be difficult / be tough / be (actually) impossible /

ser duro / ser difícil / ser (realmente) imposible

힘들면 = if be hard / if be difficult / if be tough / si ser duro / si ser dificil

보기를 = 보기 (examples, instances, cases, ejemplos, instancias, casos) + 를 [marker for object]

주다 = [infinitive of verb] give / bestow / provide / present / dar / otorgar / proporcionar / presentar

● The original meaning of «주다» is «give» or «bestow». But if it is used together with another verb, its meaning changes into «kindly do», «do as a favour» or «willing to do». It can also carry the meaning of «Please / Por favor».

줄께 = [tone of commitment] will give as a favour / be willing to provide / present kindly / dará como un favor / estar dispuesto a proporcionar / presentar amablemente

힘들면 보기를 줄께.
If it is tough for you, I am willing to provide you with some examples. /
Si es difícil para ti, estoy dispuesto a proporcionarte algunos ejemplos.

넌 = 너는 = 너 (you, tú) + 는 [marker for subject]

고르다 = [infinitive of verb] choose / pick out / select / elegir / escoger / seleccionar

고르기 = noun form of 고르다 = doing choice / picking up / lo elegir / lo escoger

고르기만 = 고르기 + **만** (just, only, simply, sólo, simplemente)

하다 = [infinitive of verb] do / act / make / hacer / realizar

해! = familiar ending for imperative mood of 하다 = Do it! / ¡Hozlo!

넌 고르기만 해! = You just pick out one! / ¡Sólo elige uno!

고민할 필요도 없게 해줄께.

고민하다 = [infinitive of verb] be in agony / suffer from anguish / distress oneself / estar en agonía / sufrir angustia / angustiarse

고민할 = adjective form of 고민하다

필요도 = 필요 (necessity, necesidad) + 도 [marker] (neither, not even, ni, ni siquiera)

있다 = [pronunciation] 읻다 → 읻따 = [infinitive of verb] there is / be / exist / stay / remain / stand / hay / estar / existir / quedarse / permanecer / pararse

없다 = [pronunciation] 업다 → 업따 = [infintive of adjective] there is no / not exist / be absent / be without / no hay / no existir / estar ausente / estar sin

없게 = [pronunciation] 업께 = adverb form of 없다 = to be without / absently / ser sin / estar sin / ausentemente

하다 = [infinitive of verb] do / act / make / hacer / realizar

하여 주다 = 해주다 = do [kindly, eagerly, as a favour] / willing to do / hacer amablemente [con guto] / dispuesto a hacer

하여 줄께 = **해줄께** = familiar ending with a tone of commitment of 하여 주다

고민할 필요도 없게 해줄께.
I will do it for you even without any need to distress yourself. /
I promise that there will be no stress at all for you.

Lo haré por ti incluso sin necesidad de angustiarte. /
Te prometo que no tendrá ningún estrés.

< Line 8 > 뭘 고를지 몰라 준비해봤어. 둘 중에 하나만 골라, Yes or Yes.

(네가) = 너 + 이가 = 너 (you, tú) + 이가 [marker for subject]
● The above subject is omitted. Este sujeto se omite.

뭘 = 무엇을 [무어슬] = 무엇 (what, something, qué, algo) + 을 [marker of object]

고르다 = [infinitive of verb] choose / pick out / select / elegir / escoger / seleccionar

고를지 = [pronunciation] 고를찌 = a noun-type conjugation of 고르다 = will choose / get to [come to, become to] pick out / be going to select / elegirá / llegar a escoger / ir a seleccionar

● «noun form» can be regarded as a noun, «adverb-form» can be regarded as an adverb, while «a noun-type conjuation» or «an adverb-type conjugation» is regarded as a verb.

● In Korean, when two verbs combine, there is a tendency that the first verb does either a noun-type or an adverb-type conjugation. By doing so, the first verb serves like an object for the second verb [in case that the second verb is a transitive verb], or modifies the second verb like an adverb [in case that the second verb is an intransitive verb].

모르다 = [infinitive of verb] not know [aware, realize, notice, understand, learned] / no saber [aprendí] / desconocer / no darse cuenta

몰라(서) = because I do not know / as I am not sure about / porque no sé / como no estoy segura de

뭘 고를지 몰라(서) = Because I do not know what you are going to pick out / As I am not sure about your choice / Porque no sé lo que vas a elegir / Como no estoy seguro de tu elección

준비 = [noun] preparation / readiness / pre-arrangements / preparación / preparativos

하다 = [infinitive of verb] do / act / make / hacer / realizar

하여보다 = 해보다 = have a try (at) / give a shot / attempt to / carry out / tratar / intentar

하여보았다 = 해보았다 = [pronunciation] 해보앋따 = past tense of 하여보다 / 해보다

하여보았어 = 해보았어 = **해봤어** [해봐써] = familiar ending of 하여보았다 / 해보았다

준비해봤어. = [pronunciation] 준비해봐써

I gave a shot to prearrange options for you. /
Dime una oportunidad para arreglar opciones para ti.

둘 중에 하나만 골라! Yes or Yes. = [pronunciation] 둘 쭝에 하나만 골라!

Pick out only one from these two! / ¡Escoge sólo uno de estos dos!

< Line 9 > 네 마음을 몰라 준비해봤어. 하나만 선택해, 어서. Yes or Yes.

네 = 너의 = 너 (you, tú) + 의 [marker for possession] = of you / your / tu

마음을 = 마음 (mind, heart, feelings, caring heart, mente, corazón) + 을 [marker for object]

모르다 = [infinitive of verb] not know [aware, realize, notice, understand, learned] /
no saber [aprendí] / desconocer / no darse cuenta

몰라(서) = because I do not know / as I am not sure about / porque no sé /
como no estoy segura de

네 마음을 몰라(서) = As I am sure about your mind / Como no estoy seguro de tu mente

준비해봤어. = I gave a shot to prearrange options for you. /
Dime una oportunidad para arreglar opciones para ti.

하나만 선택해, 어서! Yes or Yes. = Choose only one, quick! / ¡Elige sólo uno, rápido!

< Line 10 > '싫어'는 싫어. "나 아니면 우리?" 선택을 존중해. '거절'은 거절해.

싫다 = [pronunciation] 실타 = [infinitive of verb] dislike / hate / disgutar / odiar

싫어 = [pronunciation] 실어 → 시러 = [answer in Korean] "No, I don't want" /
"No, no quiero."

'싫어' = your answer "I don't want." / tu respuesta "No quiero."

'싫어'는 싫어

I don't want your answer "I don't want." / No quiero tu respuesta "No quiero".

"나? 아니면, 우리?" = "Me? If not, us?" / "¿Yo? Si no, ¿nosotros?"

(너의) = 너 (you, tú) + 의 [marker for possession] = of you / your / tu

선택을 = 선택 (choice, pick, selection, elección, selección) + 을 [marker for object]

존중하다 = [infinitive of verb] respect / esteem / respetar / estimar

존중해 = familiar ending of 존중하다

(너의) 선택을 존중해. = I respect your pick. / Respeto tu elección.

선택하다 = [pronunciation] 선태카다 = [infinitive of verb] choose / pick out / select / elegir / escoger / seleccionar

선택해! = [pronunciation] 선태캐 = imperative mood of 고르다 = do choose! / select! / ¡elija! / ¡seleccione!

하나만 선택해, 어서! Yes or Yes. = Choose only one, quick! / ¡Elija sólo uno, rápido!

거절은 = [pronunciation] 거저른 = 거절 (refusal, rechazo) + 은 [marker for subject]

거절하다 = [infinitive of verb] refuse / rechazar

거절해 = familiar ending of 거절하다 = [answer in Korean] "I refuse." / "Rechazo."

'거절'은 거절해. = I refuse your answer "I refuse." / Rechazo tu respuesta "Rechazo."

< Line 11 > 선택지는 하나. 자, 선택은 네 맘. It's all up to you.

선택지 = [pronunciation] 선택찌 = [noun] option / choice / opción / elección

선택지는 = [pronunciation] 선택찌는 = 선택지 + 는 [marker for subject]

하나 = [noun] one / una

선택지는 하나 = Your option is just one. / Tu opción es sólo una.

자, = [interjection] well / uh / bueno

선택은 = [pronunciation] 선태근 = 선택 (choice, selection, elección, selección) + 은 [marker for subject]

네 = 너의 = 너 (you, tú) + 의 [marker for possession] = of you / your / tu / tus

● Many Korean speakers including Twice pronounce 네 as 니. That is not correct.

231

맘 = 마음 = [noun] mind / heart / feelings / caring heart / mente / corazón

자, 선택은 네 맘 = Well, the selection is on your mind. /
Bueno, la selección está en tu mente.

**< Line 12 > 둘 중에 하나만 골라! Yes or Yes. 진심일까? Do not guess.
진심이니? Do not ask.**

둘 중에 하나만 골라! Yes or Yes. = [pronunciation] 둘 쭝에 하나만 골라!
Pick out only one from these two! / ¡Escoge sólo uno de estos dos!

진심 = [noun] sincerity / earnestness / seriousness / true heart / sinceridad / seriedad /
corazón sicero
이다 = [infinitive of marker that conjugates] be / ser
일까? = [soliloquy questioning] Is it that ~? / I wonder if ~ / ¿Es eso lo que ~? /
Me pregunto si ~
이니? = familiar questioning of 이다 = Is it that ~? / ¿Es eso lo que ~?

진심일까? Do not guess. = I wonder if he is sincere. Do not guess. /
Me pregunto si es sincero. No adivinar.

진심이니? Do not ask. = Are you sincere? Do not ask. / ¿Eres sincero? No preguntes.

< Line 13 > 애매한 좌우 말고, 확실히 위 아래로 (대답해).

애매하다 = [infinitive of adjective] be noncommittal / be ambiguous / be vague /
be hesitant / ser no comprometido / ser ambiguo / ser vago / ser vacilante
애매한 = present form of 애매하다 = noncommittal / ambiguous / vague / ambiguo
좌우 = [noun] left and right / izquierda y derecha
말다 = [verb] quit doing / refrain from doing / not do any longer / dejar de hacer / no hacer
말고 = quit doing, and / refrain from doing, and / dejar de hacer, y / no hacer, y

확실하다 = [pronunciation] 확씰하다 = [infinitive of adjective] be sure [certain,
affirmative] / estar seguro [cierto, afirmativo]
확실한 = [pronunciation] 확씰한 = adjective form of 확실하다 = sure / certain / affirmative /
seguro / cierto / afirmativo
확실히 = [pronunciation] 확씰히 = [adverb] surely / certainly / seguramente / ciertamente

위 아래로 = [adverb phrase] 위 (up, top, high) + 아래 (down, bottom, low) + 로 (to, toward, a, hacia)

애매한 좌우 말고, 확실히 위 아래로 (대답해).
(Answer me) not ambiguously left and right, but affirmatively up and down /
(Contéstame) no ambiguamente izquierda y derecha, sino afirmativamente arriba y abajo

< Line 14 > There's no letters, N & O. 지워버릴래 오늘부로.

지우다 = [infinitive of verb] erase / rub out / efface / eliminate / forget / borrar / eliminar / olvidar
지워버리다 = stronger expression of 지우다
지워버릴래 = familiar ending for commitment of 지워버리다
오늘부로 = 오늘 (today, hoy) + 부로 (as of, from, a partir de) = as of today / a partir de hoy

지워버릴래 오늘부로. = I surely will erase them as of today. /
Seguramente los borraré a partir de hoy.

< Line 15 > 복잡하게 고민할 필요 없어. 정답은 Yes, Yes 요.

복잡하다 = [pronunciation] 복짜파다 = [infinitive of adjective] be complicated [complex, intricate] / ser complicado [complejo, intrincado]
복잡한 = [pronunciation] 복짜판 = [present tense] complicated / complex, intricate / complicado / complejo / intricado
복잡하게 = [pronunciation] 복짜파게 = adverb form of 복잡하다 = complicatedly / intricately / complicadamente / intrincadamente => [figuratively] headachingly / too much seriously / de [por] dolor de cabeza / demasiado en serio

고민하다 = [infinitive of verb] be in agony / suffer from anguish / distress oneself / estar en agonía / sufrir angustia / angustiarse
고민할 = adjective form of 고민하다 = to be in agony / to distress oneself / angustiándose
필요 = [noun] need / necessity / requirement / necesidad / requisito
있다 = [pronunciation] 읻다 → 읻따 = [infinitive of verb] there is / be / exist / stay / remain / stand / hay / estar / existir / quedarse / permanecer / pararse
없다 = [pronunciation] 업다 → 업따 = [infintive of adjective] there is no / not exist / be absent / be without / no hay / no existir / estar ausente / estar sin
없어 = [pronunciation] 업써 = familiar ending of 없다

● In Korean, a 'verb' means an action and an 'adjective' means a situation or status. In case of «없다 (no exist)», it is always an adjective. However, «있다 (be, exist, estar)» can be either a verb or an adjective.

- 그는 방에 없다. = He is not in the room. He is not to be found in the room. = [status]

- 그는 방에 있다. = He is in the room. He is staying in the room. = [action]

- 그는 자고 있다. = He is sleeping. = [action]

- 꽃이 피어 있다. = A flower has bloomed. It is in the status of being bloomed. = [status]

복잡하게 고민할 필요 없어.
You don't need to distress yourself suffering from headache. /
No necesitas angustiarte sufriendo de dolor de cabeza.

정답은 Yes, Yes 요.

정답은 = [pronunciation] 정다븐 = 정답 (correct answer, respuesta correcta) + 은 [marker for subject]

이다 = [infinitive of marker that conjugates] be / ser

이요 = **요** = somewhat polite ending of 이다

입니다 = [pronuciation] 임니다 = polite ending of 이다

정답은 Yes, Yes 요.
The correct aswer is Yes, Yes. / La respuesta correcta es Sí, Sí.

< Line 16 > 없던 이기심도 자극하는 너의 눈과 널 향한 호기심이 만나서 타올라, 타오른다. My heart burn, burn, burn. You better hurry up.

없다 = [pronunciation] 업다 → 업따 = [infintive of adjective] there is no / not exist / be absent / be without / no hay / no existir / estar ausente / estar sin

없던 = [pronunciation] 업떤 = past tense of 없다 = that did not exist / que no existía => not to be exposed / sleeping / no estar expuesto / durmiendo

이기심 = [noun] egoistic mind / selfishness / mente egoísta / egoísmo

도 = [marker for emphasis] even / as well / but also / not even / incluso / también / así como / ni siquiera

자극하다 = [pronunciation] 자그카다 = [infinitive of verb] stimulate / spur / evocate / estimular / evocar

자극하는 = [pronunciation] 자그카는 = present adjective form of 자극하다 = stimulating / that spurs / que estimula / evocando

너의 = **너의** = 너 (you, tú) + 의 [marker for possession] = of you / your / tu / tus

눈과 = 눈 (eyes, ojos) + 과 (and, y)

없던 호기심도 자극하는 너의 눈과
your eyes that stimulate my sleeping egoistic mind, and /
tus ojos que estimulan mi mente egoísta dormida, y

널 = 너를 = 너 (you, tú) + 를 [marker for object]

향하다 = [infinitive of verb] aim at / head for / face toward / dirigirse hacia / dar a / caer a

향한 = present adjective formo of 향하다

(나의) = 나 (I, yo) + 의 [marker for possession] = of me / my / mi

호기심이 = [pronunciation] 호기시미 = 호기심 (curiosity, inquisitiveness, curiosidad) + 이 [marker for subject]

만나다 = [infinitive of verb] meet / encounter / come across / run into / hallar / encontrarse

만나서 = meet each other, and / by encountering / as a result of coming across / through running into / conocerse, y / por encontrar / como resultado de cruzar

타오르다 = [infinitive of verb] burn / blaze / flare up / arder / rehervir / conflagrarse / llamear

타올라 = poetic ending of 타오르다

타오른다 = soliloquy or familiar ending of 타오르다

없던 호기심도 자극하는 너의 눈과 널 향한 (나의) 호기심이 만나면서 타올라, 타오른다.
We are blazing up as a result that my curiosity toward you have come acrossed with
your eyes that stimulate my sleeping egoistic mind. /
We are blazing up as a result that your eyes that stimulate my sleeping egoistic mind have
come acrossed with my curiosity toward you.

Estamos ardiendo como resultado de que mi curiosidad hacia ti se ha cruzado con
tus ojos que estimulan mi mente egoísta dormida. /
Estamos ardiendo como resultado de que tus ojos que estimulan mi mente egoísta dormida
se ha cruzado con mi curiosidad hacia ti.

< Line 17 > 조금 쉽게 말하자면, 넌 뭘 골라도 날 만나게 될거야.

조금 = [adverv] a little (bit) / slight / a short while / pequeño / un poco / gota / ligero / breve / rato

쉽다 = [pronunciation] 쉽따 = [infinitive of adjective] be easy / be simple / be plain / ser fácil / ser simple / ser claro

쉽게 = [pronunciation] 쉽께 = adverb form of 쉽다 = easily / simply / plainly / fácil / simplemente / claramente

말하다 = [infinitive of verb] say / tell / talk / speak / state / decir / hablar / referir

말하자면 = if say / if tell / if tell / if talk / if speak / if state / si decir / si hablar / si referir

조금 쉽게 말하자면 = If I say a bit (more) easily, / Si digo un poco (más) fácil,

넌 = 너는 = 너 (you, tú) + 는 [marker for subject]

뭘 = 무얼 = 무엇을 = 무엇 (what, which one, something, qué, algo) + 을 [marker for object]

고르다 = [infinitive of verb] choose / pick out / select / elegir / escoger / seleccionar

골라도 = whatever choose / regardless of picking out / incluso si elegir / aunque escoger

넌 뭘 골라도 = whatever you choose / regardless which one you pick / incluso si lo que elijas / independientemente de cuál escojas / aunque cuál escojas

날 = 나를 = 나 (I, yo) + 를 [marker for object]

만나다 = [infinitive of verb] meet / encounter / come across / run into / hallar / encontrarse

(하게) 되다 = [infinitive of verb with another verb] come to / get to / ir a / llegar a

만나게 되다 = come to meet / get to encounter / ir a hallar / llegar a encontrar

될 = (future) adjective form of 되다 = that will come to / that will get to / que viene a / que llegará a

것이다 = [pronunciation] 거시다 = 것 (the thing that ~, the fact that ~, el hecho que ~, lo que ~) + 이다 (be, ser)

거야 = familiar ending of 것이다

날 만나게 될 거야 = [pronunciation] 날 만나게 될 꺼야

come to meet me / get to see me / ir a encontrarme / llegar a verme

넌 뭘 골라도 날 만나게 될 거야. = [pronunciation] 넌 뭘 골라도 날 만나게 될 꺼야.

Regardless which on you pick out, you will come to see me. /
Regardless which on you pick out, (it is the fact that) you will get to see me.

Independientemente de cuál escojas, llegarás a encontrarme. /
Independientemente de cuál escojas, (es el hecho que) te volverás a verme.

< Line 18 > 뭐 좀 황당하긴 해도, 억지라고 해도 절대 후회하지 않게 해줄게.

뭐 = [interjection] well / uh / bueno

좀 = 조금 = [adverv] a little (bit) / slight / a short while / pequeño / un poco / gota / ligero / breve

황당하다 = [infinitive of adjective] be absurd / be preposterous / ser absurdo / ser injustificado

황당하기 = noun form of 황당하다

황당하긴 = 황당하기 + 는 [maker for subject]

하다 = [infinitive of verb] do / act / make / hacer / realizar

해도 = although do [act, make] / aunque hacer [realizar]

황당하긴 해도 = although it is absurd / even if it is preposterous / aunque es absurdo / incluso si es absurdo

뭐 좀 황당하긴 해도,
although it might be a little absurd / even if it seems slightly preposterous /
aunque podría ser un poco absurdo / incluso si parece un poco injustificado

억지 = [pronunciation] 억찌 = [noun] inordinate insistence / immoderate claim / insistencia excesiva / recalmación inmoderarda

(이)라고 하다 = [verb phrase] say / talk / decir / hablar

억지라고 해도 = even if you say that it is an inordinate insistence / even though it might seem to be an immoderate claim

incluso si dices que es una insistencia excesiva /
aunque pueda parecer una recalmación inmoderarda

절대 후회하지 않게 해줄게.

절대 = [pronunciation] 절때 = [noun, also used as adverb] never / absolutely / completely / nunca / absolutamente / plenamente

● In Korean, the pronunciation of the first consonant just after 'ㄹ' tends to become hard. However, this is not usually applicable within a word. Exceptions are mostly Sino-Korean words like 《절대》 which is pronounced as 《절때》.

후회하다 = [infinitive of verb] regret / repent / feel sorry / arrepentirse / sentir arrepentido

후회하지 = a noun-type conjugation of 후회하다

아니 하다 = 안 하다 = 않다 = [pronunciation] 안타 = not do / no hacer

하지 않게 = [pronunciation] 하지 안케 = adverb form of 아니 하다 = (in order) not to do / (in order) never to do / (para) no hacer / (para) nunca hacer

후회하지 않게 = (in order) not to regret / (in order) never to remorse / (para) no arrepentirse

하다 = [infinitive of verb] do / act / make / hacer / realizar

하여 주다 = 해주다 = do [kindly, eagerly, as a favour] / willing to do / kindly let do / hacer amablemente [con guto] / dispuesto a hacer / amablemente te dejaré hacer

하여 줄께 = **해줄께** = familiar ending with a tone of commitment of 하여 주다

절대 후회하지 않게 해줄께. = [pronunciation] 절때 후회하지 안케 해줄께
I will kindly let you never regret it. / I will never make you feel sorry. / Amablemente dejaré que nunca te arrepientas. / Nunca te haré sentir arrepentido.

< Line 8 > 뭘 고를지 몰라 준비해봤어. 둘 중에 하나만 골라, Yes or Yes.

뭘 고를지 몰라(서) = [pronunciation] 뭘 고를찌 몰라(서)
Because I do not know what you are going to pick out /
As I am sure about your choice / Porque no sé lo que vas a elegir /
Como no estoy seguro de tu elección

준비해봤어 = [pronunciation] 준비해봐써
I gave a shot to prearrange options for you. /
Dime una oportunidad para arreglar opciones para ti.

둘 중에 하나만 골라! Yes or Yes. = [pronunciation] 둘 쭝에 하나만 골라!
Pick out only one from these two! / ¡Escoge sólo uno de estos dos!

< Line 9 > 네 마음을 몰라 준비해봤어. 하나만 선택해, 어서. Yes or Yes.

네 마음을 몰라(서) = As I am sure about your mind / Como no estoy seguro de tu mente

준비해봤어 = [pronunciation] 준비해봐써
I gave a shot to prearrange options for you. /
Dime una oportunidad para arreglar opciones para ti.

.

하나만 선택해, 어서! Yes or Yes. = Choose only one, quick! / ¡Elige sólo uno, rápido!

< Line 10 > '싫어'는 싫어. "나 아니면 우리?" 선택을 존중해. '거절'은 거절해.

'싫어'는 싫어 = [pronunciation] '시러'는 '시러'
I don't want your answer "I don't want." / No quiero tu respuesta "No quiero".

"나? 아니면, 우리?" = "Me? If not, us?" / "¿Yo? Si no, ¿nosotros?"

(너의) 선택을 존중해 = I respect your pick. / Respeto tu elección.

거절'은 거절해 = [pronunciation] 거저른 거절해
I refuse your answer "I refuse." / Rechazo tu respuesta "Rechazo."

< Line 11 > 선택지는 하나. 자, 선택은 네 맘. It's all up to you.

선택지는 하나 = Your option is just one. / Tu opción es sólo una.
자, 선택은 네 맘 = Well, the selection is on your mind. /
Bueno, la selección está en tu mente.

< Line 19 > Maybe not (no, no). Maybe yes, (no no).
좀 더 선명하게 네 마음을 내게 보여봐.

좀 = 조금 = [adverv] a little (bit) / slight / a short while / pequeño / un poco / gota /
ligero / breve / leve
더 = [adverb] more / further / aditionally / más / de nuevo
선명하다 = [infinitive of adjective] = be clear [clear-cut, distinct] /
ser claro [bien definido, distinto]
선명하게 = adverb form of 선명하다 = clearly / clear-cut / distinctly / claramente /
bien definido

네 = 너의 = 너 (you, tú) + 의 [marker for possession] = of you / your / tu
마음을 = [pronunciation] 마으믈 = 마음 (mind, heart, feelings, caring heart,
mente, corazón) + 을 [marker for object]
내게 = 나에게 = 나 (me, mí) + 에게 (to, a) = to me / a mí
보이다 = [infinitive of verb] be seen / look / look like / be found / verse / mirarse
보이어 = 보여 = a noun-type conjugation of 보이다

239

(해)보다 = [infinitive of verb] have a try / give a shot / attempt to / carry out / venture to / probar / tratar / intentar / llevar a cabo / atreverse

보여 보다 = try to show / attempt to show / tratar de mostrar / intentar mostrar

보여 보아 = **보여 봐** = familiar ending for imperative mood of 보여 보다

좀 더 선명하게 네 마음을 내게 보여봐.
Try to show me your heart a little more clearly! /
¡Trata de mostrarme tu corazón un poco más claramente!

< Line 20 > 귀 기울여 봐! 무슨 소리가 들리지 않니? It' simple. Y E S, Hey.

귀 = [noun] ear(s) / oreja(s)

귀 기울이다 = [pronunciation] 귀 기우리다 = [verb phrase] listen carefully / listen with care / escuchar cuidadosamente / escuchar con atención

귀 기울여 = [pronunciation] 귀 기우려 = a noun-type conjugation of 귀 기울이다

(해)보다 = [infinitive of verb] have a try / give a shot / attempt to / carry out / venture to / probar / tratar / intentar / llevar a cabo / atreverse

봐! = familiar ending for imperative mood of 보다

귀 기울여 봐! = Try to listen carefully! / Try to listen with care! /
¡Trate de escuchar atentamente! / ¡Trate de escuchar con atención!

무슨 = [determiner] what / what kind of / some kind of / qué / qué tipo de / algún

소리가 = 소리 (sound, sonido) + 가 [marker for subject]

들리다 = [infinitive of verb] hear / be heard / oírse / escuchar / ser escuchado

들리지 = a noun-type conjugation of 들리다

아니 하다 = 안 하다 = 않다 = [pronunciation] 안타 = not do / no hacer

않니? = [pronunciation] 안니? = [tag questioning] You do, don't you? / haces, ¿no?

무슨 소리가 들리지 않니?
Don't you hear any kind of sound? / You hear some sound, don't you? /
¿No escuchas ningún tipo de sonido? / Escuchas algún sonido, ¿no?

< Line 21 > 둘 중에 하나만 골라! Yes or Yes. 하나만 선택해, 어서. Yes or Yes.

둘 중에 하나만 골라! Yes or Yes. = [pronunciation] 둘 쭝에 하나만 골라!
Pick out only one from these two! / ¡Escoge sólo uno de estos dos!

하나만 선택해, 어서! Yes or Yes. = Choose only one, quick! / ¡Elige sólo uno, rápido!

< Line22 > 하나 더 보태서 Yes or Yes or Yes. 골라 봐! 자, 선택은 네 맘.

하나 = [noun] one / uno

더 = [adverb] more / further / aditionally / más / de nuevo

보태다 = [infinitive of verb] add (up) / plus / append / añadir /adicionar / adjuntar

보태서 = by adding (up) / appending, thus / por añadir / agregando, entonces /
a través de la adición

하나 더 보태서 **Yes or Yes or Yes.** = By adding up one, thus Yes or Yes or Yes. /
Agregando uno, entonces Sí o Sí o Sí.

고르다 = [infinitive of verb] choose / pick out / select / elegir / escoger / seleccionar

(해)보다 = [infinitive of verb] have a try / give a shot / attempt to / carry out /
venture to / probar / tratar / intentar / llevar a cabo / atreverse

봐! = familiar ending for imperative mood of 보다

골라 봐! = Try to pick out! / ¡Trate de escoger!

선택은 네 맘 = The selection is on your mind. / La selección está en tu mente.

< Line 8 > 뭘 고를지 몰라 준비해봤어. 둘 중에 하나만 골라, Yes or Yes.

뭘 고를지 몰라(서) = [pronunciation] 뭘 고를찌 몰라(서)
Because I do not know what you are going to pick out /
As I am sure about your choice / Porque no sé lo que vas a elegir /
Como no estoy seguro de tu elección

준비해봤어 = [pronunciation] 준비해봐써
I gave a shot to prearrange options for you. /
Dime una oportunidad para arreglar opciones para ti.

둘 중에 하나만 골라! = [pronunciation] 둘 쭝에 하나만 골라!
Yes or Yes. = Pick out only one from these two! / ¡Escoge sólo uno de estos dos!

< Line 9 > 네 마음을 몰라 준비해봤어. 하나만 선택해, 어서. **Yes or Yes.**

네 마음을 몰라(서) = As I am sure about your mind / Como no estoy seguro de tu mente

준비해봤어 = [pronunciation] 준비해봐써
I gave a shot to prearrange options for you. /
Dime una oportunidad para arreglar opciones para ti.

하나만 선택해, 어서! Yes or Yes. = [pronunciation] 하나만 선태캐, 어서!
Choose only one, quick! / ¡Elige sólo uno, rápido!

< Line 10 > '싫어'는 싫어. **"나 아니면 우리?"** 선택을 존중해. '거절'은 거절해.

'싫어'는 싫어.
I don't want your answer "I don't want." / No quiero tu respuesta "No quiero".

"나? 아니면, 우리?" = "Me? If not, us?" / "¿Yo? Si no, ¿nosotros?"

(너의) 선택을 존중해 = I respect your pick. / Respeto tu elección.

거절'은 거절해 = I refuse your answer "I refuse." / Rechazo tu respuesta "Rechazo."

< Line 11 > 선택지는 하나. 자, 선택은 네 맘. **It's all up to you.**

선택지는 하나 = [pronunciation] 선택찌는 하나
Your option is just one. / Tu opción es sólo una.

자, 선택은 네 맘 = [pronunciation] 자, 선태근 네 맘
Well, the selection is on your mind. / Bueno, la selección está en tu mente.

< Line 23 > 하나만 선택해, 어서. **Yes or Yes.**

하나만 선택해, 어서! Yes or Yes. = [pronunciation] 하나만 선태캐, 어서!
Choose only one, quick! / ¡Elige sólo uno, rápido!

Review of Adjective Forms & Principals of Pronunciation

< 1 > 먹고 있는 것 = [pronunciation] 먹꼬 읻는 걷 → 먹꼬 인는 걷 = **[present progressive]**
something that (I am) eating / something that (they are) eating /
algo que estoy comiendo / algo que están comiendo

● All the vowels and four consonants (ㄴ, ㄹ, ㅁ, ㅇ) are voiced sounds, which are soft. All the other consonants are voiceless sounds. A consonant that directly contacts with any voiceless consonant becomes hard (or fortis), if it is applicable. [ㄱ → ㄲ] [ㄷ → ㄸ] [ㅂ → ㅃ] [ㅅ → ㅆ] [ㅈ → ㅉ]

  - [먹고] The ㄱ of '고' is located between the voiceless ㄱ and the voiced ㅗ. Therefore, this ㄱ bcomes hard. [먹다 (eat) → 먹따] [먹고 → 먹꼬] [먹지 → 먹찌] [먹세 → 먹께] [먹도록 → 먹또록]
  - 'ㅁ' is also a voiced sound. However, for 'ㅁ' this rule does not apply in a verb. [감다 (shut, coil up) → 감따] [감고 → 감꼬] [감지 → 감찌] [감게 → 감께] [담다 (put in, hold) → 담따] [담고 → 담꼬] [담지 → 담찌] [담게 → 담께]

● In case of nouns and adverbs, even 'ㅁ' follows the rule of voiced and voiceless sounds. That means that in a noun- or an adverb-word the first consonant after 'ㅁ' does not become hard.
  - [사람들 (people)] [담배 (cigarette)] [김장 (kimchi-making)] [곰돌이 (teddy bear)]
  - [쉬엄쉬엄 (with frequent rests)] [주섬주섬 (piece by piece)]

< 2 > 먹는 것 = [pronunciation] 먹는 걷 → 멍는 걷 = **[present]**
something that (I, they) eat frequently [usually, these days]
algo que como [comen] con frecuencia [por lo general, en estos días]

● Sometimes «먹는 것» includes [incluye] «먹고 있는 것».

● All the vowels and four consonants (ㄴ, ㄹ, ㅁ, ㅇ) are voiced sounds, which are soft. Any consonant that is between these voiced (or soft) sounds becomes soft as well.

  - 먹는 것 → 먹는 걷 → 멍는 걷 [consonants between vowels become soft]
  - [가다 (go)] [가고] [가지] [가게] [가도록]
  - [말다 (quit)] [말고] [말지] [말게] [말도록]

< 3 > 먹고 있던 것 = [pronunciation] 먹꼬 잍떤 걷 = **[past progressive]**
something that (I was) eating / something that (they were) eating /
algo que estaba comiendo / algo que estaban comiendo

< 4 > 먹던 것 = [pronunciation] 먹떤 걷 = **[past]**
something that (I, they) used to eat frequently [usually, then]
algo que solía [solían] comer con frecuencia [por lo general, entonces]

● Sometimes «먹던 것» includes [incluye] «먹고 있던 것».

< 5 > 먹을 것 = [pronunciation] 머글 걷 → 머글 껃 = **[(future) adjective form]**
something to eat / algo de [para] comer
something that (I) will eat / algo que voy a comer
something that (they) will eat / algo que comerán

● In case of «(future) adjective forms», sometimes it is more natural to translate them into the present tense or the infinitive form in English.

< 6 > In spite of the rule of voiced and voiceless sounds, the pronunciation of the first consonant after '르' tends to become hard. Please note that this mostly applies between two independent words.

- [먹을 것 (something to eat) → 머글 걷 → 머글 껃] [할 것 (to do) → 할 껃]
- [며칠 밤 (several nights) → 며칠 빰] [열 배 (ten times) → 열 빼]
- [둘 중에 (between those two) → 둘 쭝에] [어릴 적 (when young) → 어릴 쩍]
- [할 수 있다 (can do) → 할 쑤 읻따] [갈 수 없다 (cannot go) → 갈 쑤 업따]

● Here are other examples:

다가와 준 **거**야 = [pronunciation] 다가와 준 **거**야 = [past] (You) came close nicely.
다가와 줄 **거**야 = [pronunciation] 다가와 줄 **꺼**야 = [future] (You) will come close nicely.

다가와 준 **거**야 = 다가와 준 것이야 = [pronunciation] 다가와 준 **거**시야
다가와 줄 **거**야 = 다가와 줄 것이야 = [pronunciation] 다가와 줄 **꺼**시야

● «지» was originally an independent word, whose meaning is «uncertainty», «probability» or «whether». Now it is combined with a verb for a noun-type conjugation.

- 먹을지 (whether to eat) = 먹을 [(future) adjective form] + 지 [찌]

- 발견할지 (whether to discover) = 발견할 [(future) adjective form] + 지 [찌]

● The above «지» does not become hard when it comes after 'ㄴ' instead of 'ㄹ'.

- 먹는지 (whether eats) = 먹는 [present adjective form] + 지 → [멍는지]
- 먹은지 (whether ate) = 먹은 [past adjective form] + 지 → [머근지]
- 먹었는지 (whether has eaten) = 먹었는 [present perfect form] + 지 → [머건는지]
- 먹었었는지 (whether had eaten) = 먹었었는 [past perfect form] + 지
  → [머거썬는지 → 머거썬는지]

● The Korean language has only three tenses which are the present, the past and the future. However, the language has expressions equivalent to the various tenses of European languages.

● Within a word, the pronunciation of the first consonant just after 'ㄹ' does not become hard.

- [얼굴 (face)] [몰골 (look)] [골고루 (evenly)] [골방 (small room)] [갈비 (rib)]
- [질질 (dragging)] [골골 (suffering)] [덜덜 (shivering)] [달달 (rattling)]
- [살살 (softly)] [실실 (silly)] [슬슬 (lightly)] [부글부글 (simmering)]
- [끌다 (pull), 끌고, 끌지] [밀다 (push), 밀고, 밀지] [말다 (quit), 말고, 말지]
- [달다 (be sweet), 달고, 달지]

● Exceptions within a word are mostly Sino-Korean words. That means that Sino-Korean words has a tendency to become hard right after 'ㄹ' even in a word.

- [절대 (absolutely) → 절때] [굴삭기 (excavator) → 굴싹끼]
- [결심 (resolution) → 결씸] [결정 (decision) → 결쩡] [말단 (the end) → 말딴]
- cf.: [결국 (decision) → 결국], not [결꾹]

< 7 > 'The Suffix for plural form [들]' and 'Markers' are not independent words. They are included in a noun (or pronoun) word. Therefore, they follow the rule of voiced and voiceless sounds. This is kind of a universal rule which applies to both «within a word» and «between two independent words».

- [싹들 (sprouts) → 싹뜰] [잎들 (leaves) → 입뜰] [꽃들 (flowers) → 꼳뜰]
- [나무들 (trees)] [문들 (doors)] [별들 (stars)] [꿈들 (dreams)] [창들 (windows)]

● Here are examples that rule of voiced and voiceless sounds are applicable to Markers.

- [싹도 (sprout also) → 싹또] [맛도 (taste also) → 맏도 → 맏또]

- [잎과 (leaf and) → 입과 → 입꽈] [꽃과 (flower also) → 꼳과 → 꼳꽈]
- [문도 (door also)] [오늘도 (today also)] [꿈과 (dream and)] [창과 (window and)]

● And '들' and 'Markers' don't become hard after 'ㄹ', because this rule is applicable only between two independent words.

- 얼굴들과 = 얼굴 (face) + 들 [plural] + 과 [marker for connection] (and)
- 별들과 = 별 (star) + 들 [plural] + 과 [marker for connection] (and)
- 별들도 = 별 (star) + 들 [plural] + 도 [marker for affinity] (also, as well)
- 꽃들도 = 꽃 (flower) + 들 [plural] + 도 (also) → «꼳뜰도», not «꼳뜰또»
- 사람들같이 = 사람 (person) + 들 [plural] + 같이 (also) → «사람들가치»

● Some words have hard sounds in it all the time and have nothing to do with rules.

- [할까? (Should we do it?)] [할께! (I will do it.)] [골똘히 (intently)]
- [실뜨기 (cat's-cradle)] [굴뚝 (chimney)] [선뜻 (readily) → 선뜯]

< 8 > When two independent words combine, the first consonant of the second word becomes hard. And, in case of vowels, a sound-linking (or liaison) is not allowed.

- 별빛 = 별 (star) + 빛 (light) = [pronunciation] 별빋 → 별삗
- 김밥 = 김 (laver) + 밥 (rice) = [pronunciation] 김밥 → 김빱
- 꽃밭 = 꽃 (flower) + 밭 (garden) = [pronunciation] 꼳받 → 꼳빧
- 꽃잎 (petal) = 꽃 (flower) + 잎 (leaf) = [pronunciation] 꼳닙 → 꼰닙
- 은행잎 = 은행 (ginko) + 잎 (leaf) = [pronunciation] 은행닙, not «은행입»
- 한여름 = 한 (high) + 여름 (summer) = [pronunciation] 한녀름, not «하녀름»
- 풀잎 = 풀 (grass) + 잎 (leaf) = [pronunciation] 풀닙 → 풀립
- 맛없다 (be tasteless) = 맛 (taste, flavor) + 없다 (not exists) = 맏 + 없다 = [pronunciation] 맏업다 → 마덥다 → 마덥따, not «마섭따»
- 맛있다 (be tasty) = 맛 (taste, flavor) + 있다 (exists) = 맏 + 있다 = [pronunciation] 맏읻다 → 마딛다 → 마딛따, not «마싣따»

< 9 > When 'ㅎ' combines with a consonsant, the consonant becomes aspirated.
[ㄱ + ㅎ → ㅋ] [ㄷ + ㅎ → ㅌ] [ㅂ + ㅎ → ㅍ] [ㅈ + ㅎ → ㅊ]

● Too complicated? No worries! Even if you don't follow these rules, there will be no problem in communicating. Here, the rules are for your better understating of Korean pronunciations.

https://pagemasterpublishing.ca/by/kyle-lee/

To order more copies of this book, find books by other
Canadian authors, or make inquiries about publishing
your own book, contact PageMaster at:

Para solicitar más copias de este libro, encontrar libros de otros
autores canadienses o hacer consultas sobre la publicación de
su propio libro, comuníquese con PageMaster en:

PageMaster Publication Services Inc.
11340-120 Street, Edmonton, AB T5G 0W5
books@pagemaster.ca
780-425-9303

catalogue and e-commerce store
PageMasterPublishing.ca/Shop

Lightning Source UK Ltd.
Milton Keynes UK
UKHW031200120921
390378UK00005B/112